The Sociology Manual

Study Skills for Sociology at A level and beyond.

Nik Jorgensen.

The Author:

Nik Jorgensen is Head of Sociology and Senior Lecturer in the School of Humanities at Blackburn College. He was formerly a Tutor in Sociology for the Open University and is a member of the Association of Social Science Teachers.

Editors:

Bren Abercrombie and Janet Day.

Acknowledgements:

The author wishes to thank the many students who made comments and suggestions, took part in interviews and gave examples of their work. He is also indebted to Michael Haralambos for early advice and suggestions, to John Hughes and Nick Abercrombie of the Department of Sociology, Lancaster University, to Pat McNeill of the ATSS, who provided information on Sociology courses, to Irene André who typed the manuscript, to Judith Isherwood for advice and guidance, and to Jan Jorgensen, who contributed to Chapters 8 and 9, and commented on early drafts.

The publishers wish to thank Pamela Ebdon and Pamela Kitching for assistance.

First published 1987 by

Framework Press Ltd.
St. Leonard's House
St. Leonardgate
Lancaster LA1 1NN

The Sociology Manual

ISBN 1 85008 085 2

Illustrations by Christopher Stephens

Cover design by John Angus

Typeset by Blackpool Typesetting Services Ltd., Blackpool

Printed by Redwood Burn Ltd., Trowbridge, Wiltshire

For Jan

CONTENTS

Page

INTRODUCTION 1

Chapter 1 **STARTING YOUR SOCIOLOGY COURSE** 5
A. **Preparing to Study** 5
B. **The Study of Sociology** 8
C. **The Language of Sociology** 14
D. **Critical Thinking in Sociology** 16

Chapter 2 **RESOURCES FOR SOCIOLOGY** 21
A. **The Importance of Resources** 21
B. **Written Sources** 22
C. **Numerical Data as a Resource** 38
D. **Supplementary Sources** 46
E. **Daily Life and Experience—Cultivating your Sociological Imagination** 55

Chapter 3 **READING** 59
A. **Types of Reading** 60
B. **SQ3R Method** 60
C. **Difficulty of Subject Matter** 62
D. **Developing your Reading Speed** 66
E. **Expanding your Vocabulary** 67

Chapter 4 **NOTE-MAKING** 69
A. **Class Notes** 70
B. **Notes from Reading** 73
C. **Storage of Notes/Retrieval System** 86

Chapter 5 **WRITING SOCIOLOGY ESSAYS** 87
A. **What is an Essay?** 89
B. **Coursework Essays** 90
C. **Interpreting/Understanding the Question—Question Analysis/ Decoding/Dismantling** 93
D. **Research** 97
E. **Contents of an Essay** 98
F. **Planning your Essay** 98
G. **The 'Audience' for an Essay** 101
H. **Writing the Essay** 102

Page

Chapter 6 **ALTERNATIVES TO ESSAY QUESTIONS** 113
A. **Stimulus—Response Questions** 114

Chapter 7 **REVISION** 125
A. **Revision as Rehearsal** 125
B. **Using Past Questions and Examination Papers as a Revision Aid** . 128
C. **Revision Activities** 128
D. **Revision Syndicates** 128
E. **Revision Activity** 129

Chapter 8 **EXAMINATION TECHNIQUES** 133
A. **The Day Before** 133
B. **Exam Day** 133
C. **Problems that may Arise in the Examination** 137
D. **Exam Do's and Don'ts** 140

Examination Board Abbreviations

AEB	The Associated Examining Board Stag Hill House Guildford SURREY GU2 5XJ
Cambridge	University of Cambridge Local Examinations Syndicate Syndicate Buildings 1 Hills Road CAMBRIDGE CB1 2EU

* Denotes 'Reproduced by permission of University of Cambridge Local Examinations Syndicate'

JMB	Northern Universities Joint Matriculation Board MANCHESTER M15 6EU
London	University of London School Examinations Department Stewart House 32 Russell Square LONDON WC1B 5DN
Oxford	University of Oxford Delegacy of Local Examinations Ewert Place Summertown OXFORD OX2 7BZ

NOTE:
The author wishes to thank all the above Examining Boards for their co-operation and for the use of examination questions and extracts from examiners' reports. The advice given in this book on answering examination questions is solely the responsibility of the author and has not been provided or approved by the examination boards.

INTRODUCTION

Background Notes

The aim of this book is to help you develop effective study skills for an advanced Sociology course. The guidance given is based on my experience of teaching in Further and Higher Education and a series of interviews with a representative sample of past and present students. In these interviews we explored the difficulties encountered in studying what can at times be a complex and demanding discipline. This students' eye view is an essential part of this book and I am grateful to the people concerned for taking part.

The use of the word 'Manual' in the title does not imply that you will be given instructions on the 'dismantling' of Sociology as a subject, as you would a car, motorbike or sewing machine. That would be an impossible task. Psychological and related research evidence on study skills has been incorporated wherever appropriate, but it is not the intention that such research findings are used in a definitive way or as a concrete set of rules for studying Sociology. The study of Sociology or any advanced subject cannot simply be likened to a mechanical process such as learning to drive a car.

The aim is to give constructive advice and helpful hints on how to study Sociology effectively, which includes techniques which have been used by successful students. The emphasis is on flexibility, thus enabling you to choose and adapt those methods which suit you best as an individual student.

Examples of students' work are included where appropriate to indicate good and not so good approaches, the standard varying from high pass grade levels to low or borderline fail levels. I would like to thank the students concerned for being willing to subject their work to the critical gaze of others.

How to use this book

The Sociology Manual is not a replacement for textbooks or accompanying course reading. It should be used along with such material. You are not required to read and work through all the contents in the initial stages of your course. Certain sections could profitably be worked at in the first few weeks, for example, the sections on Resources (Chapter 2), Reading (Chapter 3), Note-Making (Chapter 4), and Essay Writing (Chapter 5), whereas other sections can be left until later on in the course, for example those on Revision or Exam Preparation (Chapter 7) and Examination Techniques (Chapter 8). Some sections can be read and worked at and returned to at times when a particular problem is faced or a skill needs developing.

Exercises and activities to give you practice in developing skills are included where appropriate, the intention being that you complete them to aid your progress through the course.

The need for study skills

The main aim of this book is to enable you to develop efficient study skills to help you become a more effective student of Sociology. It has often been assumed by teachers and students that the skills of studying develop naturally and that the good student does not require help or guidance. In my view this assumption is incorrect. Compare the skill of studying properly with that of learning to swim. Very young children can float and manoeuvre themselves around in water quite happily, but is this an effective method of swimming? There comes a stage when elementary instruction in rudimentary swimming strokes would help the child become a much more effective swimmer. The same idea can be applied to studying, where many students are left to 'sink or swim', particularly in the early stages of an advanced course, when guidance on study skills could make the student's task much easier.

Even when lower level courses such as GCE O levels or GCSEs have been recently followed, many students find themselves at a loss on advanced courses, where the necessity for independent study and self discipline in one's approach to the course is much greater.

Why study skills for Sociology?

> "I prefer dictated notes. This is what we got all the time at school. You know where you are then, don't you?"
> 16 year old 1st year A level student.

There are several guides available which give good general advice on study skills for students of various disciplines or subjects (See *Further Reading* p.4). So why is there a need for a *Sociology Manual* specifically dealing with study skills for Sociology? The main reason is that in the same way a general car manual is only of use in explaining the general principles of how cars work and is not of use for specific details concerning a particular make or model, so it is with study skills for Sociology. Reading sociology books effectively, writing essays, developing a sociological imagination, being analytical and critical in your approach to the study of society, and other features of the course, are all specific skills which relate solely to this subject.

Do external examinations constrain active learning on Sociology courses?

Some critics see examinations as an unnecessary constraint which can lead to 'parrot-fashion' learning or the regurgitation of 'packages' of knowledge. Consider the following statement:

> 'The system of teaching and examination inevitably constrains the sociological activity of students. Thus for the most part sociology students read what they are told to. It is in this sense that the development of sociology education has been teaching rather than learning-centred, and more authoritarian in its values as opposed to democratic.'
> C.J. Margerison, I. Campbell, A. Dawson, 'An action-centred Sociology course' in *The British Journal of Sociology, Volume 22,* pp.441-447

ACTIVITY

Do you agree with the above comment? If you agree, write down what may be a more 'democratic' form of sociology education. Discuss this with your teacher and other students. Perhaps a class discussion on this theme could be arranged.

EXERCISE

Devise a table comparing the advantages and disadvantages of external examinations.

Advanced courses which are solely assessed by exams can lead to intensive, structured and teacher-directed approaches, where the student can become too dependent on set textbooks or class material. This will lead to moderate overall performance at best. Students who recognize that the resources for advanced study should not be restricted to one or two basic sources such as text-books, and who also develop the ability to research for wider and more detailed knowledge in their subjects, will be successful throughout the course as well as in the examinations. (Guidance on appropriate resources for Sociology is given in Chapter 2).

Summary

It is the aim of this book to help you become more active, independent and self-directed in your approach to study. You should use this book as follows:

1. to develop your ability to study effectively from the beginning of the course;
2. as a reference source throughout the course, whenever particular difficulties are encountered e.g. in writing essays or in preparation for exams.

Consider the diagram on the next page, which shows how good study techniques can lead to more efficiency, resulting in more time being available to you:

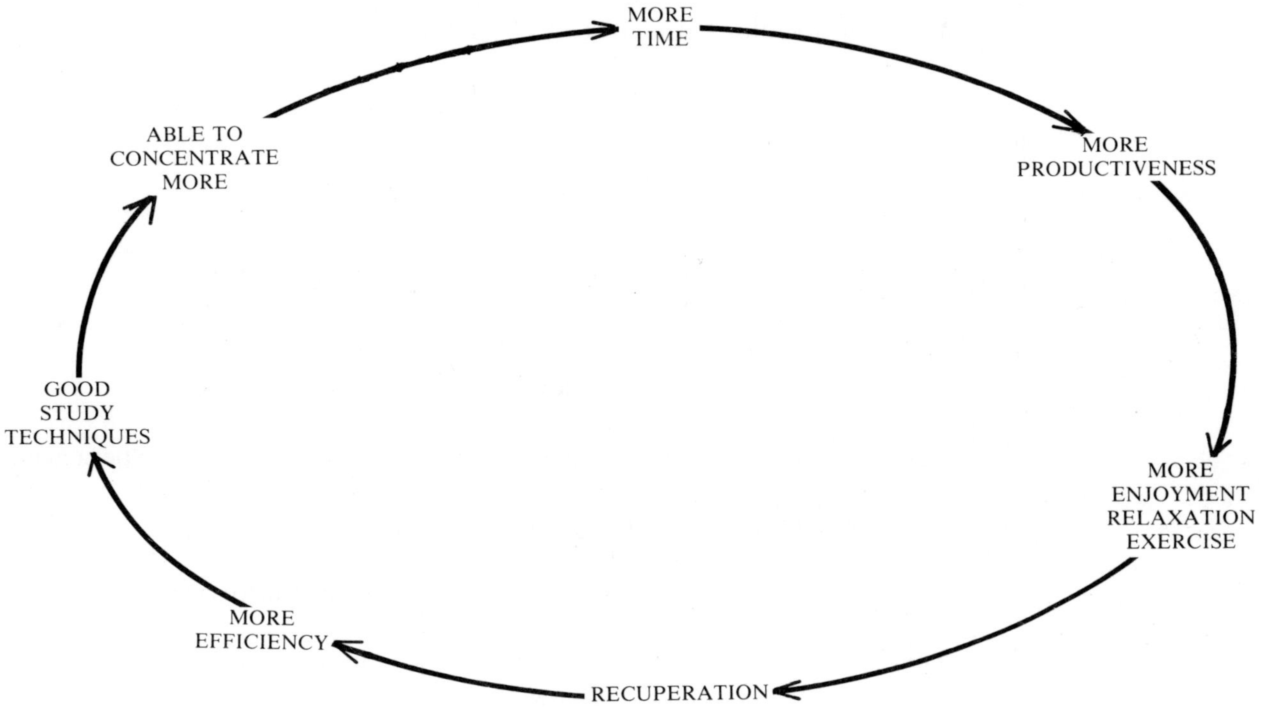

Fig.1. STUDY SKILLS FEEDBACK LOOP
How Study Skills can help your study of Sociology

EXERCISE

Consider your previous experience of courses of study. Write down:

1. whether you were an *active* or *passive* participant;
2. the activities you carried out when studying, e.g. taking dictated notes, reading;
3. proportionately how much time was spent on the above activities;
4. suggestions as to how learning may be improved if carrying out a similar course;
5. any activities you devised yourself which you found particularly useful, e.g. revision exercises or a card index system.

The skills of studying productively

The successful Sociology student *CONQUERS* inefficiency in study.

C	oncentration	— High levels of this needed
O	organization	— Need to prepare, plan, think ahead
N	otemaking	— Don't just listen or read—record
Q	question analysis	— The ability to decode essay or exam questions is a crucial skill
U	using textbooks, course material, wider sources, mass media, experience	
E	xam techniques, essay writing, stimulus-response questions	
R	evision	— The preparation for exam 'performance'
S	ociological imagination	— You should incorporate this throughout the course

Further Reading

The following are examples of useful general guides on study techniques which you can consult as necessary:

Casey, F., *How to Study; A Practical Guide* (Macmillan Education, London, 1985)

Coles, M., and White, C., *Strategies for Studying* (Collins Educational, London, 1985)

Fisher, Cassie W., and Constantine, T., *Student's Guide to Success* (Macmillan, London, 1977)

Harman, C., and Freeman, R., *How to Study Effectively* (National Extension College, Cambridge, 1984)

Maddox, H., *How to Study* (Pan Books, London, 1963)

Neill Wright, G.G., *Study* (English Universities Press, London, 1963)

Rowntree, D., *Learn How to Study* (Macdonald, London, 1970)

CHAPTER 1

STARTING YOUR SOCIOLOGY COURSE

A. PREPARING TO STUDY

Motivation

It is a good idea to consider your reasons for joining a course before you enrol. Consult the diagram and make sure your motivation is of a high level with sound reasons for joining, based on advice and guidance from appropriate teachers and tutors as well as careers specialists.

MOTIVATION LEVEL	REASONS FOR JOINING COURSE	COMMENT
HIGH	(1) I am interested in the subject (2) I read the syllabus and course information (3) I looked through an introductory textbook (4) I talked with tutors about the subject	All good sound reasons; more so if (1)–(4) all applied before enrolling
MEDIUM	(5) I had a careers interview and was told Sociology fits in with my longer term career ambitions (6) Sociology seems to be about people and I eventually want to work with people	A reasonable starting point but need to do (2)–(4) before enrolling. Never start a course before finding out about the subject
	(7) It's a subject I haven't studied before so I might as well have a go	Need to find out more: see (1)–(4). Interest could develop
	(8) I need a third A level and this is the only one that fits in with my timetable	Get further advice from tutors.—Should not enrol on any course purely on this basis.
LOW	(9) I've heard that Sociology's a left wing subject and I'm politically on the left	Mistaken conception—need to do some preliminary reading
	(10) I really wanted to do History but I only got a D in my O level, so I'll do Sociology instead	Consult History tutor—possible O level resit? and then A level History?
	(11) I've been told Sociology's a soft option—common sense and waffle should get me through	Misconception—Sociology as rigorous and demanding as other advanced subjects.

If your motivation level is low and reflected in some of the reasons (8)–(11) in the diagram, it is essential that you seek further advice. You will not do very well in any subject about which you have misconceptions or which you just drift into. With further advice and guidance it could well turn out that you become interested in Sociology and eventually do well.

Planning and organizing a study timetable

To be successful on an advanced course, you need to spend on average 6–8 hours per week in private study in addition to the time you spend in class. This can vary at different stages, for example more time will have to be spent when essays are due or in the exam preparation and revision periods. If you are a full-time student, make sure your timetable for your subjects includes both class times and free periods, the majority of which should be used for private study and the remainder for recreation, relaxation and sporting activities which, as the study skills feedback loop in the Introduction indicated, is an important part of your preparation for study.

Daytime free periods which are allocated for private study can be short, sometimes an hour or less. It is often tempting to spend this time with friends, but you should avoid this temptation. Providing that you allow yourself a mid-morning and mid-afternoon break (15–20 minutes) you can profitably use short private study periods for activities such as:
—tidying up class notes
—analysing coursework essay titles
—reading and making notes from articles or sections from books
—keeping abreast of current affairs through reading newspapers, magazines or journals
—making answer plans for homework essays.

Of course, some activities such as essay writing (see Chapter 5) are better carried out in more prolonged sessions, so you would have to reserve full mornings, afternoons or, more usually, evenings. Do remember, however, that the quality of your essays and coursework as well as your progress as a student could well depend on the amount of back-up activity and preparation carried out during your short daytime private study periods, so use your time wisely rather than in endless cups of coffee and chatter!

A weekly timetable for a full-time A-level student could be as follows—

	MON.	TUES.	WED.	THURS.	FRI.	SAT.	SUN.
A.M.	9–10 TUTORIAL 10.30–12 SOCIOLOGY	9–10.30 PSYCHOLOGY 10.30–12 PRIVATE STUDY	9–10 PSYCHOLOGY 10.30–12 SOCIOLOGY	9–10 PRIVATE STUDY 10.30–12 ECON./SOC. HISTORY	9–10.30 ECON./SOC. HISTORY 11–12.30 PRIVATE STUDY	PART-TIME JOB AT TESCO'S	LOOK AHEAD TO NEXT WEEK. ESSAYS TO COMPLETE? PREP?
P.M.	1.30–2.30 PRIVATE STUDY 3–4.30 ECON./SOC. HISTORY	1.30–3 ECON./SOC. HISTORY 3–4 PRIVATE STUDY	SPORT/ RECREATION	1.30–3 PSYCHOLOGY PRACTICAL 3–4.30 SOCIOLOGY	1.30–3 SOCIOLOGY/ 3–4.30 PSYCHOLOGY		REST/ WALK THE DOG
EVENING	PRIVATE STUDY/ HOME-WORK	PRIVATE STUDY/ HOME-WORK	YOUTH CLUB – YOGA BADMINTON	PRIVATE STUDY/ HOME-WORK	LEISURE/ RECREATION TV	LEISURE/ RECREATION TV	TV/ READ A BOOK/ RECORDS

Allow for flexibility—you may prefer to study more at weekends.

Part-time students—less time available. Need to concentrate work into weekends and/or evenings.

Some students prefer to work early in the morning and others late into the night, two contrasting student types who have been described as "larks" or "night owls". You may have to decide which you are by finding out the times of day or night when you are best able to concentrate and are at your most receptive, and then you can organize your private study accordingly.

Until you settle into your course, you need to have a flexibility of approach in organizing your study hours, so that you avoid setting impossible targets which can create anxiety. Be realistic, don't waste time and, so long as you have satisfied yourself that you have profitably used your study time, you can reward yourself with a well-earned period of rest and relaxation.

Study environment

Your college or school will probably provide daytime facilities for study in the library or allocated study areas. For work at home, a quiet, warm and reasonably comfortable room free from distractions is desirable. A desk, some bookshelves or somewhere to file and store your books and course material so they are easily accessible is recommended. Your room need not necessarily be like a monastic cell, but be aware that private study can often require high levels of concentration and motivation, so a room full of audio equipment, a TV set, posters and so on could be a source of distraction. Clearly, the most important thing is that your interest, involvement and motivation in your course(s) is high so there is less likelihood of your mind wandering. When things become difficult, use a system of rewards such as playing a record or having a cup of coffee after a period of concentrated effort. You should aim to study for a minimum period of 20 minutes and a maximum period of 3 hours with hourly breaks, depending on the task and the level of difficulty of what you are studying.

Background noise

Most research on study would suggest that a quiet room to work in is desirable, but some students prefer to work with a low level of background music. In this case it could well be that if you are used to a noisy environment most of the time: traffic; jukeboxes in pubs etc. complete silence could be distracting.

Public Libraries

Some students find it difficult to work at home, either because the facilities for study are not available, or, as several adult female students have told me, they find themselves involved in household or child care activities. (Later in your course you could well explore why this may relate more to *female* than *male* students).In this case, either the home of a friend or relative with a spare room could be utilized, or the public library or local college library which are often open in the evenings and for parts of the weekend. One highly innovative student of mine with three energetic young children made herself a study space in a cupboard under the stairs!

If private study facilities are a problem, consult your teachers or tutors, who may well be able to help you.

Equipment for study

A desk or table top with an upright chair and some nearby storage facilities and bookshelves are recommended. Second hand filing cabinets can sometimes be purchased from second hand shops or office equipment suppliers. A filing system for handouts, notes, essays, course materials could prove very useful.

Ring binder files and A4 size paper are sometimes provided free or can often be purchased cheaply through college or school offices.

As well as ordinary writing pens, coloured pens and highlighter pens are particularly useful when making notes or stressing particular sections of books. Making your study material colourful and diagrammatic will make retrieval of information much easier later on.

Summary

It is important when starting your course to consider facilities for private study, as it is in such an environment that most of your productive work will be carried out. If you can have a comfortable, distraction-free study environment, you will probably find you get much more done in the available time and so produce more effective work. This means more free time for leisure activities and relaxation which benefits your overall performance.

B. THE STUDY OF SOCIOLOGY

Who studies sociology?

Perhaps more than any other subject, Sociology is taken by a wide range of students in relation to age and background. When Sociology became available as an Advanced level subject in 1966, it was mainly studied by older students in Further Education and Adult Colleges, often on a part-time evening basis. In recent years, however, Sociology has been increasingly studied by 16 to 19 year old students in school sixth forms, Tertiary and Sixth Form Colleges.

Initially there was resistance in some quarters to making Sociology available to younger students, as it was thought that the study of Sociology required maturity in outlook and experience of life outside the classroom. Yet there have been many able students of Sociology in the younger age group who have taken to the subject and done well. With regard to experience of life outside the classroom, there are key areas of sociological concern, which most younger sociology students have experienced. They have lived in families, some possibly experiencing the divorce of parents and living in one-parent families; they have had experience of at least eleven years schooling; and some have worked, either part-time in Saturday jobs or during school holidays.

ACTIVITY

There are two and a half to three times as many female Sociology students as there are male ones. Why do you think this is? (If you have difficulty with this question you may return to it later in the course after studying the Sociology of Gender). *Clue:* This ratio would be dramatically different on a Physics course.

Previous experience of studying Sociology

The majority of students at advanced levels have not studied Sociology before the age of sixteen. Even when GCE O level or GCSE Sociology has been taken, Sociology is not usually a subject which has been followed throughout one's school career. So you have not got the 'base' of knowledge to build on that you have with other subjects such as Mathematics, English, History, French or Sciences. However, in a more indirect sense Sociology does have a 'base' in that all new students of the discipline have experienced the subject matter of Sociology by virtue of being members of society themselves. This can, as one famous founding father of Sociology, Max Weber, emphasized, have advantages, in that we all possess an insider's perspective on the subject matter. There are disadvantages, however, in that our view of society can be somewhat blinkered by our experience and we may find it difficult to be objective. Another sociologist, Peter Berger, points to the need for the good sociologist to become an alien in his or her own familiar society, as such familiarity can breed inattention to what is going on sociologically. These themes will be dealt with in more detail in later sections, but for the moment consider the following:

ACTIVITY

In a cartoon Popeye and Bluto are babysitting and Bluto grabs Sweet Pea the baby from Popeye, saying he knows all about babies, as he was one himself once!

Discuss in pairs how this might be of relevance to the difficulties of studying Sociology?

Sociology as a discipline

> 'Sociology is better understood as a series of questions on the nature of society with no set answers, than as a set of agreed findings.'
> Mike O'Donnell, *A New Introduction to Sociology* (Harrap, London, 1981) p.7

> 'Other subjects deal with facts, Sociology is all opinions'
> (1st year student).

Probably one of the earliest things you will realize in your study of Sociology is that it is a discipline which is full of controversy and conflicting viewpoints. Sociology appears to have a diversity of approaches to its subject matter which is not encountered to the same extent in other subjects. Not only do sociologists disagree about a number of theoretical approaches or perspectives, but they have conflicting views on whether Sociology could or should be scientific, what are the appropriate methods to employ, whether to study large numbers of people or a few, and so on. A glance at some of the more recently established textbooks will endorse this and some even point to this diversity of approach by the use of the word 'Perspectives' in their titles. Put simply, to the newcomer it might appear that Sociology is a mess, a view endorsed in the following quote:

> 'Its arguments fail to come to firm conclusions, its inquiries do not close off avenues of dispute, its studies do not fit together in neatly cumulative ways, and it has no fundamentals to speak of.'
>
> Anderson, Hughes and Shorrock, *The Sociology Game* (Longman, London, 1985) p.x

However, the authors do add that this situation is typical of more disciplines than one might imagine, including scientific ones, a theme which is looked at in more detail in later sections.

To the student, this initial appearance of uncertainty can have both positive and negative aspects. On the positive side, Sociology can be seen as a stimulating and challenging subject, which encourages argument and debate. In this sense the study of Sociology is an exciting endeavour. However, it can also be expected that there will be negative aspects, in that the new student feels unsettled and unsure, more particularly so if he or she is used to an educational environment where 'facts' and 'answers' have constantly been provided.

It would seem that Sociology is more prepared than most disciplines to introduce controversy at advanced level rather than at degree level or beyond. It does at times seem to teachers of Sociology that the expectation from advanced students is high in comparison with other subjects, in that students are confronted from the outset with complex and sophisticated arguments and debates, some of which are at the forefront of knowledge in the subject.

A factor to be taken into account here, however, is the difference in all subjects when you move from the more structured lower level work to advanced levels, where controversy and differing explanations are brought in. The possibility of explaining the world in different ways has at this stage to be grasped both in scientific and non-scientific subjects.

At advanced level, all subjects introduce students to controversy and different viewpoints. In Biology the student is made aware that Darwin's 'Laws' of Evolution are far from clear cut and uncontroversial; Physics students learn of Heisenberg's 'Uncertainty Principle' in Quantum Mechanics (which states that it is impossible to measure the position and momentum of a particle simultaneously with more than strictly limited precision); Economics students discover that Economists disagree as to the causes of inflation or the way to reduce high levels of unemployment; Psychology students find that there are Behaviourist Psychologists who have different views from Cognitive and Humanist Psychologists; and so on. Advanced students are therefore generally made aware that their subjects do not simply involve learning an accepted body of knowledge. Rather, they are introduced to a world of arguments, debates and differing interpretations of what is or is not important or correct in a subject.

ACTIVITY

Consider any other subjects you may be studying. Are you assuming that you are about to be presented with a set of facts about which there is no controversy? Discuss this with the subject tutor and consult your textbooks. You will probably find that this is not the case in any subject at advanced level. So it would appear that your initial impressions of uncertainty in Sociology also apply to the study of other advanced subjects.

Is Sociology different in approach from other subjects?

Where Sociology may be seen as different from other disciplines is in the more direct political inferences that can arise when society is examined critically. A sociological study of inequalities of opportunity between different social groups such as men and women, blacks and whites, and the middle and working classes can obviously lead to the making of political judgements as to how these inequalities may be ended. Other subjects, on the other hand, may give the impression of being non-political, objective or neutral, this being particularly the situation in the pure sciences such as Physics and Chemistry. However, even this is debatable, as a historical and sociological study of scientific progress would show. The knowledge of the scientific laws of navigation in the 15th and 16th Centuries enabled imperial powers such as Britain, Portugal and Spain to traverse the globe, not just for the purposes of discovery and peaceful trade but for plunder and wealth which enhanced the global political power of such countries. In more recent times the political issues concerning the scientific development of nuclear energy are well known.

Coping with controversy

So what do the points raised in the foregoing section mean for you as a new student of Sociology? You need to get away from a way of thinking which concerns itself with *the* correct approach, expecting clear cut answers to questions, or the seeking of 'facts' about the nature of society.

You have to approach Sociology with an interested, enquiring and open frame of mind, which is aware that uncertainties and controversy will be encountered.

Facts

> 'Truth is never pure and rarely simple'
> Oscar Wilde, *The Importance of Being Earnest* (1895) Act 1

> 'There are no "raw facts" in science; there are only facts within a specific conceptual framework'
> Berger and Kellner, *Sociology Re-interpreted* (Penguin Books, Harmondsworth, 1981), p.43

Facts are true statements supported by evidence, but the question of evidence can be crucial, as in most subjects new evidence is constantly being unearthed which can either support or challenge accepted facts. Some facts can change over a period of time in the light of experience, testing and the addition of more knowledge. For example, it was once scientific 'fact' that the earth was flat, that you could make gold from base metals and that the solar system revolved around the Earth, all of which have been disproved in the light of new evidence. Some 'facts', and this is particularly true of Sociology, are the product of interpretation and are subjective rather than objective. If you consider official statistics on crimes such as burglary and robbery, these may appear to be accurate, precise and factual accounts of the amounts of this type of law breaking activity. However, as you will discover in your course, this is not necessarily the case, since statistics are produced by the police and related agencies as a result of members of the public reporting such events. It could well be that some crimes are not reported for a variety of reasons. For example, the victims of robbery might be embarrassed at their inability to safeguard their property, judge the sum of money too small to bother about, or simply not want the police to be involved in their problems. So the 'fact' of the amount of crime revealed by the statistics is clearly open to question.

REMEMBER

Facts can be changed in the light of new evidence and in isolation do not tell us much about the world.

Consider the following comparison of a scientific approach to facts and a sociological one:

(1) FACTS AND MEDICAL SCIENCE

The Proposition 'Many people who smoke get cancer and heart disease' is correct and can be supported by evidence, but in isolation such a statement may be of little use. Further questions could be raised in the light of statements such as, 'Some people who don't smoke develop cancer or heart disease'. What is required is an examination of factors like the *probability* of a smoker compared to a non-smoker getting cancer or heart disease. The "why?" questions in relation to the statement above are even more difficult to answer and need the careful weighing of evidence and the analysis of related variables such as diet or stress, before a satisfactory explanation of the causes of diseases such as cancer can be given.

It will be noted as you proceed through your course that explanations in terms of probabilities, the weighing of evidence and the analysis of related variables, as in the example above, typify the work of the sociologist.

As a comparison consider the following:

(2) FACTS AND SOCIOLOGY

In 1984 there were 158,000 divorces granted in the United Kingdom compared to 27,000 in 1961. (Source: *Social Trends,* 1986).

As with the statements about smoking, such a statement only raises further questions.

It might be inferred from this statement that the institution of marriage and family life are more unstable today than in the past. However, when you study this topic in your Sociology course, you will find that this is not necessarily the case. For example, some sociologists would argue that it is the greater ease of divorce in recent times which make the rate higher than in the past. Correspondingly, the portrait of stable family life earlier in the century could well be incorrect, as historians have shown (Reference: Michael Anderson, 'How much has the family changed?', New Society (27 October, 1983)

You will find that the 'fact' of high divorce rates leads to argument and debate amongst sociologists as to the interpretation of the reasons for the statistics, which could include, besides the increased availability of divorce, the changed position and role of women in society, and changed attitudes to divorce. You will also discover if you study the sociology of the family that a high percentage of divorcees remarry, so the 'fact' of rising divorce rates does not necessarily lead you to conclude that the institution of marriage is breaking down.

REMEMBER

Facts lead invariably to interpretation, opinion, evaluation and judgement, activities which should be a constant feature of your Sociology course.

Now do the following exercise:

EXERCISE

TWO VIEWS ON RAPE

The facts and fears of crime

Crime in Britain is a serious—and, in some parts of the country, an acute problem. Fear of crime even more so. But, in the midst of another week of headlines, panics and instant solutions, it is more than ever necessary to hang on to some facts and to a sense of perspective.

Fact number one: Britain is not a rape-torn society. Last year, according to the figures that were issued yesterday, there were 1,842 recorded rape offences in the entire country. That is 1,842 too many, but it is not, overall, a large total. It does not justify the claims that rape is widespread. The overwhelming majority of women in this country are not at risk from rape. Nor does the increase of 29 per cent in the total compared with 1984 necessarily imply that rape is spreading as rapidly as may appear. Part of the increase in recorded rapes is attributable to an increase in publicity about what are seen as more sympathetic police rape handling procedures introduced since 1983. There may also be other reasons why raped women are more ready to report the assault. This is not to say there has been no increase in real terms. But it is to say that the wilder headlines this morning have at least as much to do with selling newspapers and creating a climate of fear as they have to do with objective risk assessment.

Some critics will respond: "Of course the figures are low. Women are afraid to report rapes." That claim is undoubtedly true—as it is with almost all crime. But, again, a sense of proportion is needed. The frequently made claim that one in every six women in the country has been raped is simply unreliable and is based on unsound research techniques. What is probably true is that the official figures understate rape by about half and that, in particular parts of the inner cities (as the recent

Islington crime survey shows), the statistical threat of rape and other forms of assault (as distinct from harassment) is much higher still. Taking harassment into account, more than half the women in these areas are at risk each year. As a result of this combination of threats, a majority of women in such areas fear the outdoors and as many as a quarter are too afraid ever to go out at night. In reality, therefore, the problems affecting most women are harassment and fear, rather than rape. It's fine to ensure, as the Government and the Lord Chief Justice have done, that rapists are heavily sentenced. We support that both because rape is horribly serious in itself and because long sentences give clear messages to the public. But the current concern about anonymity rules for defendants is, in policy terms, irrelevant. Undoubtedly there is scope for some procedural improvement in police and court handling of rape cases. For the most part, however, public opinion needs no convincing about the seriousness of rape and the law is not deficient. The real problem is to tackle harassment and, through that, fear.

Fact number two: yesterday's crime figures offer what could be one of the most important messages of encouragement in recent years. Domestic burglary, one of the commonest crimes affecting ordinary people, has been rising and spiralling out of control for years. In 1985, however, it was down—by 4 per cent nationally and by 11 per cent in London. How can this be? The quotient of wickedness in the population has not changed. Unemployment hasn't been reduced. The housing crisis is no less acute than it was before. The reason is simple. A sensible publicity campaign has been launched by the Home Office, giving practical crime prevention suggestions and backed by community neighbourhood watch schemes and by greater police resources. The result is the first serious inroad into everyday crime for many years. It isn't perfect and it may yet stumble and slide, but at long last crime policy makers can say: This seems to work.

They will get no help from the rape-obsessed Fleet Street tabloids, but the Government ought now to learn the lessons of its modest achievements on burglary and try to apply them to sexual harassment. First, it needs to give a lead, by coordinating and cajoling rival services and professions into a joint approach. Second, it needs to persuade the public that there are practical things which they themselves can do to lessen the threat. Third, it needs to pressurise the police to divert resources into effective anti-harassment strategies and away from methods which alienate the public. Above all, the message should be that crime is preventable. But it can't be prevented by slogans.

Guardian Leader article, 14 March, 1986

Letter in Reply, 18 March, 1986

Sir.—I was astounded and angered by the off-hand, dismissive tone of your leader's discussion of rape (March 14 1986). Taking the figure of 1,842 as being an understatement of "about half", you reject all recent claims of a much higher hidden figure as being "simply unreliable". Clearly it is difficult to gain accurate figures as to the extent of rape but your statement that "the overwhelming majority of women in this country are not at risk from rape" is an irresponsible and literally inaccurate conclusion.

My reading of the contemporary literature, which has come from a range of important monitoring and research projects, is that reported rapes represent around ten per cent of actual rapes. Broader evidence now available from rape crisis centres, incest victims' support groups, women's refuges and campaign groups involved in counselling women who have been the victims of rape and incest suggests that even the figure of ten per cent is an overestimate.

What your leader fails to recognise is that a high proportion of rapes, again the figure is contentious, are committed by men known to their victims. These include husbands (although their rapes are not recognised in law), partners, fathers, boyfriends, relatives and "friends". My experience of these cases shows clearly that women rarely report such cases because they are pressured into protecting someone "close" to them and also because they believe, with good reason, that it will be assumed that they contributed to their own rape.

In these cases women are forced to have sex against their will in situations which could never lead to prosecution. The consequence is that they do not even consider reporting as a possibility.

Women who live outside the "conventional" boundaries of marriage know only too well that, if they report a rape and the case goes before the courts, it will be their sexuality which will be doubted and scrutinised. The Attorney General's now infamous statement of contributory guilt over the murders of prostitutes by Peter Sutcliffe is representative of a long tradition of similar statements made by judges and senior police officers.

Your Leader argues that women's fear of rape or sexual assault, despite the harassment experienced by women in the home, at work, on public transport, in leisure activities and in schools, is largely unfounded. There is no appreciation at all that sexual harassment, supported by the attendant imagery of pornography and "knife movies", is on the same continuum of violence against women as sexual assault and rape. Women do not need to be told this—they live it. It was well exemplified by Clare Short's appalling treatment meted out by baying Tory MP's during the Commons' debate over nudity in daily newspapers.

Yours sincerely,
Phil Scraton.
Centre for Studies in Crime and Social Policy,
Edge Hill College.

Show how the two sides use 'facts' to support their arguments.
Examine the difficulties presented by the use of such 'facts'.

Sociological perspectives

It has been suggested that there is not one unified approach or body of knowledge which is accepted by all sociologists. This can be confusing for the new student. The previous section looked at matters relating to facts in Science and Sociology and showed how 'facts' are often subject to interpretation and the raising of questions to be debated and researched. So 'facts' in themselves, whether about crime rates or divorce trends, become less certain to the student than they may have been formerly. The advice given was that the new student has to learn to cope with uncertainty and develop an enquiring and open mind. A related issue to this concerns the use of several perspectives in Sociology, this approach being particularly stressed by the largest examining board, the AEB.

COMPLEMENTARY PERSPECTIVES

Perspectives can either be complementary or conflicting. They are complementary where each perspective is seen simply as one of several ways of looking at the same thing, that is society and the social world, but from a slightly different angle of vision. This is where the use of perspective is similar to that in Art, where each perspective or angle of vision helps to make a complete picture. So sociologists studying the family may look at various aspects of the family, for example, the 'problem' of the working wife and mother or the role of the family in relation to socialization and social control of children. These two different emphases are both based on a common assumption that there is a dominant type of family and that the family is necessary in society. In this way the two approaches or perspectives can be seen as complementary.

CONFLICTING PERSPECTIVES

Perspectives can be seen as conflicting when one perspective cannot co-exist with another, because to accept one is to deny the other. So biblical versions of Creation and the Coming of Man are in contradiction with biological and scientific versions of the same events. In Sociology, the study of the family from a feminist perspective would conflict with traditional sociological approaches. Feminist sociologists would stress the exploitation and oppression of women within the family, which leads to questions concerning the necessity of the family if women are ever to lead full lives, offering equality of opportunity with men.

Another feature of using perspectives is that they can oversimplify and create boundaries which in reality do not exist. A recent report by A level examiners complained of the 'ritualistic incantations of the perspectives response which amounts to little more than crude juxtaposition'. This indicates dissatisfaction with students who apply a simplistic perspectives 'formula' to every question, usually involving three main approaches, functionalist, conflict and interactionist. This indicates that the student is unaware that sociologists often tackle common theoretical problems. Many sociologists do not believe that one 'theoretical package' or perspective is adequate for explaining the complexity of the social world.

However, this is not to deny that perspectives in Sociology can have their uses as a way into the examination of a sociological topic or phenomenon, which can be complex and difficult to analyse without an organizing principle provided by a perspective.

ACTIVITY

Consider other subjects you may be studying. Are there a number of approaches or is *one* approach suggested?

EXERCISE

Use the introductory chapter of your textbook to find out what are the major perspectives in Sociology and briefly summarize their main themes.

C. THE LANGUAGE OF SOCIOLOGY

The vocabulary of Sociology (jargon)

> 'It's only words'
>
> The Bee Gees

> 'Sociologists invent the words that mean industrial disease'
>
> Dire Straits

Of all academic subjects, Sociology seems to be the discipline which is most often singled out for criticism with regard to the language used, which is sometimes disparagingly referred to as jargon or mere gobbledegook. Most of the dictionary definition quoted reflects this negative view of jargon. The satirical magazine 'Private Eye' often pokes fun at the over-complex use of language and jargon in the professions with its 'Pseuds' Corner' column as well as more specifically at the medical profession in 'A Doctor Writes'.

> *Jargon* (Dictionary Definition: Chambers' 20th Century Dictionary)—'Chatter, twittering: confused talk: slang: artificial or barbarous language: the terminology of a profession, art, group, etc'.

EXERCISE

'A Sociologist Writes'

Shaking hands—a symbiotic salutation ritual which is common in primary interactional meetings between two societal members as a display in the affective domain.

Write your own versions of 'A Sociologist Writes' for other everyday activities:

e.g. Posting a letter
Taking the dog for a walk
Going to a party/disco
A football match.

A Doctor writes
Crossing your legs

AS A Doctor, I am often asked "Doctor, can crossing my legs be a health hazard?"

Well, at present we Doctors still know comparatively little about the potentially dangerous effect of leg-crossing on *translimbus limbus normalis* as it is known to the medical profession.

What happens normally is that the patient raises one leg (it could be either, depending on the circumstances) and rests it on top of the other.

A patient may perform this motion up to a hundred times during the course of a normal waking day.

Generally speaking crossing your legs is a perfectly safe and healthy procedure. But there may be cases when prolonged leg-crossing could lead to serious side effects e.g. paralysis and death.

If you are at all anxious about crossing your legs, you should seek expert advice.

In Sociology, a famous attack on overcomplicated language was launched by C. Wright Mills in his book *The Sociological Imagination*. He provides a 'translation' of the writings of the American sociologist Talcott Parsons, which condenses three paragraphs from Parsons' book *The Social System* into two sentences.

The need for jargon or precise terminology

> 'The charge that many sociologists write in a barbaric dialect must also be admitted with similar reservations. Any scientific discipline must develop a terminology. This is self-evident for a discipline such as, say, Nuclear Physics that deals with matters unknown to most people and for which no words exist in common speech. However, terminology is possibly even more important for the social sciences, just because their subject matter *is* familiar and just because words *do* exist to denote it.'
> Peter L. Berger, *Invitation to Sociology* (Penguin, Harmondsworth, 1970), p.25.

In the above passage, Berger points to the need for jargon in scientific subjects and also to the acceptance of its usage in a field like Nuclear Physics. However, as Berger suggests in his last sentence, there is, if anything, a greater need for precise terminology when a discipline has as its subject matter the familiar and everyday. To illustrate this, consider the example of the word 'family'. Now it could be seen at a glance that everyone 'knows' what a family is. Most of us are born into a family, and live and die within a family. But what does a 'family' mean?

Consider the following:
Is it our parents and brothers and sisters living at home?
Does the word family mean more than this? What about aunts, uncles, grandparents, cousins?
Don't we also belong to the wider human family?
Sometimes managers tell their workers that 'we all belong to one big happy family in this factory'.

The single word 'family' can contain several layers of meaning which can relate to context and so on. So when sociologists study the family in society, they need to be very clear on this and ask questions such as 'What type of "family" are we dealing with here?'

D. CRITICAL THINKING IN SOCIOLOGY

'The world is not what it appears to be'
Berger and Kellner, *Sociology Re-interpreted* (Doubleday, Garden City, N.Y., 1981), p.12

Reconsider some of the points raised in the earlier section on facts. The aim was to try to get you into a critical frame of mind when any 'facts' are considered, whether they are scientific, such as making a statement about the connection between smoking, cancer and heart disease, or sociological, such as the relation between divorce rates and family stability.

Sociology, in company with other academic subjects, employs what Berger and Kellner have termed a 'debunking angle of vision' where there is a constant attempt to question assumptions about the social world. In Sociology three types of critical thought can be identified:

(1) Critical thinking about society

This is where you would be expected to develop an analytical and critical approach to your examination of society. Consider the following table which compares individualistic, naturalistic and sociological explanations of poverty, industrial conflict, suicide, marriage and woman's role. The first two types of explanation may well reflect a common view but are they based on clear evidence and sound analysis?

EXERCISE

Table 1.1

Explanation of:	Individualistic	Sociological
Poverty	People who are poor are so because they are afraid of work, come from 'problem families', are unable to budget properly, suffer from low intelligence and shiftlessness.	Contemporary poverty is caused by the structure of inequality in class society and is experienced by those who suffer from a chronic irregularity of work and low wages.
Industrial conflict	Industrial conflict is caused by the interference of influential individuals or 'agitators' in the work-place.	Industrial conflict only occurs and is only sustained because of the existence of widespread grievances among the work-force.
Suicide	The most individual of all acts committed by a person of unsound mind.	The frequency, location, and type of suicide is governed primarily by social factors such as religion, family and marriage patterns and not individual factors.

Table 1.2

Explanation of:	Naturalistic	Sociological
Marriage	It is only natural that a man and woman should live together for life because they fall in love and want to raise children.	Monogamy is only one form of marriage, predominant in Western society. For example, polygyny (a man with more than one wife) and polyandry (a woman with more than one husband) also exist in other societies. Marital patterns depend on a variety of economic and social factors. The eligibility of marriage partners depends on the class and status position of the individuals.
Woman's role	It is important that the woman should be at home to raise her children because this satisfies her maternal instinct and the children's need for a mother.	Women stay at home because it is a widespread social expectation that the home is the correct place for them to be and because of limitations on the opportunity to do otherwise. Socialisation of children is just one function of the institution of the family which could be performed in non-familial contexts.

T. Bilton et al, *Introductory Sociology* (Macmillan, London, 1981)

Look closely at each of the individualistic or naturalistic explanations and make criticisms in the light of the sociological explanations. What questions would the sociologist level at the person explaining things in individualistic or naturalistic terms?

So at the sociological level other forms of explanation are offered which move away from blaming the individual for his/her poverty, suicide or from seeing things like marriage and woman's role as 'natural'. Sociologists examine in an analytical manner such factors as the way society works to reward some as compared to others or to reinforce one particular view of marriage and woman's role.

(2) Critical thinking about Sociology

As you become more involved in the study of Sociology, you will be encouraged to examine society critically in the way outlined above, and you will also be expected, with encouragement from your teacher, to think critically about different sociological approaches or perspectives, as discussed earlier. In connection with this, some sociologists describe Sociology as an *argumentative* subject, which is more akin to Philosophy, than to *knowledge* subjects like Linguistics or Physics. (For further discussion of this theme see Anderson, Hughes and Sharrock, *The Sociology Game* (Longman, London, 1985))

Consider a further example from the Sociology of the family. One perspective that has dominated sociological theorizing about the family in society is that of functionalism. This presents a stereotypical view of the nuclear family, comprising a male breadwinner, a housewife and dependent children. This relatively small stable unit is seen as ideally suited to 'fit' the needs of an advanced industrial society, where a geographically and socially mobile work force is required. Other features of this model of the family stress its functions of socializing the young (parents bring up children to conform to the dominant norms and values of society) and its role in stabilizing adult personalities (the family provides a safe retreat from the pressures and strains of the everyday world).

The first thing to reflect on when considering such a model is whether its implied harmony and stability conform to the reality of family life. Think of your own house at breakfast time, when everyone may be going out to school, college or work! Is the assumption that all families have two parents correct?

EXERCISE

A significant proportion of wives and mothers go out to work. Use a statistical reference work like *Social Trends* (available in most libraries) to find out the percentage who do.

You would also need to examine other sociological approaches to the family, such as Marxism and Feminism. What is their view on the family? Put simply, Marxists stress the ideological nature of the family and its role in reproducing capitalist values, and feminists concentrate on the exploitative aspects of women's role within the family as unpaid houseworkers and child carers.

A consideration of different sociological models of the family shows, therefore, that as well as needing to think critically about the way society works, you are expected to be able to think critically about differing sociological approaches or perspectives. Do they provide satisfactory explanations of the phenomena being examined? Are there alternative explanations? This should be the type of thought which develops during the course.

(3) Critical thinking about common sense and experience

In the early stages of the course, where some of your previous assumptions about society may be challenged, it is hard not to fall back on common sense and experience. We are all members of society and have experience of life which is important to us and is a part of our sense of identity and self-esteem. Therefore you may react defensively when sociological views are seen to undermine your experience.

One problem is the tendency for some students to generalize from the individual to the societal level. A student may say: 'My dad does all the housework and cooking in our house', and use this as a basis to challenge sociological views which suggest that it is women who perform the majority of such activities. The student needs to adopt a critical frame of mind, reappraising such experience and raising questions concerning whether the father's behaviour at home is sociologically typical or untypical and why this is the case. A number of interesting explanations could emerge:

Mum and Dad may have reversed roles, Dad deciding to stay at home while Mum goes out to work, OR Dad's household activity may be connected with his own experience with his parents, OR Dad has studied Sociology and he thinks it right that he should participate in household activity!

Part of the problem for new students, as was discussed in the earlier section on 'facts', is in coming to terms with Sociology as a *probabilistic* discipline rather than a discipline which makes definite statements and provides facts or laws about human societies. So in the example of the houseworking father, the student generalizing from a personal experience is arguing from a faulty logical position.

So the situation above involves the following process of reasoning:

(1) SOCIOLOGICAL STATEMENT
The majority of people doing household tasks and caring for children are female.

(2) STUDENT'S STATEMENT BASED ON EXPERIENCE
'My father does the household tasks and childcare in our home.'

(3) WRONG ASSUMPTION WHICH MISSES THAT SOCIOLOGICAL STATEMENT IS PROBABILISTIC
Therefore Statement (1) is incorrect.

(4) FURTHER SOCIOLOGICAL QUESTIONS ARE REQUIRED TO CLEAR UP THE MISCONCEPTION
How typical is your father?
Is there role reversal? e.g. father redundant, mother going out to work.
One parent family?

EXERCISE

Construct a similar chain of reasoning focusing on a student whose mother has a better job and earns more than a father.

In connection with using personal experience in the early part of your course, it must always be remembered that Sociology makes probabilistic statements as follows:

"In the majority of cases . . .
"In 75% of cases . . .
"In general . . .

Such probabilities will always allow for exceptions which could relate to your individual experiences, but in the case of Sociology 'the exception does not disprove the rule'. This is a vital point to bear in mind.

Conclusion

This chapter has outlined some of the main difficulties encountered by students in the early stages of a Sociology course. As well as having the right motivation for the course and organizing yourself for the requirements of advanced study, you need to be prepared to encounter a discipline which will not provide neat 'packages' of knowledge to be learned. Sociology confronts uncertainty and controversy from the outset and involves debates and arguments between differing approaches, perspectives or viewpoints. Sociology may undermine taken-for-granted views of the social world which you had previously held. Once you have understood this, you will be well prepared to proceed with the course and you should find much that is stimulating and challenging, which will soon overide any early feelings of uncertainty.

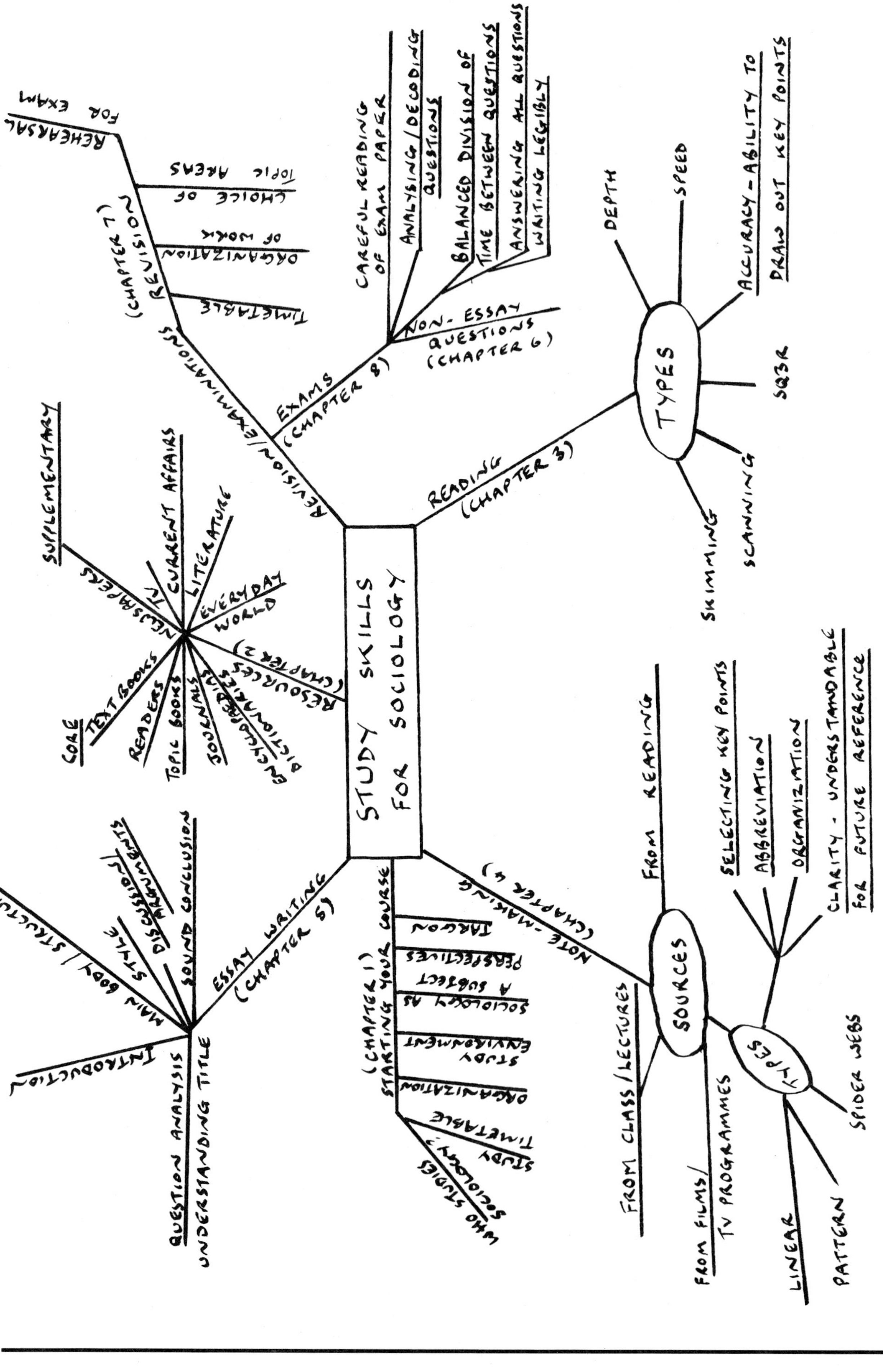
STUDY SKILLS FOR SOCIOLOGY
READING (CHAPTER 3)
TYPES
DEPTH
SPEED
ACCURACY – ABILITY TO DRAW OUT KEY POINTS
SQ3R
SCANNING
SKIMMING
REVISION/EXAMINATIONS
REVISION (CHAPTER 7)
TIMETABLE
ORGANIZATION OF WORK
CHOICE OF TOPIC AREAS
REHEARSAL FOR EXAM
EXAMS (CHAPTER 8)
NON-ESSAY QUESTIONS (CHAPTER 6)
CAREFUL READING OF EXAM PAPER
ANALYSING/DECODING QUESTIONS
BALANCED DIVISION OF TIME BETWEEN QUESTIONS
ANSWERING ALL QUESTIONS
WRITING LEGIBLY
RESOURCES (CHAPTER 2)
SUPPLEMENTARY
NEWSPAPERS
TV
CURRENT AFFAIRS
LITERATURE
EVERYDAY WORLD
CORE TEXT BOOKS
READERS
TOPIC BOOKS
JOURNALS
ENCYCLOPAEDIAS
DICTIONARIES
ESSAY WRITING (CHAPTER 5)
INTRODUCTION
MAIN BODY/STRUCTURE
STYLE
DISCUSSIONS/ARGUMENTS
SOUND CONCLUSION
QUESTION ANALYSIS
UNDERSTANDING TITLE
STARTING YOUR COURSE (CHAPTER 1)
JARGON
PERSPECTIVES
SOCIOLOGY AS A SUBJECT
STUDY ENVIRONMENT
ORGANIZATION
STUDY TIMETABLE
WHO STUDIES SOCIOLOGY?
NOTE-MAKING (CHAPTER 4)
SOURCES
FROM READING
FROM CLASS/LECTURES
FROM FILMS/TV PROGRAMMES
TYPES
LINEAR
PATTERN
SPIDER WEBS
SELECTING KEY POINTS
ABBREVIATION
ORGANIZATION
CLARITY – UNDERSTANDABLE FOR FUTURE REFERENCE

RESOURCES FOR SOCIOLOGY

CHAPTER 2

A. THE IMPORTANCE OF RESOURCES

> 'There appears to be a continued reliance on only one or two basic texts. The better candidates stood out as those who had had access to a wider variety of resource material . . .'
> (JMB Examiners' Report:
> A level Sociology, 1985)

The subject matter of Sociology, human society, is in several senses all around you, so Sociology should not be seen as something to be learned solely from a textbook. Textbook sources are essential as basic guides to major sociological themes and issues, but the more successful students are able to gather information more widely, thus fostering their 'sociological imagination'.

This chapter points to the wealth of material that is available for an advanced course. The aim is to guide you through some of the available resources so that you can eventually become adept at acquiring information not just from class material but from a wide variety of sources which include newspapers, magazines, television and even novels. Familiarize yourself with what is available and where to obtain it as early in the course as possible.

It has been indicated in the last section that success in advanced study requires independence and self-direction on the part of the student. This means developing the ability to research and acquire information and knowledge without the need for a teacher or tutor to be constantly directing you. Teachers are able to give advice and guidance on some of the available resources and where to look for them, but increasingly the onus should be on students to research actively and pursue their studies independently. This is why the effective use of private study periods is so essential if good progress is to be made through the course.

In the twenty years or so since Sociology has been available as an A level subject, resources such as textbooks, readers, topic books and journals have increased in number dramatically. The Sociology sections of bookshops and libraries now contain a wide range of material for students. In one sense this wealth of material is to be welcomed, but in another the sheer quantity can at times be overwhelming. This chapter aims to introduce some of the resources that can be used, but before this it is necessary to refer to an important aspect of your activity as a student, and that is the use of the library as a resource and study centre.

The Library

Treat the library as your workshop as well as a resource centre. Full-time students will probably receive a copy of an introductory textbook as well as other resources such as readers and topic books. This will be insufficient for advanced study, so the fullest use possible should be made of the library throughout the course. Familiarize yourself with the library as soon as possible. Find out:

1. The location of the library
2. Is there an information leaflet?
3. Opening hours: Do these include evenings or weekends? Such times can be useful for private study, particularly when facilities at home are limited. If your college or school library does not open in the evenings or at weekends, many Public Libraries do, so also consider making use of this facility.
4. Is there a plan of the layout of the library? Where is the Sociology and related Social Sciences section?
5. How many books can you borrow and for how long?
6. Library services: Ask the Librarian. These could include:
   photocopying facilities;
   reservation of books (If a book is not immediately available ask if it can be reserved);
   inter-library loans (If a book is not stocked by the library, it can be obtained for a small fee from a national interlending network to which most libraries belong.)

Don't just see the library as a place for borrowing books, use it as an information and working centre. Research and explore topics covered in class. Look for studies referred to by your teacher and read and make notes from them. You may be able to locate studies which are not referred to in textbooks or standard literature. Read serious daily newspapers such as 'The Guardian' or 'The Times'. Most libraries stock them. Read and make notes from magazines and journals such as 'New Society' for up to date material.

LIBRARY CLASSIFICATION SYSTEM

Most libraries use the Dewey Decimal system of classification for their non-fiction works. This is divided into ten broad general groups of subjects as follows:

000 General—reference books
100 Philosophy
200 Religion
300 Social Sciences
400 Languages
500 Science
600 Technology (Applied Sciences)
700 The Arts
800 Literature
900 General Geography and History

Each of these ten main classes are further subdivided into ten, so that the Social Sciences class 300 covers Sociology under 301. Decimal points are then used to classify further subdivisions:

e.g.	301	Sociology
	301.4	Social Structure
	301.42	Marriage and the Family
	301.421	Structure and Functions of the Family
	301.4212	Nuclear Family

and so on, so that the longer the number after the decimal point the more specific the subject.

All libraries have indexes of their stock, most commonly a card index, but in recent years microfiche systems have been increasingly introduced. Ask your librarian for advice on the use of these. Indexes are either author indexes, which are used if you are looking for a specific author and book title, or subject indexes, which can be used when researching a particular topic area. For example, if you were writing an essay on poverty in relation to social class, you could look in the index and find the appropriate reference number on Poverty: Social Class which is 301.441. You could then seek information on the shelves featuring this number.

FINAL COMMENT

Familiarize yourself with and find out as much as possible about the organization of the library as soon as you can. Effective use of the library is a vital part of your development as a student.

B. WRITTEN SOURCES

Textbooks

You will need at least one basic textbook for the duration of the course, as this provides your initial reference point for finding out about particular themes or topic areas. In recent years a number of good introductory Sociology texts have become available. The following are some examples of the better known ones:

Haralambos, M., *Sociology: Themes and Perspectives* (University Tutorial Press, Slough, 1985) (2nd Edition)

O'Donnell, M., *A New Introduction to Sociology* (Harrap, London, 1981)

Bilton, T. (et al.), *Introductory Sociology* (Macmillan, London, 1981)

McNeill, P. and Townley, C., *Fundamentals of Sociology* (Hutchinson, London, 1981).

Earlier textbooks were either criticized for being too academic for A level students or for concentrating on a particular approach or perspective, rather than emphasizing the diversity of approaches which characterize the subject.

All of the so called 'new generation' of textbooks mentioned above provide good sound introductions to Sociology. Most are written by experienced teachers and stress the diversity of Sociological approaches or perspectives and the argumentative nature of the discipline.

IS MORE THAN ONE TEXTBOOK NECESSARY?

You should use one textbook as your central source when starting to investigate a particular topic or theme, so you need to read it thoroughly, making notes or, if it is your own, underlining key points or sections as you make your way through the book. Most textbooks try to cover the major areas of the syllabus such as the origins of Sociology, Sociology in relation to science, key theoretical debates and methods in Sociology as well as dealing with key topics such as the family, education, work and technology, women's changing roles, inequality and stratification, power and politics, and urbanization, crime and deviance. However, one important drawback, if only one textbook is used, is that you may become over-reliant on it and not look elsewhere. Remember that there are a number of approaches to Sociology and there are debates and arguments as to the interpretation of these, so it is always useful to read sections on a topic in other textbooks to find differences of interpretation and emphasis. Another feature of the main textbooks is that in any particular one some sections of the syllabus may be omitted or given a fairly superficial coverage.

Most of the newer texts stress the interdependence and overlap between key topic areas and the core theoretical and methodological debates which relate to them. It is these latter which new students have difficulty 'unravelling' in the early stages of the course.

You will probably find that copies of alternative textbooks are available either through your teacher or in the library, so make sure you avail youself of them as much as possible.

EXERCISE

Go to the library and consult as many introductory Sociology textbooks as possible, comparing their contents, chapter headings and indexes. Are there any significant differences in approach or subjects dealt with? Make a note of them. Another useful exercise is to compare an older Sociology textbook (for example Steven Cotgrove, *The Science of Society,* (Allen and Unwin, London, 1978)) with a more recent one. Note how the subject has been changing in recent years with reference to approaches, key concerns and topic areas.

Topic books

In recent years a number of topic books have been published. Some cover in more detail topic areas also found in basic textbooks, such as Gender, Religion, or Sociological Theory and Methods. Others cover topic areas such as Health and Social Policy, Development or Race Relations, which are recent additions to the Sociology syllabus. Topic books provide useful supplementary reading, giving extra depth and detail to topics which are sometimes introduced in textbooks at a fairly basic level. Another feature of recent topic books is that they are written specifically for the A level student.

The main disadvantage of topic books is that they could give an impression of self-containment, which may lead to the topic being seen in isolation from other sociological areas. In this regard general textbooks have an advantage as they point to the overlap and interconnectedness between various topic areas. Examples of some currently available topic books are:

Clarke, E.A. and Lawson, T., *Gender: an Introduction* (University Tutorial Press, Slough, 1985).

Pilkington, A., *Race Relations in Britain* (University Tutorial Press, Slough, 1984).

Jones, P., *Theory and Method in Sociology* (University Tutorial Press, Slough, 1985).

Trowler, P. and Riley, M., *Topics in Sociology* (University Tutorial Press, Slough, 1984).

Frith, S., *The Sociology of Youth* (Causeway Press, Ormskirk, 1984).

Foster-Carter, A., *The Sociology of Development* (Causeway Press, Ormskirk, 1985).

Glover, D., *The Sociology of the Mass Media* (Causeway Press, Ormskirk, 1985).

Marsh, I., *Sociology in Focus: Crime* (Longman, Harlow, 1986)

Ball, S., *Sociology in Focus: Education* (Longman, Harlow, 1986)

Readers

A Reader is a collection of short articles and book extracts, which can either be from original sources written by key figures in the development of Sociology, extracts from empirical research studies, or material from unusual or previously unavailable sources. Such collections are useful as a resource, in that they give the student a chance to read original material rather than second or third hand accounts. However, condensed versions of or short extracts from original works may lead to misrepresentation of the author's central ideas, so that editors of such readers have to be careful with the extracts they use, in order that they provide an accurate reflection of the main points and issues of the original.

Readers provide supplementary material which helps to add depth to your knowledge of a topic as well as the experience of reading original sociological writers. It is recommended that you have access to at least one of the following:

O'Donnell, M. (ed), *New Introductory Reader in Sociology* (Harrap, London, 1983)

Butterworth and Weir (eds), *The New Sociology of Modern Britain* (Fontana, Aylesbury, 1984) (3rd Edition)

Thompson, K. and Tunstall, J. (eds) *Sociological Perspectives* (Penguin Books, Harmondsworth, 1971)

Bocock, R. (et al) (eds) *An Introduction to Sociology* (Fontana, Aylesbury, 1980)

O'Donnell's Reader is particularly useful, as he introduces each reading with a short explanatory passage, as in the following example:

21 A.H. Halsey: Changes in the British Occupational and Class Structures and in the Distribution of Income and Wealth

The following passage from A.H. Halsey's *Change in British Society* reviews changes in occupational structure and in the distribution of income and wealth during the twentieth century. His analytical framework is broadly Weberian. Two groups receive less attention than needed: the upper class and women. Halsey tends to concentrate on the upper middle class (professional and managerial stratum), sometimes referred to as just the middle or service class, the lower middle class, and the manual working class. The wealth and power of the upper class does not depend on occupation but on private (often inherited) property and capital and social connections. Their economic, social and political position is controversially examined by Anthony Giddens in the third extract in this section (see also Marx and Engels: Class Conflict, Section 1, reading 2). Women, too, are relatively neglected here for the (surely inadequate) reasons Halsey gives (p.134). We include two extracts on the place of women in the occupational and stratificational systems in the next section (readings 26 and 27).

Halsey is quite wide-ranging and subtle in his treatment of inequality: he allows for the operation of the informal economy in discussing 'affluence' and his analysis of trends in the distribution of income and wealth is complex enough to discredit any notion that redistribution from the rich to the poor has indisputably occurred. Usefully, he introduces the dimension of the liberal-Marxist ideological debate in his analysis of the latter point. He also discusses the relative ineffectiveness of State intervention in fiscal policy (mainly taxation), the social services, and occupational welfare in bringing about greater equality.

On one matter, Halsey's material is badly in need of updating. His unemployment chart shows the number of people out of work was moving towards one million by 1976. In February 1982, the number of unemployed was over three million. If we also include the increasing numbers of relatively low paid people in the 1980s, then the number of poor has become significantly greater than in 1976.

(Reading 21 from A.H. Halsey, *Change in British Society* (Oxford University Press, 1978), pp.24–39.)

M. O'Donnell, *New Introductory Reader in Sociology* (Harrap, London, 1983)

Original Sociological Sources (1) Empirical research studies

'. . . weaker scripts on the whole were short on reference and data.'
(Cambridge Examiners' Report: A level Sociology, 1984)*

'. . . arguments used in answering the questions must be supported by empirical evidence.'
(Cambridge Examiners' Report: A level Sociology, 1984)*

Published accounts of original research can provide insights into the way professional sociologists go about their work. In addition, they are sometimes a useful counter to the approach offered in some mainstream texts, which may give the impression that sociologists can always be neatly categorized in terms of one of three main sociological perspectives or one particular method of research. A perusal of some research studies will show that labels as to a sociologist's perspective or methodological orientation are often difficult to apply.

An illustration of this is provided by the work of Dr Eileen Barker, who studied a religious sect nicknamed 'The Moonies', the official title of which is the Unification Church. In the following extract she points to the issues arising from considerations of theoretical approach and methods of research:

ACTIVITY

Read the following passage and note how Eileen Barker raises questions concerning the difficulty of carrying out sociological research. Use your books to find out what is meant by 'verstehen'.

> There is in sociology a time honoured dichotomy between those schools that focus on interpretive understanding and those that stress more behaviourist, positivistic or scientific approaches. What was to be my approach? Should I perhaps become an ethnomethodologist and investigate the taken-for-granted Moonie world, or should I regard Moonies as rats and dispassionately watch them running about their mazes, dismissing from my mind any notions of meaning or conscious purpose that could not be covered by stimulus/response or the more sophisticated operant-conditioning models of behaviour? Or perhaps I should forget about individuals as such and search only for structures and functions at a societal level? Would I adopt a philosophical anthropology that asssumed we are complicated but nonetheless determined, reacting robots: or are we free, initiating creators, capable of self determination? Whom would I believe when it came to descriptions of the Unification Church? Who was more trustworthy, the brainwashed Moonies themselves or the sceptical critics? Would I learn more as an outsider or an insider? What was the true reality and how could I get to know about it? Was I to be guided by fact or theory or both? But then, which theory, and how was I to get at the facts?
>
> I began to realize that there could be no one answer. Several of the perspectives seemed to be necessary while none was sufficient for my purposes. I was convinced that without having a methodology as scientific as possible one would be unlikely to produce a sociological contribution that would add anything to all the claims and counter-claims which already existed. But it also seemed that without *verstehen*, or in other words some kind of empathic understanding, one could not hope to find one's data in the first—or in the last—place.

Open University D207 Media Booklet (1982), p.6, Research Project 1, Eileen Barker, 'Sect and Society'

However, some research studies display their theoretical leanings or perspective more clearly. Theoretical orientation is clearly presented in the following extract from Westergaard and Resler's *Class in a Capitalist Society* (Penguin Books, Harmondsworth, 1976):

> 'Our perspective is Marxist. And our aim has been to present an interpretation of the class structure of Britain—as an example of contemporary Western capitalist societies—which is both Marxist and anchored in empirical fact.' Source: p.ix, Preface.

THE USEFULNESS OF RESEARCH STUDIES

Some questions on examination papers specifically ask you to explore a sociological issue based on a research study you have read. Detailed knowledge of a number of studies is useful for adding to your understanding of the topic researched, e.g. gender and schooling, race and ethnicity, the lives of workers in a factory, changing attitudes to class and so on. More indirectly, a thorough knowledge of a number of research studies is useful for the insights gained into issues of theory and method which are central to Sociology. If you are on a two year course, a good time to read some sociological research studies is during the summer term and vacation at the end of the first year. Other opportunities could be during private study periods or evenings and weekends.

It is useful to compile a table or a card index system, so that when you have read a study you can enter up the details for future reference. Also you should make notes as you carry out your reading (see Chapter 4).

USING A RESEARCH STUDY

Some studies are easier to read and make notes on than others. A study of professional criminals, carried out by Professor Laurie Taylor of York University, provides a witty and entertaining account of his encounters with the criminal underworld, where he is introduced to conmen, fraudsters, bank robbers and shoplifters by his friend, the former bank robber, John McVicar. (L. Taylor, *In the Underworld* (Unwin Paperbacks, Hemel Hempstead, 1985))

The study itself raises a number of issues, some connected with its aim to appeal to a wider audience than sociologists. It is certainly more readable than many sociological studies, as it is full of amusing stories, anecdotes and descriptions of criminals' activities, which make the book very entertaining.

When reading such a work, always do so in a critical frame of mind, raising questions such as:
'How objective was Laurie Taylor in his research?'
'Was there exaggeration and distortion?'
Such questions concern themselves with the relationship between theory and method in Sociology, themes which you will explore in detail during your course. Compare the following extracts A and B, one from Taylor's study which highlights a long standing problem of 'involvement' in studies of this kind and the other a much earlier study by William Whyte into street gang life, where similiar problems of method and involvement are encountered.

ACTIVITY

The first extract illustrates the difficulties some sociologists face when they become involved with research.

Extract A

'That's all very well, *Professor* Taylor, but why didn't you let the police know that a crime was about to be committed?'

'Well, you see, *I* thought that . . .'

'Surely, you were aiding and abetting?'

'Oh no. Not really. You see, I was just standing there in the street.'

'Your presence was quite enough to give encouragement. "Look", they could say to themselves. "How can this be wrong? Here's a Professor of Criminology, standing by and watching us get on with it!"'

'Well, I can only say . . .'

All this was last November, after a talk in Nottingham at a college of higher education. I was sitting, uncomfortably, in a corner of a seminar room, while some visiting policemen who'd been at my lecture took it in turns to complain about my romanticism—my complicity.

Eventually I managed to produce an answer. 'Look, they'd have commited the crime anyway. Whether I'd have been there or not. They completely ignored me. Looked through me. I couldn't have stopped them if I'd wanted to. And if I had reported the matter to the police, it wouldn't have led to their detection. I had no idea where they were going or whose cheques they were carrying. By the time they were found, they'd have been clean. What's more, any such call to the police would have meant the end of the project. Absolutely no more introductions by John and so no chance whatsoever to discover anything of interest about the tactics and style of a group of criminals about whom we know so little.

'What's more, what's more it wasn't as though anyone was going to get hurt. The whole point about traveller's cheques is that the owner is quickly and fully compensated when they go missing. Banks themselves are well able to stand the loss: not only do they charge for the travellers cheque service, but of course they make substantial revenue from the short-term investment of all the hard cash they get from the sale of the cheques. So naturally they wish to keep them as attractive as possible by making them so easy to use. The fact that illegitimate users find them almost as readily negotiable is just a small cost to set against the overall benefits. If I also tell you that this was the only time I was ever in a position like this during twelve months of research, wouldn't you say that this one small incident might be condoned. Wouldn't you?'

But unfortunately, by the time I'd put all that together, the policemen had long since gone home, and I was at least half way round the Doncaster by-pass on the way back to York.

L. Taylor, *In the Underworld* (Unwin Paperbacks, Hemel Hempstead, 1985)

What perspective is Laurie Taylor using?

Extract B

As I began hanging about Cornerville, I found that I needed an explanation for myself and for my study. As long as I was with Doc and vouched for by him, no one asked me who I was or what I was doing. When I circulated in other groups or even among the Nortons without him, it was obvious that they were curious about me.

I began with a rather elaborate explanation. I was studying the social history of Cornerville— but I had a new angle. Instead of working from the past up to the present, I was seeking to get a thorough knowledge of present conditions and then work from present to past. I was quite pleased with this explanation at the time, but nobody else seemed to care for it. I gave the explanation on only two occasions, and each time, when I had finished, there was an awkward silence. No one, myself included, knew what to say.

While this explanation had at least the virtue of covering everything that I might eventually want to do in the district, it was apparently too involved to mean anything to Cornerville people.

I soon found that people were developing their own explanation about me: I was writing a book about Cornerville. This might seem entirely too vague an explanation, and yet it sufficed. I found that my acceptance in the district depended on the personal relationships I developed far more than upon any explanations I might give. Whether it was a good thing to write a book about Cornerville depended entirely on people's opinions of me personally. If I was all right, then my project was all right; if I was no good, then no amount of explanation could convince them that the book was a good idea.

Of course people did not satisfy their curiosity about me simply by questions that they addressed to me directly. They turned to Doc, for example, and asked him about me. Doc then answered the questions and provided any reassurance that was needed.

I learned early in my Cornerville period the crucial importance of having the support of the key individuals in any groups or organizations I was studying. Instead of trying to explain myself to everyone, I found I was providing far more information about myself and my study to leaders such as Doc than I volunteered to the average corner boy. I always tried to give the impression that I was willing and eager to tell just as much about my study as anyone wished to know, but it was only with group leaders that I made a particular effort to provide really full information.

My relationship with Doc changed rapidly in this early Cornerville period. At first he was simply a key informant—and also my sponsor. As we spent more time together, I ceased to treat him as a passive informant. I discussed with him quite frankly what I was trying to do, what problems were puzzling me, and so on. Much of our time was spent in this discussion of ideas and observations, so that Doc became, in a very real sense, a collaborator in the research.

This full awareness of the nature of my study stimulated Doc to look for and point out to me the sorts of observations that I was interested in. Often when I picked him up at the flat where he lived with his sister and brother-in-law, he said to me: "Bill, you should have been around last night. You would have been interested in this." And then he would go on to tell me what had happened. Such accounts were always interesting and relevant to my study.

Doc found this experience of working with me interesting and enjoyable, and yet the relationship had its drawbacks. He once commented: "You've slowed me up plenty since you've been down here. Now, when I do something, I have to think what Bill Whyte would want to know about it and how I can explain it. Before, I used to do things by instinct."

However, Doc did not seem to consider this a serious handicap. Actually, without any training he was such a perceptive observer that it only needed a little stimulus to help him to make explicit much of the dynamics of the social organization of Cornerville. Some of the interpretations I have made are his more than mine, although it is now impossible to disentangle them.

W.F. Whyte, *Street Corner Society* (Chicago Press, Chicago, 1943)

A useful extract which raises issues concerning participant observation as a method of research.

How might a scientific (or Positivist) sociologist respond to the passage? Would he/she favour such research?

The 'perspective' in such studies is interactionist and the methods used are in-depth informal interviews and participant observation. Critics of such approaches in Sociology would point to their lack of objectivity, highly descriptive content, small numbers of people studied and to the difficulty of making generalizations from such research. A comparison of such studies with others like Westergaard and Resler's *Class in a Capitalist Society* or Wilmott and Young's *The Symmetrical Family* would show alternative approaches in theory and method as well as different levels of difficulty in reading. As you make progress through the course, you will find that you will be able to read and make notes from more challenging and complex studies, but at first it is advisable to select studies which you find interesting and easy to read.

REFERENCES—some suggestions for reading:

Earlier Studies (somewhat dated, once regarded as 'classics' in their fields, but can still be profitably studied).

1. Whyte, W.F., *Street Corner Society* (Chicago Press, Chicago, 1943)—Study of Italian slum life in Boston, USA.
2. Dennis, N. (et al), *Coal is our Life* (Eyre and Spottiswoode, London, 1956)—Study of mining community in Yorkshire pit village.
3. Wilmott, P. and Young, M., *Family and Kinship in East London* (Penguin Books, Harmondsworth, 1957)—Community study of working class in East End. Looked at effects on family life of breakdown of traditional communities.
4. Goldthorpe, J. (et al), *The Affluent Worker* (3 volumes) (Cambridge University Press, Cambridge, 1968 and 1969)—Study of car workers. Examined 'embourgeoisement thesis'.
5. Tunstall, J., *The Fishermen* (MacGibbon and Kee, London, 1962)—Study of trawler-men in Hull, an 'extreme' occupation.
6. Jackson, B. and Marsden, D., *Education and the Working Class* (Routledge and Kegan Paul, London, 1962)—Study of 'successful' working class grammar school pupils in Huddersfield.
7. Lockwood, D., *The Blackcoated Worker* (George Allen and Unwin, London, 1958)—Study of changing nature of clerical and office work. Are such workers now 'working class'?
8. Townsend, P., *The Family Life of Old People* (Penguin Books, Harmondsworth, 1963)—Study of old age and poverty.
9. Kerr, M., *The People of Ship Street* (Routledge and Kegan Paul, London, 1958)—A community study of a working class street in Liverpool.
10. Gavron, H., *The Captive Wife* (Penguin Books, Harmondsworth, 1966)—Study of wives and mothers at home.

More recent studies

1. Taylor, L., *In the Underworld* (Unwin Paperbacks, Hemel Hempstead, 1985).
2. Pryce, K., *Endless Pressure* (Penguin Books, Harmondsworth, 1979)—Study of black West Indian community in St Paul's district of Bristol.
3. Stanworth, M., *Gender and Schooling* (Hutchinson, London, 1983)—Study of sexual divisions in the classroom.
4. Rutter, M. (et al), *15,000 Hours* (Open Books, London, 1979)—Study of effects of different comprehensive schools on children.
5. Oakley, A., *The Sociology of Housework* (Martin Robertson, London, 1974)—Study of middle and working class housewives.
6. Nichols, T. and Beynon, H., *Living with Capitalism* (Routledge and Kegan Paul, London, 1977)—Study of workers in a chemical factory.
7. Beynon, H., *Working for Ford* (Allen Lane, London, 1973)—Study of car workers at Ford's Halewood plant.
8. Oakley, A., *Subject Women* (Fontana Paperbacks, London, 1982)—Study of women's experience in society today.
9. Wilmott, P. and Young, M., *The Symmetrical Family* (Penguin Books, Harmondsworth, 1973)—Study of changes in family life.
10. Glasgow University Media Group, *Bad News* (Routledge and Kegan Paul, London, 1976)—Content analysis of Television news reportage to investigate possibility of bias.

Research studies you have read can be referenced as follows:

(1) As a Table

TITLE	AUTHOR	SUBJECT/TOPIC	THEORETICAL APPROACH	METHODS	BRIEF SUMMARY (SEE NOTES ALSO)
'The Making of a Moonie' (BLACKWELL, LONDON, 1985)	Eileen Barker	Religion Sects Youth	Various (See notes)	Questionnaires In-depth Interviews Participant Observation	found that Moonies not 'irrational' – valid reasons for joining. Seek 'answers' Moonies provide in world full of problems
'The Sociology of Housework' (ROBERTSON, LONDON, 1974)	Ann Oakley	Women, Housewives, Work	Feminist	Interviews Questionnaires	Housework an unpaid 'job' as any other. V. long hours. Tied in with identity of woman.
'Endless Pressure' (PENGUIN, HARMONDSWORTH 1979)	Ken Pryce	Youth, Race, Community, Urban issues Conflict	Various mainly conflict	Participant Observation	Study of black community, found (pre-1979 riots) many strains, alienation

(2) In a Card Index

AUTHOR	TITLE
Laud Humphreys	The Tea-Room Trade (DUCKWORTH, LONDON, 1970)

Study of homosexual (male) encounters in public places i.e. public lavatories

Theoretical Approach: Phenomenological / Interactionist

Methods: Interviews, Partial participant observation (acted as a lookout)

Study shows stereotypes of such people as 'perverts' / 'deviants' incorrect. Many – married, some with children. Sample included middle class professionals – 'pillars of the community'.

Note:
Always record your reading as shown in the above examples. This can act as a 'key' in to your more detailed notes.

More detailed advice and guidance on reading Sociology books is given in Chapter 3, but at this point it is necessary to stress the importance of being able to scan and pick out relevant information and make good notes, which can be referred to on future occasions. Many studies have introductory chapters where the aims of the research are spelt out, concluding chapters where a summary is provided and appendices which sometimes deal with problems of research methods—see the following examples. These help the reader to gain an insight into the study, when there may be insufficient time to read the complete work thoroughly.

Some studies have in their appendices useful passages or summaries of the problems arising when research is carried out, as in the following example:

Appendix

Method of Study

The main method adopted for the research on which this study is based was participant observation. Participant observation, because it deposits one inside the culture of the group studied and forces on one the role of involved actor and participant, affords the academic researcher a unique opportunity of getting the right leads and following through situations whereby he can replace superficial impressions with more accurate insights. By combining his outsider's perception with an insider's view of the way of life under consideration, the researcher can thus get behind the statistical shapes and patterns and explore at first hand the wide variety of adaptive responses he encounters, studying them from the value position of the people themselves, in their own terms and on their own ground. All the time he does this through prolonged, intensive direct exposure to actual life-conditions over a relatively long period of time. Not only can the findings of this intensive approach supplement and add significance to data gathered by more quantitative techniques, they can generate fruitful hypotheses which quantitative research can later refine and test.

Ken Pryce, *Endless Pressure* (Bristol Classical Press, 1979)

ACTIVITY

1 First, our investigation clearly showed that secondary schools varied markedly with respect to their pupils' behaviour, attendance, exam success and delinquency. This had been observed before, but the demonstration that these differences remained *even after taking into account differences in their intake* was new. This suggested that, contrary to many views, secondary schools *do* have an important influence on their pupils' behaviour and attainments.

2 Secondly, we found that these variations in outcome were systematically and strongly associated with the characteristics of schools as social institutions. The pattern of findings suggested that the associations reflected a causal relationship. There were indications from previous studies that this might well be the case but it had not previously been systematically demonstrated by comparing different secondary schools.

3 Thirdly, the research showed *which* school variables were associated with good behaviour and attainments and which were not.

4 Fourth, the pattern of findings suggested that not only were pupils influenced by the way they were dealt with as individuals, but also there was a group influence resulting from the ethos of the school as a social institution.

We may conclude that the results carry the strong implication that schools can do much to foster good behaviour and attainments, and that even in a disadvantaged area, schools can be a force for the good.

M. Rutter et al, *15,000 Hours* (Open Books, London, 1979), p.205

Note how easy it is to highlight and make notes from this extract from the concluding chapter of a study.

Find an account of a sociological research study and see if there are similar summary sections to the foregoing and make notes.

Original Sociological Sources (2) Works of the 'Founding Fathers' of Sociology

You will not be expected to read in detail the works of key early figures in the development of Sociology such as Marx, Weber and Durkheim, because their works are difficult and demanding for students at this level. Your main contact with such writings will probably be through your textbooks and Readers. It has already been suggested that second hand information has dangers of misrepresentation, so try to read a variety of summaries. More demanding and detailed treatments of the work of the Founding Fathers can be obtained from Fontana's *Modern Masters* series, which has separate volumes on Marx and Durkheim, and Tavistock's *Key Sociologists* series, which has separate volumes on all three.

More advanced reading can also be found in the following:

Giddens, A., *Capitalism and Modern Social Theory* (Cambridge University Press, Cambridge, 1971)

Fischer, E., *Marx in his Own Words* (Penguin Books, Harmondsworth, 1973)

Bottomore, T.B. and Rubel, M., *Karl Marx: Selected Writings* (Penguin Books, Harmondsworth, 1963)

Gerth, H.H. and Mills, C.W. (eds), *From Max Weber, Essays in Sociology* (Routledge and Kegan Paul, London, 1948)

Aron, R., *Main Currents in Sociological Thought*, Volumes 1 and 2 (Penguin Books, Harmondsworth, 1968, 1970)

If you wish to sample original works try the following:

Marx, K. and Engels, F., *The Communist Manifesto* (Penguin Books, Harmondsworth, 1967) Penguin edition with introduction by A.J.P. Taylor

Durkheim, E., *Suicide: A Study in Sociology* (Routledge and Kegan Paul, London, 1970)

Weber, M., *The Protestant Ethic and the Spirit of Capitalism* (Allen and Unwin, London, 1952).

Books of stimulus-response material

1. Haralambos, M., *Sociology : A New Approach* (Causeway Press, Ormskirk, 1984)
2. North, P.J., *Understanding Evidence* (Longman, London, 1984)
3. Burgen, A.D., *Comprehension Exercises in Sociology* (Thornes, Cheltenham, 1982)
4. Clarke, E.A. and Lawson, T., *Stimulus Questions in A-level Sociology* (University Tutorial Press, Slough, 1984)
5. Myers, D., *Stimulus Response Questions in Sociology* (Longman, London, 1984)

The first three are primarily aimed at O level students, but can sometimes be useful for higher level work as an introduction to the reading and analysis of sociological material. (4) and (5) are specifically aimed at the compulsory stimulus response question in the AEB examination.

Stimulus-response questions (see example opposite) centre around a piece of given material, such as a passage from a book, a statistical table or diagram, which is intended to provoke thought about the material's subject matter. A number of questions at various levels of difficulty are set, the answers to which range from brief definitions to more complex mini-essays. Advice on answering such questions is given in Chapter 6.

9A SKIN

Many people in Britain claim that the colour of a man and woman's skin is unimportant and that it is the 'foreign' habits and culture of coloured 'immigrants' that cause prejudice and discrimination. If these immigrants were as 'British' as the existing white population, discrimination would therefore disappear.

But what if a white Englishman were suddenly to turn brown? The following extract describes an interesting example:

. . . If they ask what difference the prejudice of white English people would make to their personal lives if their skin turned brown, they may like to reflect on the case of a Welshman, an ex-commando and former Services boxing champion, living in a Dorset town. He suffered from a kidney disease which meant that he had to seek lighter work. The disease also darkened his skin so that he was mistaken for a coloured man (Humphrey and John, 1971: 20–21). As a result he has experienced colour prejudice. 'It is not as if it happened just once. It might happen 10 times a week. I have known it to happen three times a day. Sometimes I have been stopped in the street by a stranger, who says something like: "You bloody wog, why don't you go back to the palm trees?"' He applied for work as a sales representative or insurance salesman only to learn (when they saw his face) that employers thought colour a bar: 'because I look like a Pakistani I cannot get a job' (*Guardian*, 24 July 1970). Two days later it was reported by the *Observer* that 'he is no longer to lose his home after all— although he can no longer keep up his mortgage repayments. His local council is to buy his house and rent it back to him at a rate he can afford . . . The local Lions Club has bought him a refrigerator, and paid for a course of driving lessons to help him get a job as a driver. He has been allowed to fall behind with his rates and electricity bills.'

(From *Racial Minorities* by Michael Banton, 1972)

1. What is the difference between 'prejudice' and 'discrimination'?
2. What does this passage tell us about the importance of skin colour for prejudice?
3. The man described in the passage received assistance in a number of ways. Is this the kind of assistance also generally given to 'real' Pakistanis? Give an explanation for your answer.
4. People are often surprised to hear a West Indian or an Asian talking with a strong Scouse, Cockney or Brummie accent. Account for this surprise.
5. Some white people go out of their way to be especially talkative and friendly to coloured people whom they meet at work, at parties and so on. Does this mean that they are not colour prejudiced?

A.D. Burgen, *Comprehension Exercises in Sociology* (Thornes, Cheltenham, 1982)

Dictionaries/Encyclopaedias of Sociology

Slattery, M., *The ABC of Sociology* (MacMillan, London, 1985)

Abercrombie N., Hill, S. and Turner, B., *The Penguin Dictionary of Sociology* (Penguin Books, Harmondsworth, 1984)

Mann, M., *The MacMillan Student Encyclopaedia of Sociology* (MacMillan, London, 1983)

Duncan Mitchell, G., *Dictionary of Sociology* (Routledge and Kegan Paul, London, 1980)

The International Encyclopaedia of the Social Sciences

Kuper and Kuper (ed), *The Social Science Encyclopaedia* (Routledge and Kegan Paul, London, 1985)

Such reference books are useful as a starting point for your exploration of a particular sociological theme or concept, as they provide short summaries and guides to the relevant issues. Sociological language or jargon has already been discussed and it is helpful to have access to short, clear explanations of what may seem to be complex terms. Terms which may be encountered early in the course such as positivism, functionalism and alienation can be looked up.

If you use such reference works in the early stages, you will gradually familiarize yourself with a wide variety of sociological terms, so that eventually you will gain the confidence to know a meaning and relate it to the context in which the word occurs. It is useful to have a notebook in which you compile a glossary. This can be in the form of your own brief version of new terms encountered, which can be referred to when you need to refresh your memory with a word or term.

Guides to Sociology essay-writing

Morison, M. and Pey, J., *Writing Sociology Essays* (Longman, London, 1985)

Lane, J.K., *A Practical Guide to A Level Sociology* (Nelson, Walton-on-Thames, 1985)

Writing essays is a central task for any Sociology student and Chapter 5 deals with this skill in detail. The references above also provide valuable guidance on question analysis, planning answers, the structure, content and style of an essay as well as examples of complete Sociology essays. There are possible problems with specimen answers, however, which students should bear in mind:

(1) Often such answers are of a very high standard, beyond that which could be reached by many students particularly under examination conditions.

(2) Writing style is very much an individual matter, so a specimen answer may not be of much help apart from the more technical aspects of presentation i.e. grammar, spelling, punctuation, paragraphing and so on.

(3) There are often several ways in which a particular question could be answered, all of which could be correct. Specimen answers can give the false impression that there is only one answer to a question.

(4) Students may attempt to memorize such answers so they can be reproduced in the exam, even when the question learnt is not the question asked, as the following comment notes:

> '. . . answers, however good, to questions that have not been asked will not obtain good marks'
>
> (Cambridge Examiners' Report: A level Sociology, 1984)*

If you are mindful of such dangers, specimen essays can be of use to show you how to approach a question with respect to content, points to cover and structure. They can also be used to compare with your own answer to the question set.

Journals

NEW SOCIETY

The weekly magazine 'New Society', can be a valuable source of additional information for Sociology students. It contains articles on sociological topics which can update your textbook sources, an example being an area of the syllabus like voting behaviour where, as examiners' comments have indicated, in some scripts, students fail to consider anything beyond Britain in the mid-1960's.

There are also summaries of recent research findings and book reviews, all of which can add to your stock of information. Another feature during term time is the fortnightly insert "Society Today" which is aimed specifically at GCSE and A level students. Each issue deals with a particular topic area from the syllabus.

Copies can be purchased more cheaply through a group subscription scheme, but even if you do not obtain your own copy, you should try to consult 'New Society' every week through your library. Use a regular private study period for such reading and make notes from articles or features which are relevant to your course.

'New Society' articles provide useful supplementary reading:

New Society 9 May 1985
THE RISE OF THE NEO-CONVENTIONAL FAMILY
ROBERT CHESTER
Have the old-style family, and the old-style male breadwinner, really gone? Not so—though a more subtle variant on the traditional family is emerging.

JANE FRENCH
New Society 7 March 1986
Gender and the classroom
The sexist attitudes of teachers may affect the way they treat their pupils. But the different behaviour of boys and girls in the classroom can also exert an influence.

'Society Today'—'New Society''s insert aimed at GCSE and A level students:

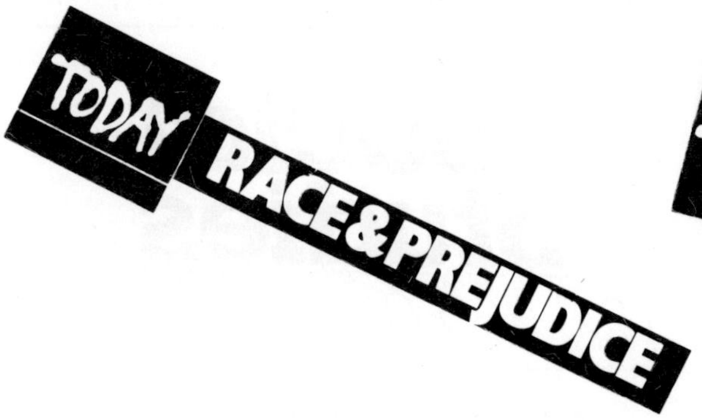
TODAY
RACE&PREJUDICE

TODAY
EDUCATION AND CLASS

EXERCISE

Example of a 'New Society' article updating textbook information on Social Mobility.
Read and make notes summarizing the key points:

Snakes and ladders

OBSERVATIONS ●

For most of us, social mobility means *upward* mobility—climbing the social ladder from the front room to the lounge to the drawing room. But in the real-life game of snakes and ladders, people slide down the snakes too—from the middle class to the working class. And some drop off entirely into unemployment. Back to square one, while the winners are already collecting their new homes, their swish cars, their foreign holidays.

In fact, the British working man's chances of climbing the ladder are as high as they have ever been. But since 1972, his chances of losing his job completely have risen steeply too. According to John Goldthorpe and Clive Payne of Nuffield College, Oxford, the chances of mobility for working class men have become "polarised" over the last decade.

It was Goldthorpe and Payne who, with Catriona Llewellyn, published a massive study in 1980 of male social mobility in the 50 or so years leading up to 1972. Now they have brought the story up-to-date, by comparing their 1972 figures with data collected in 1983 as part of the British General Election Study ("Trends in intergenerational class mobility in England and Wales 1972–83," Sociology, vol 20, No.1).

The earlier study showed that, during the middle years of the 20th century, the professional, administrative and managerial class (what Goldthorpe and Payne call the "service" class) expanded enormously, while the working class got smaller. It wasn't so much that society became more open and equal, but that economic growth changed the overall class structure, and men were able to move into jobs of a higher social and economic status than their fathers had had.

This meant that the service class came to contain many

people whose fathers had come from a lower class. In 1972, for instance, about 58 per cent of the service-class men in the survey had had fathers from the same class: the other 42 per cent had "risen" from other classes. Between 15 and 19 per cent of those in manual jobs in 1972 had slid down from a service class background. So upward movement was stronger than downward movement.

Goldthorpe and Payne say that 1972 was a watershed year: the last year of the "long boom," during which the capitalist world's economy seemed set for stable growth. In 1973, war broke out in the middle east, then oil prices rocketed, and 1974 saw international economic crisis.

But, interestingly, the strong upward trend of social mobility in Britain has continued through crisis and depression, and the working class is smaller than ever. In 1972, just under half the respondents said that they had manual jobs; by 1983, the figure was nearer one in three. And one in three had service-class jobs, compared with about one in four only eleven years previously.

What has made a difference is unemployment. Only 5 per cent of the men in the 1972 inquiry were out of work, and most saw themselves as between jobs. They expected their next job to be on the same level as their last.

But 1983 saw a changed picture. Almost 9 per cent of the sample were out of work—and, unlike the 1972 figures, that excluded those waiting to take up jobs. About 5 per cent had been out of work for more than a year. Most of these jobless men were from the manual working class—between 74 and 83 per cent, according to how "manual" jobs are defined.

It was when Goldthorpe and Payne decided to treat the unemployed as a class on their own, and ran their data through the computer again, that the new, strange and distinctive pattern emerged. In 1972, 16 per cent of the men from working class backgrounds aged between 20 and 34 had moved up the ladder into the service class, and 60 per cent had stayed in the working class. By 1983, prospects for that age group had improved: 22 per cent had moved into the service class, and only 40 per cent had stayed put. But 11 per cent had no job at all.

The chances of reward from playing snakes and ladders in Britain today may have increased, but so have the risks.

New Society, 7 March 1986

SOCIAL STUDIES REVIEW

This is published five times a year. It is specifically written for A level Politics and Sociology students and contains appropriate, up-to-date articles as well as useful features like students' essays with examiners' comments on them.

Social Studies REVIEW

The Sociology of the New Religions *Roy Wallis*

This study of the new religions which emerged in the 1960s and early 1970s focuses on their origin in traditional religion, their relevance to industrial society and their development in recent years.

In Search of the Hooligan Solution *John Williams*

This review of soccer hooliganism places the Brussels disaster in perspective, discusses current responses to the 'English disease' and looks at the uncertain future of the game.

Unemployment: Why Pick on Youth? *David N Ashton*

The social composition of the unemployed, its determinants and why young people should be hardest hit are the subject of this paper. The author goes on to contrast youth unemployment today with the problem as it existed in the last great recession in the 1930s.

Can Labour Rise Again? *Ivor Crewe*

Professor Crewe addresses the question at the centre of current political debate: can Labour recover from its disastrous performance in the 1983 general election?

The Life and Ideas of Karl Marx *John Hoffman*

The first in a series of articles devoted to political and social thought, this study charts the key developments in Marx's life and analyses the central tenets of Marxist theory.

Part-Time Working: Pragmatism or Patriarchy? *Angela Dale*

Angela Dale examines the seemingly anomalous increase in the number of women working part-time despite a general background of rising unemployment.

What is Positivism? Part One *Christopher G A Bryant*

Professor Bryant outlines the continuing debate among sociologists over the accuracy of classifying their subject as a 'science'.

Journals as a resource: Articles which have featured in recent editions of 'Social Studies Review'

Other journals

Your library may also stock quarterly journals such as 'The British Journal of Sociology' which is aimed at an academic audience, but which may occasionally feature articles and book reviews useful to you, in that they contain summaries of research findings or contributions to a debate.

The contents page shows some articles which can be very demanding for Advanced levels but articles marked (*) may provide useful reading.

The British Journal of Sociology

VOLUME XXXVII NO. 2 JUNE 1986

CONTENTS

Socialist stratification and sociological survival 157
Michalina Vaughan

Aristocracy and meritocracy in merchant banking 180
S.D. Chapman

Catch-up, distributional coalitions and government as determinants of economic growth or decline in industrialized democracies 194
Erich Weede

* Spectator violence at football matches: towards a sociological explanation 221
Eric Dunning, Patrick Murphy and John Williams

* Mugging as a moral panic: a question of proportion 245
P.A.J. Waddington

Has there been a British intelligentsia? 260
M.S. Hickox

Intellectuals and religion in Ancient Greece: notes on a Weberian Theme 269
Joseph M. Bryant

REVIEW ARTICLE

Max Weber: a monumental edition in the making 297
G. Poggi

BOOK REVIEWS

C. NUMERICAL DATA AS A RESOURCE

Graphs, Statistical Tables and Diagrams

> 'There are three kinds of lies—
> lies, damned lies and statistics.'
> Mark Twain

> 'There are two kinds of statistics, the kind you look up and the kind you make up.'
> Rex Stout

> 'I am one of the unpraised, unrewarded millions without whom statistics would be a bankrupt science. It is we who are born, who marry, who die, in constant ratios.'
> Logan Pearsall Smith

> 'He uses statistics as a drunken man uses lamp-posts—for support rather than illumination.' Andrew Lang

The following section is a brief guide to the use of numerical data as a resource for Sociology. Further advice specifically relating to answering Advanced level stimulus-response questions based on such data is given in Chapter 6.

Numerical data in the form of graphs, statistical tables or diagrams seem to be a source of difficulty for a number of students. One reason for this derives from earlier experiences of Maths. Some students say that when it comes to Maths and numerical information their minds go blank. In fact, complete innumeracy is very rare, but many students think it affects them.

To extract information from numerical data, you do not need a sophisticated grasp of formulae or to make complex calculations. All you need is the ability to see the total picture portrayed by numbers, tables and headings. Statistical tables are usually provided to indicate a trend; examples being demographic trends concerning changes in birth rates and mortality rates in the population; changes in crime rates; the numbers of working days lost through strikes; or improvements in living standards as reflected in the numbers possessing video recorders. Sociological statistics usually compare rates on a year by year basis during this century:

Households : by size

Great Britain

	Percentages					
	1961	1971	1976	1981	1983	1984
Households by size						
1 person	*12*	*18*	*21*	*22*	*23*	*25*
2 people	*30*	*32*	*32*	*32*	*32*	*32*
3 people	*23*	*19*	*17*	*17*	*17*	*16*
4 people	*19*	*17*	*17*	*18*	*18*	*18*
5 people	*9*	*8*	*8*	*7*	*7*	*6*
6 or more people	*7*	*6*	*5*	*4*	*3*	*3*
Total households	*100*	*100*	*100*	*100*	*100*	*100*
Average household size (number of people)	3.09	2.89	2.76	2.71	2.64	2.59

Source: *Social Trends 16*, 1986

You need to concentrate on the overall picture that the table is showing. What trends are indicated? What is the key information being offered? Exercises to help you gain confidence in the handling of statistics are set later in the chapter.

APPROACH STATISTICS WITH A CRITICAL FRAME OF MIND

Although they are exaggerated or humorous in intention, it is worth bearing in mind the quotes at the beginning of this Section. You should consider what is not shown by statistics, how and by whom they were compiled and for what purposes. Ask yourself whether the data is necessarily an accurate, correct or valid representation of the phenomenon dealt with.

EXERCISE

Which of the following, as represented by numerical data, are likely to be (a) the most accurate, and (b) the least accurate? (Give reasons for your answer)

Births
Crimes
Divorces
Deaths
The numbers attending Church regularly
Strikes
Marriages

What sociological issues regarding the family, industrial disputes, religious trends or crime in society may be hidden in such numerical data?

Numerical data alone are insufficient for sociological purposes. They need placing in a context and interpreting, as discussed in relation to the use of facts in an earlier section. This can lead on to discussion and debate as in the following simple example:

EXAMPLE

Church attendance

In 1851, according to a religious census, approximately 40% of the population attended Church regularly. In recent years the proportion is approximately 10%. What conclusions can be drawn from such information? A simple one may be that fewer people today are religious than in former times, but several qualifications can be made. For example, the 40% of the population who attended regularly may have done so because of social convention, pressure from family or peers, or because it was expected by their employers. The 10% of the population who attend regularly today, on the other hand, are more likely to go because they really want to. So it could be said that there are no fewer sincerely religious people today than in the past, when social pressures made people attend Church. Comparisons between different periods in the form of statistics may obscure and confuse issues rather than clarify them. You should be aware of this.

GRAPHS AND STATISTICS

Graphs can best be described as diagrammatic representations of data, and statistical tables can be seen as numerical representations of data. Both forms are useful to the sociologist and can be a vital component of a topic or theme. A graph of divorce statistics in England and Wales this century can lead to an examination of the implications of such trends for marriage and family life. A table of crime statistics can raise questions as to the nature of crime rates, types of crimes committed, categories of offenders and related matters in the sociology of deviance.

USING GRAPHS

At the end of this section you should be able to:
—understand what graphs are;
—recognize the main type of graph;
—extract information from a graph;
—apply this information to the analysis of sociological topics.

The first thing to do when considering a graph is to avoid getting distracted by the figures. Concentrate on titles and headings and ask yourself 'what is this graph telling me?' In this way you can obtain the overall sense of the information provided. When you have done this, you can get down to the details of the numbers, percentages or related information and apply them to the topic concerned.

TYPES OF GRAPH

Graphs can be presented in several forms the main ones being:

(i) *Line (or Linear) Graphs*

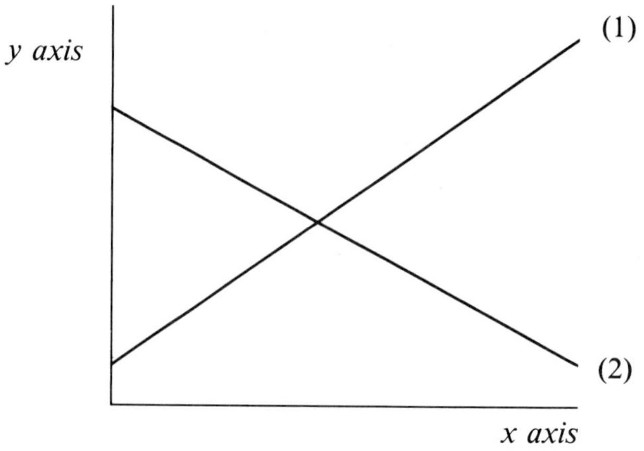

This is probably the most familiar from school Maths. Often in Sociology the x axis is used to represent years e.g. the bottom left hand corner could be the year 1870 and the bottom right hand corner the year 1985. The y axis could be divorces per annum, numbers in the UK population, crime figures and so on. A rise in the diagonal line from left to right indicates an increase in such figures (Diagonal (1)). If y represented the birth rate or the level of illiteracy in the population then Diagonal (2) would be more appropriate as a fall in the diagonal line from left to right indicates a fall in such figures.

(ii) *Pie Graphs (Charts)*

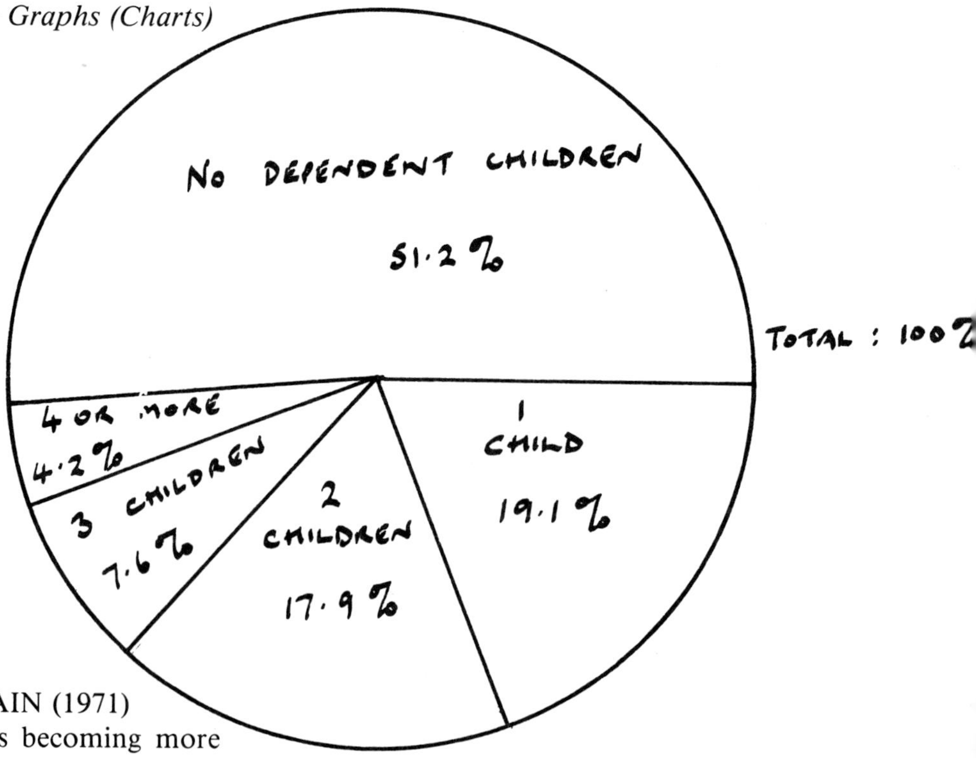

FAMILIES IN GREAT BRITAIN (1971)

This method of presentation is becoming more popular, as it is easy to extract information and in some senses it can be seen as resembling a cake (or pie) cut into slices.

(iii) *Bar Charts/Histograms*
These are similar in that information is presented in rectangular blocks but differ in that the blocks in bar charts are self contained pieces of information, whereas in histograms the data is continuous.

BAR CHART

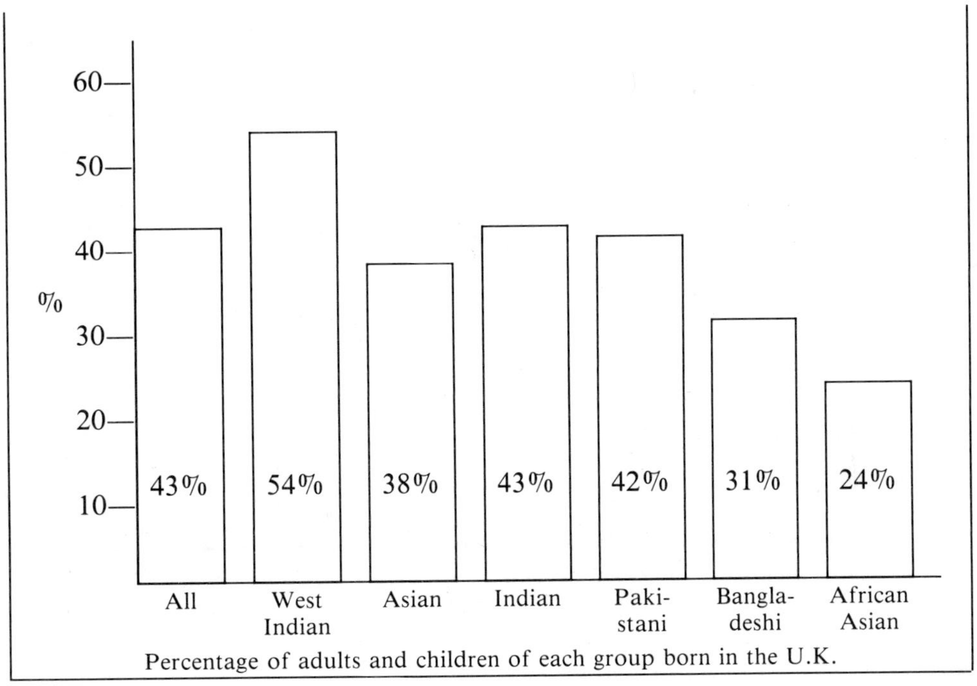

N. Abercrombie *et al*, *Contemporary British Society* (Polity, Oxford, 1987)

HISTOGRAM
Persons found guilty of, or cautioned for, indictable offences per 100,000 of the population aged 10 and over, 1960–76

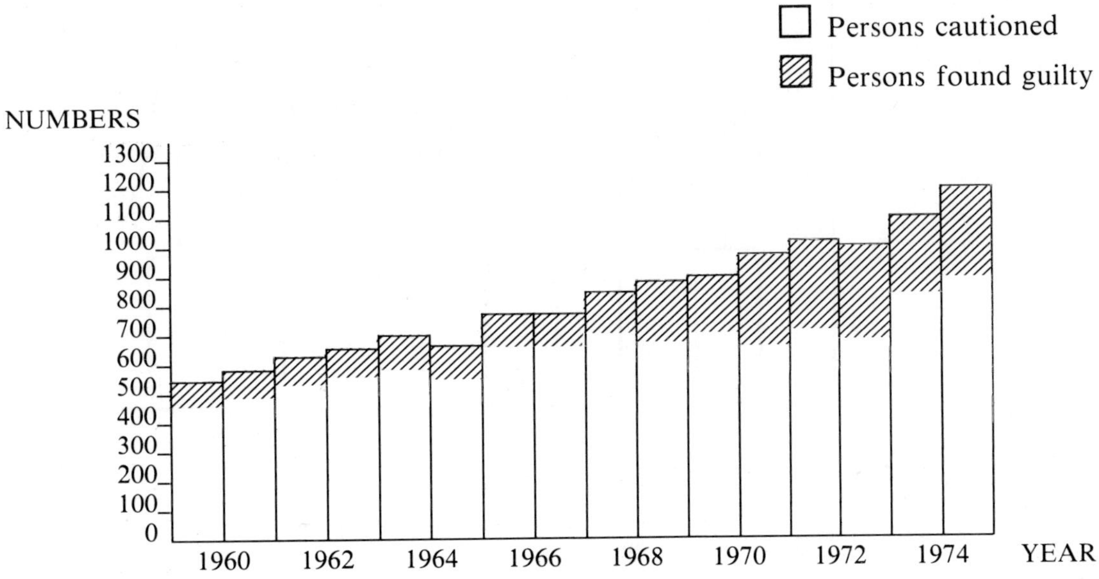

Adapted from criminal statistics—England and Wales

(iv) *Pictogram (Pictograph)*

This is becoming an increasingly popular method of data presentation. As you can see from the figure, data is represented pictorially and the pictures represent proportions which are to be compared with the size of other pictures of the same object.

Percentage of the Population Owning Their Own Houses

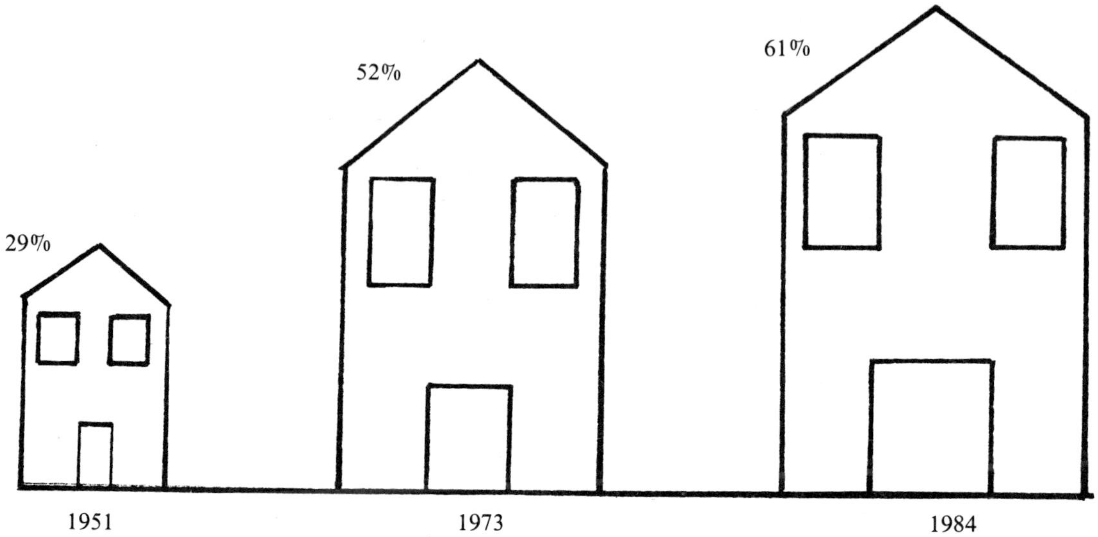

Source: *Social Trends 16*, 1986

Sometimes a figure will represent a fixed quantity e.g. 1 figure represents 10 million units, as in the diagram below. This method is now often used in demographic data presentation.

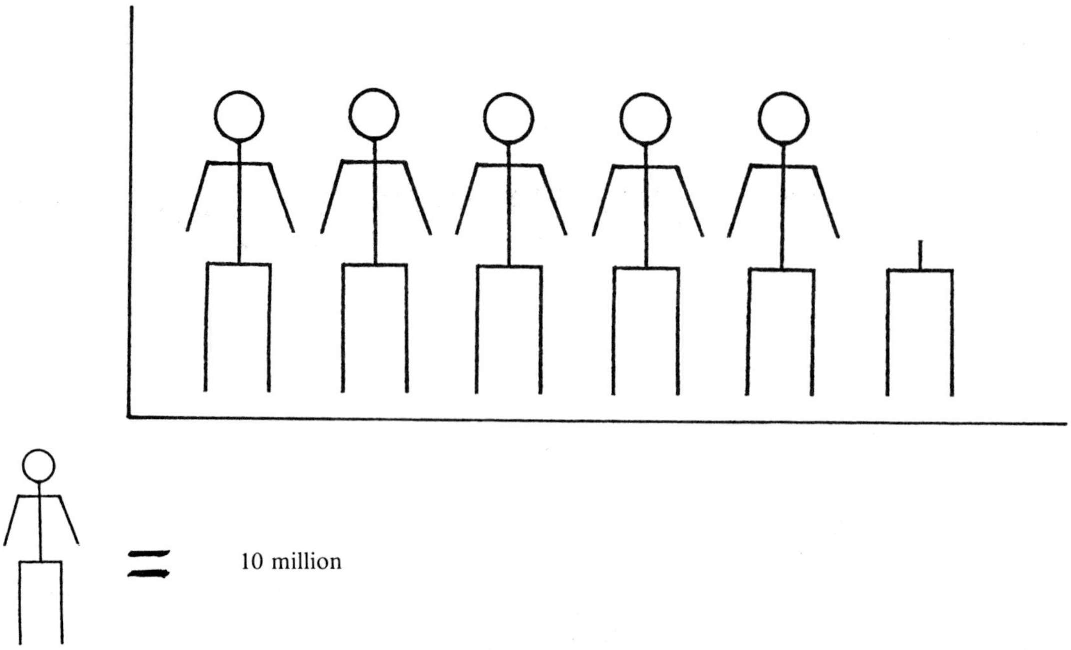

EXERCISE 1

Using the following information, draw examples of a pie graph, a bar chart and a pictograph—

Population of the U.K.

OCCUPATIONAL GROUPINGS	PERCENTAGE OF TOTAL
(i) Higher-grade professionals, administrators, managers, and proprietors.	7.7
(ii) Lower-grade professionals, administrators and managers. Supervisors and higher-grade technicians.	6.0
(iii) Clerical, sales and rank-and-file service workers.	7.4
(iv) Small proprietors and self-employed artisans. The 'petty bourgeoisie'.	12.6
(v) Lower-grade technicians and foremen. The 'aristocracy' of labour.	11.3
(vi) Skilled manual workers in industry.	27.2
(vii) Semi- and unskilled workers in industry.	22.6
(viii) Agricultural workers and smallholders.	5.2

EXERCISE 2

(More difficult. You will need to use textbooks and library resources to complete this).

1. Which of the above groups would you call (a) working class? and (b) middle class? Give reasons.
2. Which group(s) may feature in debates about—
   (a) embourgeoisement? and (b) white collar proletarianization? and why?
3. Which group(s) have proportionately (a) increased and (b) decreased in numbers this century? Give reasons.
4. A.H. Halsey, *Origins and Destinations* (O.U.P., Oxford 1980) collapses the eight occupational groupings into 3 classes. What are these and what are Halsey's reasons for doing this? Are there any problems with this? e.g. what aspects of class and inequality may be obscured?

EXERCISE 3

Consider the diagram below, which compares the different methods of data collection from the point of view of the numbers involved in the research and the personal involvement of the researcher. Read the Theory and Methods sections of a basic text book and answer the following:

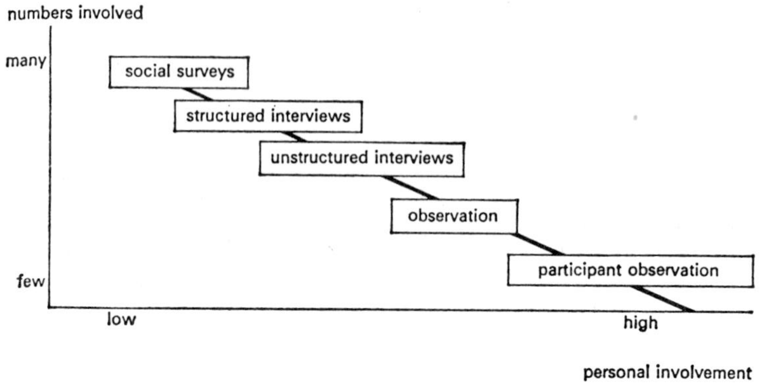

Figure 2 Relationship between number of respondents and degree of personal involvement of sociologist

Source: P. Worsley, *Introducing Sociology* (Penguin, Harmondsworth, 1977)
Reproduced by permission of Penguin Books Ltd.

1. Where in the diagram would you put (a) positivistic approaches and (b) phenomenological approaches? Give reasons.
2. Where would you put (a) quantitative data and (b) qualitative data? Give reasons.
3. Which sociological approach in 1. stresses the validity of data and which method of research is advocated?
4. How might the other approach in 1. reply to this?

EXERCISE

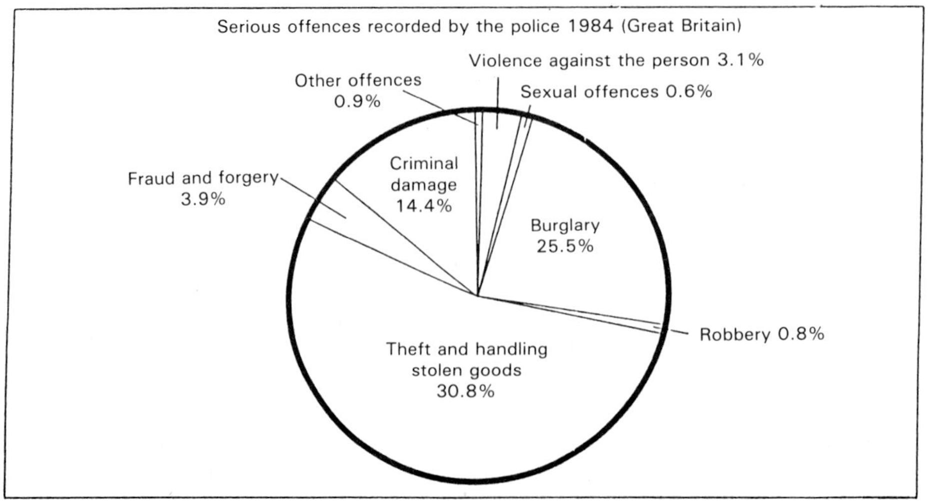

Source: *Social Trends 16,* 1986

1. The popular press devote approximately 45% of their content to crimes involving sex and violence. In the light of the information portrayed at the base of the previous page, how can this be seen as providing an unrealistic view of crime in Great Britain?
2. Which particular categories of reader do you consider to be most affected by the view of crime in the popular press?

EXERCISE

MALCOLM DEAN analyses the grim statistics of child-killing

When murder is a family affair

ALTHOUGH child-killers grab the headlines, more children are murdered by their parents than by psychopaths. Despite the fact that many of these killings are covered up by the parents and only recorded as accidental deaths, even those homicides that are recorded are sufficient to make the first 12 months of life the period in which people are statistically most likely to be murdered.

Officially, there were 506 homicides in 1983—the latest year for which we have figures—of which some 78 involved children under 16. There were 28 aged under one, 33 aged between one and five, and 17 aged between five and 16. Some 45 out of every million babies under one face death from homicide, compared with 13 per million children aged one to five, and two per million children aged five to 16.

Child killers who are unrelated to their victims fall into three crude categories: paedophiles who panic; psychopaths; and sadists. Paedophiles are usually full of remorse. Psychopaths, by their nature, do not suffer from guilt or regret. The sadistic killer, like Ian Brady convicted of the Moors murders, is in the smallest category.

The offender convicted of a serious sexual or sadistic murder of a child now faces a minimum of 20 years in prison under the new categories of lifers identified by Mr Leon Brittan in his first address to the Conservative Party conference as Home Secretary in 1983.

Leoni Keating's killer would undoubtedly be placed in such a category, having sexually assaulted the little girl before tying her hands behind her back and throwing her into a water-filled dyke.

One study made after Mr Brittan's speech suggested only about four murderers a year fall into this category. The prison statistics showed only 20 offenders who had sexually or sadistically killed children between 1965 and 1970. Of the 20, only four had been released by the time Mr Brittan set down his new 20-year minimum sentence.

Donald West, the Cambridge criminologist, said yesterday that most sadistic killers had a childhood background involving violence and aggression. "This does not explain why they become murderers, however, because many people have a similar background but do not become killers," he said.

Professor West, who was a member of the Howard League working party on Unlawful Sex and carried out his own study of sex victims, said paedophiles who kill are usually similar to other paedophiles. They were sexually inhibited and repressed, and killed in a panic when they were trying to silence the child.

He thought there was much more attention being paid now to giving children warnings about the dangers of strangers and sexual assault. A new pressure group, the Child Assault Prevention Programme, published a pamphlet earlier this year giving a practical guide to parents and teachers. It helps to show children the difference between telling tales to get somebody into trouble and getting help when someone is in trouble.

Article on child-killing—the dark side of family life, taken from 'The Guardian', 20 September, 1985.

Are the popular press stereotypes of child-killers representative? If not, what conclusions do you draw from the statistical and other information given here?

EXERCISE

Statistics on Newspaper Circulation

	July-Dec 1985	July-Dec 1984	% change (-)
Sun	4,125,480	4,083,573	1.0
Mirror	3,033,271	3,493,782	(13.2)
Daily Star	1,454,727	1,633,263	(11.0)
Daily Express	1,902,425	2,001,928	(5.0)
Daily Mail	1,815,056	1,864,471	(2.7)
Daily Telegraph	1,202,290	1,235,459	(2.7)
Guardian	487,080	471,718	3.3
Times	478,174	456,557	4.7
Financial Times	233,604	218,461	7.0
News of the World	5,103,164	4,698,341	8.6
Sunday Mirror	3,009,397	3,489,471	(13.8)
Sunday People	2,961,982	3,252,624	(8.9)
Sunday Express	2,449,246	2,542,084	(3.7)
Mail on Sunday	1,630,886	1,606,829	1.5
Sunday Times	1,251,442	1,260,357	(0.7)
Observer	735,745	744,232	(1.1)
Sunday Telegraph	686,298	712,686	(3.7)

Source: ABC

The Guardian, 27 January, '86

1. Which newspapers are increasing their sales?
2. Which newspapers' sales are declining?
3. Find out what is meant by 'popular' and 'quality' with reference to newspapers. Which of the above are popular and which quality? Can any trends in their sales be discerned?
4. Which newspapers are predominantly read by the middle and which by the working class? Give reasons why this is the case.

SOCIAL TRENDS

This is a collection of government statistics published annually by Her Majesty's Stationery Office and is available in most libraries. As the contents page illustrated (p.47) indicates it is a rich source of information showing important changes that are occurring in British society. As well as statistical tables and graphs there are useful written subsections on issues arising from the statistics.

EXERCISE

2: HOUSEHOLDS AND FAMILIES

Table 2.17 Divorce[1]: by age of wife at marriage

Great Britain Percentages and numbers

	Age of wife at marriage							All divorces (=100%) (numbers)
	Under 20	20-24	25-29	30-34	35-39	40-44	45 or over	
Year of divorce (*percentages*)								
1961[2]	*31.8*	*46.2*	*13.4*	*4.5*	*1.9*	*1.0*	*1.1*	27,018
1971[2]	*37.9*	*45.3*	*10.0*	*3.2*	*1.6*	*0.8*	*1.1*	78,922
1976[2]	*39.0*	*44.3*	*9.5*	*3.3*	*1.6*	*0.9*	*1.4*	134,823
1981	*37.7*	*43.2*	*10.4*	*3.9*	*2.1*	*1.2*	*1.6*	155,608
1983	*36.0*	*42.9*	*10.9*	*4.7*	*2.3*	*1.4*	*1.7*	160,717
1984	*34.8*	*43.3*	*11.4*	*4.8*	*2.5*	*1.4*	*1.7*	156,416

[1]See Appendix, Part 2: Divorce.
[2]Excludes divorces in Scotland to people married outside Scotland.

Source: Office of Population Censuses and Surveys

The older a couple were at marriage the less likely they are to divorce (Table 2.17). Spouses who marry in their teens are almost twice as likely to divorce as those who marry between the ages of 20 and 24. The proportion of divorces in Great Britain in 1984 where the wife was aged under 20 at marriage was 35 per cent, and the corresponding proportion where the husband was under 20 was 12 per cent. Just over half the divorces in 1984 were to men who were aged between 20 and 24 at marriage; comparatively few men marry before the age of 20.

Social Trends 16, 1986 p.40

Use your text books to find out what factors have led to the increase in divorces shown in the table. What trends concerning age can be seen in the figures? What explanations can be offered for these trends?

D. SUPPLEMENTARY SOURCES

'It is appropriate to use 'real world' events in Sociology papers . . . The examination is not, of course, an examination of current affairs but such references do illuminate answers.'
(Cambridge Examiners' Report:
A level Sociology, June 1985)*

The above comment reflects examiners' concern that students are not using wider sources of sociological information than is provided in textbooks and similar material. Sociology in this view should not be seen in isolation from daily life. This is not to argue for a return to Sociology's earlier mistaken reputation as a subject which could be studied from a basis of common sense, experience of 'life' and a reading of the popular daily newspapers. This approach has been the source of student failure in the past and is still around as the following comments indicate:

'Weak candidates . . . tended to flee from Sociology into journalism and 'common sense' on issues such as family violence, juvenile delinquency, inner cities and gender'
(Cambridge Examiners' Report:
A level Sociology, 1984)*

Contents

SOCIAL TRENDS 16, 1986

	Page
List of Tables and Charts	3
Introduction	10
Income After Retirement *G C Fiegehen, Economic Advisers' Office, Department of Health and Social Security*	13
1: Population	**19**
Population structure and changes	19
Births and deaths	24
International migration	27
World population	29
2: Households and Families	**31**
Households	31
Families	34
Marriage and divorce	37
Family building	41
3: Education	**45**
Provision for the under fives	45
School pupils	46
School leavers	50
Further and higher education	52
Educational standards of adults	57
Resources	57
4: Employment	**61**
Economic activity	61
Type of job	65
People at work	69
Unemployment	71
Special employment measures	75
5: Income and Wealth	**77**
Household income	77
Income from employment	78
Benefits	80
Taxes	84
The poverty trap	87
Low income families	88
Redistribution of income	89
Wealth	91
6: Resources and Expenditure	**93**
National resources	93
Prices	94
Consumers' expenditure	98
Methods of payment and saving	103
Public income and expenditure	105
7: Health and Personal Social Services	**107**
Some measures of the nation's health	107
Social habits and health	113
Accidents	118
Preventive medicine	120
Health services	121
Private health services	126
Personal social services	128
Resources	130
8: Housing	**133**
The housing stock	133
Characteristics of occupants	136
Housing action	138
Costs and mortgages	143
9: Transport, Communications, and the Environment	**147**
Transport	147
Communications	151
The environment	153
Resources	157
10: Leisure	**159**
Use of time	159
Social and cultural activities	160
Sport	165
Holidays	167
Resources	169
11: Participation	**171**
Voluntary and charitable activities	171
Religion	174
Trade unions	175
Political participation	177
Civic participation	180
12: Law Enforcement	**183**
Offences	183
Police and court action	186
Sentencing	190
Prisons	192
Probation service	196
Compensation	196
Legal aid	197
Civil justice	199
Public order in Northern Ireland	200
Resources	201
Appendix: Definitions and Terms	**203**
Alphabetical Index	**217**
Amendments to Social Trends 15	**224**
Articles in previous issues	inside back cover

You should be aware of the pitfalls illustrated by such comments, but nevertheless there is clearly scope for the use of insights gained from newspapers, magazines, television programmes and other sources which may not at first be seen as directly course-related. The crucial factor is *how* you incorporate such material into your sociological work. It is clearly of overwhelming importance that the basis of your knowledge of Sociology is firmly rooted in a thorough study of set texts and related course materials as well as a reading of appropriate empirical research studies, as described in earlier sections. However, the successful student needs to develop beyond such sources as the course progresses.

Supplementary sources for Sociology are those which are additional to course material. They can provide up to date examples to highlight, illustrate and make more relevant sociological themes and issues covered in textbooks. The following list gives some sources which are available and suggests how they can be used.

(1) Using newspaper material

Note how Current Affairs are incorporated in the following extract from a student's essay:

> 'In examining whether or not religion is necessarily a conservative force in society, consideration of some recent events may illustrate the debate. In the Phillipines in 1986 the Catholic Church supported protest against President Marcos, who was eventually deposed; in South Africa leading Church figures such as Bishop Tutu have vigorously opposed apartheid and in Latin America the Church is linking poverty to government oppression. Such activity can be seen as examples of the Church as a force for radicalism rather than conservatism. Closer to home the Church of England's report on the crisis in the inner cities caused dismay in the Conservative party. Also the Bishop of Durham speaks out against unemployment and Monsignor Bruce Kent is a leading figure in the Campaign for Nuclear Disarmament.'

Such use of topical examples shows the reader that the student is doing what a previously cited examiners report advocated, that is using contemporary examples to illustrate the point that the Church is not inevitably a conservative force in society.

NOTE: It is always wise for students to remember that press articles should be read critically. How factual or emotive is the writing? What bias is evident in the slant the writer takes and the language used?

ACTIVITY

A satirical portrayal of the Press in Britain.

What sociological points can be made concerning the portrait of ownership and control of the Press given in the cartoon?

In what ways might newspapers be seen as biased?

(2) **Television**

Consider the following extract from an essay on the mass media:

> 'When considering the Glasgow University Media Group's research in the *Bad News* series, which looked into bias and pro-establishment views in TV news reportage, an illustration is provided by a comparison of the way the doings of Royalty and industrial affairs are reported.
>
> The former are given a sanitized, highly deferential, showbusiness-style treatment, whereas the latter are often presented in ways that are pro-management and critical of workers. The Glasgow Group indicated this in a TV programme which featured news broadcasts on the 1985 coal dispute, where phrases like 'a Scargill Surcharge' with reference to projected increases in electricity prices as a result of the strike were used in broadcasts. The comedian Les Dawson wittily highlighted this when, in a sketch set in a training school for TV news broadcasters, he received a reprimand from the tutor when he got the instructions the wrong way round and grimaced when he reported news about Royalty and smiled approvingly as he reported a strike!'

The above example is clearly using TV sources in an unusual way and to do so requires confidence on the part of the student. Television documentaries perhaps provide safer, more factual background. In recent years there have been programmes on the lives of people in Russia ('Comrades'), and Channel 4's series 'The Heart of the Dragon' provided an excellent set of programmes on the Chinese, focusing on marriage, the family, divorce, crime, the care of the elderly, all of which gave valuable insights for students looking for comparative material from other societies. Documentaries often focus on sociological issues such as drug abuse, the world of work, racism, the police, crime, football hooliganism, women's changing role and poverty, all of which can be useful background material for your studies. A BBC Horizon programme 'Science . . . fiction?' broadcast early in 1986 questioned the objectivity of science and whether science in effect is a system of belief similar to religion or magic in previous times.

8.10 Horizon

Science . . . Fiction?
Once people looked to the Church to tell them about the world, now they look to science. Once everyone believed in heaven and hell, now most people believe in atoms and molecules, in stars and galaxies. But perhaps a time will come when these present theories are seen as superstitious myths; as the fictions of our time.
This programme tells a story which challenges beliefs people think unchallengeable. It is a story that calls into question the truths of the great project of knowledge now called science.
Narrator Alexander John
Film editor CHRISTINE PANCOTT
Horizon editor ROBIN BRIGHTWELL
Written and produced by
HILARY LAWSON

'Radio Times', BBC2, Monday, 17 February 1986

This could have been used as a basis for a sociological discussion of science in relation to society, the objectivity of scientific knowledge, and belief systems, which are all key areas of concern in Sociology courses.

OPEN UNIVERSITY PROGRAMMES
(Broadcast between February and October each year)

The relevant course references are D102 and D207, which are the Sociology-related O.U. units, one drawback being that the programmes are sometimes broadcast at awkward hours e.g. 6.25 am on Sunday mornings! The programmes are for the Open University's Degree level students but their content and presentation in short 25 minute slots is not too demanding. A good example of useful material is the two programmes focusing on Eileen Barker's research (referred to previously) into the religious sect 'The Moonies', which concentrated on the methods of research she used, such as participant observation, questionnaires and in-depth interviews. This provided a good example of a multi-method study. Schools programmes aimed at 16–19 year olds can also cover sociological topics.

FICTIONAL PROGRAMMES

Clearly, as with the Les Dawson example previously cited, great care needs to be taken, but consider the following extract from an essay, which uses *Coronation Street* to illustrate a discussion on women's role in the family:

> 'A good example of the pressures on married women today, raised by Ann Oakley in her criticisms of Wilmott and Young's 'Symmetrical Family' concept (with its emphasis on balance in male-female family roles) occurred in *Coronation Street*, when Gail Tilsley wanted to return to work and her husband, Brian, objected. Although this is fiction, it is no doubt the situation faced by numbers of women who still feel trapped in their housewife role, as was pointed out by Hannah Gavron in *The Captive Wife.*'

Again good use of the sociological imagination is being made in this extract.

(3) **Radio**

Radio does not contain the same variety of sociological sources as television, but there are occasionally series on Radio 4 focusing on sociological topics, examples being programmes on The Family, Youth Culture and Adolescence. Sometimes Radio 4 plays can be of interest. A recent one featured a girl working as a motor mechanic and neatly illustrated issues concerning women at work in scenes where she was ridiculed and undermined by male workmates, because she was a woman in a job they considered to be for men only.

(4) **Literature**

Literature can also be used to illustrate a sociological discussion as in the following extract which uses a fictional illustration to highlight points about stereotypical views of the family:

> '. . . so it would appear that mainstream functionalist approaches to the family, which stress the 'fit' between the family and the needs of an industrial society and which also implies a nuclear family 'norm' of male breadwinner and dependent wife and children at home, is an inadequate model of the modern family. A more realistic portrait would have to incorporate the diversity of family types in modern industrial societies. The extended family still exists, one parent families and reconstituted or step families after divorce are all aspects of modern family life. Perhaps the somewhat chaotic family situation in *The Secret Diary of Adrian Mole* is more true to life, despite humorous exaggeration, than conventional functionalist approaches with their implication of harmony and stability in the family unit.'

EXERCISE

Read the following extract from a novel about the American car industry and then read a section on work from a textbook particularly concentrating on the concept of alienation.

The stairway at factory floor level was close to a section of assembly line where early subassemblies were welded onto frames, becoming the foundations on which finished cars would rest. The din at this point was so intense that men working within a few feet of one another had to shout, heads close together, to communicate. Around them, showers of sparks flew upwards and sideways in a pyrotechnic curtain of intense white-blue. Volleys from welding machines and rivet guns were punctuated by the constant hiss of the power tools' lifeblood—compressed air. And central to everything, focus of activity like an ambling godhead exacting tribute, the moving assembly line inched inexorably on . . .

. . . Zaleski knew, as did most others who were close to auto plants, that few people who worked on factory production lines for long periods had ever intended to make that work a lifetime's occupation. Usually, when hired, they looked on the job as temporary until something better came along. But to many—especially those with little education—the better job was always out of reach, for ever a delusive dream. Eventually a trap was sprung. It was a two-pronged trap, with a worker's own commitments on one side—marriage, children, rent, instalment payments—and on the other, the fact that pay in the auto industry was high compared with jobs elsewhere.

But neither pay nor good fringe benefits could change the grim, dispiriting nature of the work. Much of it was physically hard, but the greatest toll was mental—hour after hour, day after day of deadening monotony. And the nature of their jobs robbed individuals of pride. A man on a production line lacked a sense of achievement; he never made a car; he merely made, or put together, pieces—adding a washer to a bolt, fastening a metal strip, inserting screws. And always it was the identical washer or strip or screws, over and over and over and over and over and over and over again, while working conditions—including an overlay of noise—made communication difficult, friendly association between individuals impossible. As years went by, many, while hating, endured. Some had mental breakdowns. Almost no one liked his work.

Thus, a production line worker's ambition, like that of a prisoner, was centred on escape. Absenteeism was a way of partial escape; so was a strike. Both brought excitement, a break in monotony—for the time being the dominating drive.

Alex Hailey, *Wheels* (Pan Books, London, 1973), p.29-31

If possible consult empirical studies of the car industry, such as Goldthorpe and Lockwood's *The Affluent Worker* and Huw Beynon's *Working for Ford*. Compare the approaches in the readings. What evidence is there for 'alienation' in the novel extract? Compare the attitudes to work of a car worker with that of a doctor. Goldthorpe and Lockwood use the term 'instrumental orientation' to describe the attitudes to work of workers in the car industry. In the light of your reading and the above extract, what do you understand by this term?

(5) **Photographs**

Visual resources such as photographs have not been used greatly on Sociology courses, but it is an area that could develop in the future. Economic and social history textbooks of the modern period often contain photographs portraying people as they have lived and worked in recent times.

FAMILY PHOTOGRAPH ALBUMS

Have your father and mother any photographs of when they were young, showing them at work, school or in family groups? What about your grandparents? Have they any similar photographs? What did your grandmother do during the War? She could well have worked in an occupation which was formerly seen as male such as a munitions factory, a shipyard or in agriculture. (See photographs of Land Army 'girls' in the Second World War).

World War 2, Land Army 'girls'. New occupational role for women. Note their masculine style of dress.

Early gender stereotyping?—note the role played by the little boy as compared to the little girl.

Wedding photographs can often contain good insights into family life in former times. Were families larger then? How old were the bride and groom? Was the wedding in a Church or Registry Office?

As well as family life, old photographs of leisure activities, people at work, schoolfriends at school, the houses people lived in, the transport they used, the pubs they drank in can all provide vital links with our recent past. This can help make textbook accounts of recent changes in contemporary society come to life.

NEWSPAPERS and JOURNAL PHOTOGRAPHS

These often contain evidence which could be of sociological interest.

EXERCISE

Photograph courtesy Maggie Murray, Format Photographers Ltd.

Compare the women in this photograph from 'New Society', 7 March, 1985: 'Society Today' with those in the Land Army during the War (above). Which photograph reinforces stereotypes of women and which challenges them? Give reasons.

PHOTOGRAPHS in SOCIOLOGY TEXTS

Apart from book cover illustrations or occasionally to illustrate a section of text, photographic sources have been little used so far. A recent attempt to combine photographs with a sociological portrait of life in factories in the West Midlands in the 1970's is Hedges and Beynon's *Born to Work* (Pluto Press, 1982). Consider the following examples:

EXERCISE

Why may this photograph indicate Goldthorpe and Lockwood's 'instrumental orientation' to work i.e. work seen as a means to an end?
Why would you not expect a doctor or a manager to act as the woman in the photograph is doing?

Pay Day!

EXERCISE

Women factory workers—note the shopping bags. What does this indicate about women's role in society? Would you expect to see male factory workers with shopping bags?

Women's Dual Role

Photographs courtesy Nick Hedges

(6) **Popular magazines and journals**

Such sources can be used either when they contain articles of sociological interest (see example below) and reports of attitude surveys into sociological areas or as source material. In the latter case, a useful exercise is to examine popular women's magazines. Consider the way women are predominantly portrayed, particularly in advertisements. Many feature women as ideal housewives and only show them involved with household tasks and child care. How does this compare to the lives of most women, when they form 40% of the labour force and 65% of mothers go out to work? Such popular magazine sources can be used to gain insight into how women are stereotyped by the mass media.

An examination of the ways in which men are stereotyped in magazines could be useful as a comparison.

Your husband, according to the experts, is more promiscuous than you are, less emotional, much more confident with money, but incapable of coping with the common cold. Science fiction or sex fact? Jill Eckersley investigates

Does Sex Make All The Difference?

'Options' magazine, October, 1985

E. DAILY LIFE AND EXPERIENCE—CULTIVATING YOUR SOCIOLOGICAL IMAGINATION

The prevailing value system in Sociology teaching highlights the teacher as the man of knowledge who transmits this knowledge by means of a lecture to his students. By implication it is assumed these students are not knowledgeable or experienced in the areas being discussed. Teaching and learning are therefore separated out.'

C.J. Margerison, I. Campbell, A. Dawson—'An Action-Centred Sociology Course' (article in *The British Journal of Sociology* Vol. 22, 1971, pp.441–447.)

Of all your supplementary sources for Sociology this is the one that is most fraught with danger. As has been stated, common sense and anecdotal Sociology are to be avoided. However, there are ways in which experience can be used to illustrate or support a particular sociological argument or point. Consider how this occurs in the following extract from an essay:

> 'The view that the extended family has declined or disappeared is not supported by its continuing existence in working class communities such as exist in mining areas in Yorkshire and South Wales. This was highlighted during the 1984 miners' strike, where strong support came from extended family members. (Good use made of TV sources here?) Another factor to consider is the family organization of some of the ethnic minority groups in Britain, particularly Asians, where culture and religion stress family commitments and responsibilities. My own family could be seen as an example: I live with my parents, brothers and a sister (the nuclear family) but my grandparents also live in my house (so we are an extended family). In the same neighbourhood lives my older married brother with his wife and family and I have aunts and uncles and several cousins close by. So my family type is clearly extended and compares with the extended families described in Wilmott and Young's 1950's study of working class communities in East London.'

Another example of a student using experience to illustrate a sociological discussion occurs in this extract:

> 'With regard to inequality of opportunity for girls as compared to boys, my experience at school when I wished to do an O level in Technical Drawing is an example. The male teacher was reluctant to accept me at first, but did so after my parents came to see the headteacher. The teacher's reaction after this was one of ridiculing my mistakes with the additional intimation to the rest of the class that this was only to be expected of a girl. Such an example shows how changes in legislation concerning discrimination are insufficient, because such social attitudes are so deeply rooted. These are the hurdles women face in education, work and other aspects of their lives relating to careers and opportunities generally.'

Consider carefully the two examples above. At first glance they may appear to be breaking one of Sociology's 'Ten Commandments', 'Thou shalt not use personal experience'! But look at the way in which the students use their experiences of family life and schooling. Such experience has been used to illustrate and add to the sociological discussion, which shows the students are using Sociology as 'a tool for making sense of the world around them', which a Chief Examiner has indicated he would like to see. When experience is being used, provided it is of relevance and supports a sociological argument, it can be very effective.

EXERCISE

In the first weeks of the course, you could consider your own personal experiences of family life, school, work (even part-time or 'Saturday jobs') and see how these relate to sociological approaches, as the students did in the extracts above.

The skill of highlighting sociological discussion with experience may well not develop until later in the course, when you have a more thorough grasp of sociological themes and issues.

> C. Wright Mills started his book, *The Sociological Imagination*, with the words: 'Nowadays most men feel their . . . lives are a series of traps.' That was fifteen years ago. Mills is now dead and people are increasingly bewildered by the events that punctuate the path of their lives. Their minds are dominated by recrimination and regret. Little has happened, since Mills wrote his book, to suggest that the imagination of sociologists has helped matters. That these 'scientific' examiners of society have failed to make clear the issues that so deeply affect people's lives, is a condemnation of them and their art. At best, they have written with 'the profession' over their right shoulder, and produced sociology for sociologists: an absurdity which cuts the writer off from the subjects of his writing.
>
> In writing *Working for Ford* I have tried to overcome this contrived isolation. I have never worked for Ford. I have told the story of other people's experiences, some of which I shared, as an outsider. An outsider who was accepted inside. These pages are the product of that hesitant mutuality. They are made up of the activity and conversation of men and women in the pub, the factory, on the picket-line or in their homes, combined in an attempt to describe the lives that people lead when they work on the shop floor of a large car factory; to outline the crises they encounter and the way in which they try to make sense of them and the world they live in. The names are their names and the book is written for them in the hope that they, and others like them, will be able to identify parts of themselves in the story and perhaps, thereby, see more clearly the way they are going.
>
> H. Beynon, *Working for Ford* (Allen Lane, London, 1973), Preface.

The above quotation indicates the need for the sociologist to observe and listen to people as they go about their daily lives. Conversations in bus queues, doctors' waiting rooms, pubs, supermarkets, workplaces and on street corners can be a rich source of information as to how people live. I can remember overhearing two elderly women in conversation in a doctor's waiting room. One had recently been burgled and her friend asked if the police had been helpful. The burglary victim replied that she had not contacted the police as not much of value had been stolen and she did not want them 'prying into her affairs'. If a student had been studying the debate in Sociology about the use of official crime statistics, the two women's conversation would have fitted in well with the aspect that a significant proportion of crimes are unreported. In this way the world of the textbook meets everyday life in a meaningful way.

Conclusion

This chapter has provided some examples of the wealth of resources that are available for Sociology. Textbooks and similar materials are essential as the basis of your knowledge, but it is strongly advocated that you do not rely on these as your sole source of information. To grasp Sociology's essence, you need to explore and research widely, develop your sociological imagination by using supplementary sources, and take an interest in current affairs and the changes occurring in society. In this way Sociology should take on a more exciting dimension than that of a subject which has to be learned and worked at in an abstract academic manner.

EXERCISE

HUMOUR AS A RESOURCE

What sociological points can you draw out of this Posy cartoon?

Posy Simmonds, *Very Posy* (Jonathan Cape, London, 1985), reprinted from 'The Guardian', 1984

CHAPTER 3

READING

> 'There is an art of reading, as well as an art of thinking, and an art of writing.'
> Isaac D'Israeli

> 'Continuity of thought upon one single thing, and the suppression of every source of distraction, multiply in an extraordinary way the value of time.' Alfieri

Preliminary exercise

Before reading this chapter do the following:
Consult your textbook and read the introduction or the first section of Chapter 1. Note:

What do I find difficult about this passage?
Do I read quickly or slowly?
Do I read every word and try to grasp its meaning before continuing?
Do I find it easy to concentrate?
Do I read a passage once and try to remember as much as I can?

Now work through the rest of the chapter and then return to this exercise and evaluate your initial approach to reading. In the light of what has been covered do you see room for improvement?

Reading is an active rather than a passive activity, i.e. you need to be alert and enquiring as well as using high levels of concentration and effort. Effective reading means effective study.

If you can read efficiently and productively, you have the advantage of being able to read more widely, thus adding greater depth and detail to your knowledge of Sociology. There are differences between reading for pleasure and reading for study. When we read for pleasure we are usually highly motivated, which means we can concentrate and read effortlessly without being distracted. It is often easy to be distracted from study reading. 'Forget that, come and have a coffee' is often hard to resist!

It is insufficient to read and hope you can remember what you have read at a later date. You should always have some method of recording your reading, such as highlighting or making notes of important points (see Chapter 4). The ability to read sociological material effectively is an important skill which you need to develop from the outset of your course. Examiners can easily recognize students who have limited their reading to pre-digested material from one or two basic sources, their dissatisfaction with this being indicated in the following comment:

> 'Examiners . . . have started to get concerned about an apparent over reliance on texts for both theoretical summaries and synopses of research. Candidates would gain a great deal from reading studies for themselves'
> (JMB Examiners' Report: A level Sociology, 1984)

What has been your approach to reading in the past? Consider these two examples:

STUDENT (A)
Reads bare minimum for essays, e.g. class notes and handouts, short sections from textbooks one or two nights before an essay deadline. Private study periods often spent talking with friends in common room.

STUDENT (B)
Reads widely, uses library, does a lot of preparatory reading for essays, classwork. Reads basic texts, readers, topic books, empirical studies, journals, reference works, statistical sources. May end up with more information than necessary for an essay or a piece of work, but has made notes and files them in relevant sections for future use.

Clearly student A has not moved away from the approach which might fit the requirements for lower levels of study, but if this is continued through an advanced course, a low grade pass is the best that can be hoped for. Student B, on the other hand, will benefit from reading widely and, if this is combined with the other skills outlined in this book, such as the correct interpretation of questions, notemaking and essay writing, he or she will attain a high pass grade.

A. TYPES OF READING

(1)	SKIMMING	A newspaper can be read in this way, by quickly looking through the pages and only stopping to read the occasional article.
(2)	SCANNING	More purposeful than skimming. You may be looking for your name on a notice board to see your exam result, or if you have been picked for a team. We scan a telephone directory when we are looking for someone's number.
(3)	WORD-BY-WORD (sub-vocalization)	This is where we need to follow something methodically e.g. reading a set of instructions on how to assemble a piece of furniture. Sub-vocalization is where you read as if there were a voice in your head. When applied to study, word by word reading and sub-vocalization is painstaking and slow and wastes much time. You should try quickly to grasp the overall sense of a group of words or sentences to be more effective in your reading.
(4)	LIGHT READING	Reading a popular novel can be seen as light reading, but obviously there are different levels of difficulty and it depends on the purpose. For example reading a novel for English Literature study is different from reading a novel you take on holiday.
(5)	STUDY READING	The most difficult of all. Often requires high levels of motivation and concentration. Needs to be 'worked at' i.e. reading accompanied by reflection, thought, analysis, criticism—notes made, summaries, points highlighted and emphasized, arguments and discussions understood.

We are all reasonably adept at types (1)–(4). The problem is in applying the best of such skills to study reading, type (5).

B. SQ3R METHOD

A well-known method which can help to develop good study reading skills is the SQ3R method. This is often cited in study skills handbooks as an example of a systematic approach to good reading practice. The method was originally devised to help American college students and was found to be successful.

WHAT IS SQ3R?
SQ3R is a five stage approach to study reading, comprising a survey or skimming stage (S), a question stage (Q), a reading stage (R), a recall or recite stage (R2), and a review or revise stage (R3).

(1) SURVEY/SKIMMING ('getting the gist')

This is the process of getting the overall gist of a chapter, a section or an article fairly rapidly. Before you start reading, note the title, author and date of publication. If you are reading a book, look at the 'blurb' (potted summary) on the cover. Consult the introductory and concluding chapters, appendices, the index to see the topics covered, and also the bibliography to see the sources the book was based on. Note chapter headings and subheadings, and skim through the pages and paragraphs quickly. Many students omit this important preparatory and gist-gathering stage and laboriously work their way through a piece of reading without first standing back and getting an overall picture of what is to be read. This should lay the foundation for the detailed work in the following stages.

(2) QUESTION

This stage involves considering the piece of reading you have just surveyed and making a list of questions to guide you through the more detailed reading in the third stage, and establish the purpose of your reading.
What are the main points that the writer wishes to make?
What theory, approach, idea or research is being described?
What is the angle/bias/attitude with which the points are presented?
What does this reading add to my pre-existing knowledge?

(3) READ

Read the key passages once fairly quickly to add more detail to your initial survey and skimming. Then read again, this time either making notes (see Chapter 4), using headings, sub-headings and numbered points or, if the reading material is your own, you can save time by underlining or highlighting key sections and writing comments or reference points in the margins.

(4) RECALL or RECITE

Once the read stage is completed, you can reflect on the passage covered and attempt to recall in note form or recite verbally the key ideas so that you strengthen your understanding. If this is difficult, return to your notes or the marked passage, using these as a trigger to complete the gaps in your knowledge.

(5) REVIEW/REVISE

Go through your notes again more methodically and add to or amend them as necessary, so they can be referred to and understood at later stages of the course. Make cross-references to related work in this area.

The five stage SQ3R study reading method may seem at first glance to be very time consuming, but with practice you should eventually be able to use this naturally as part of your standard approach to study reading. If this method is employed effectively, you will develop a much firmer base for your acquisition of knowledge through reading than formerly.

EXERCISE

Read the following extract from O'Donnell, applying the SQ3R five stage method. How would you have read such a passage previously?

Which method do you now judge to be a more effective approach to reading?

How Working Class Kids Get Working Class Jobs: An Observational Study
Paul Willis' book is entitled *Learning to Labour*, but its real concern is manifested in its sub-title: *How working class kids get working class jobs*. Willis describes a harsh collision between the tough working class 'lads' who are the subject of his study and the highly middle class world of the educational system. The 'lads' seldom even begin to struggle for examination success which not only requires a kind of mental discipline foreign to their experience but is unlikely to be of much use in the kind of manual jobs most of them expect to get. The lads tend to find the conformist behaviour of the 'lobes', as they call more hard-working pupils, a matter for mockery and amusement.

The school experience of the lads fails significantly to alter the course of their lives. Schools are middle class institutions in that they are run by middle class people (teachers) and because success in them requires conformity to middle class values, such as academic commitment, and middle class goals, such as a career. Comparing the lads to the lobes, Spansky, one of the lads, says:

> I mean, what will they remember of their school life? What will they have to look back on? Sitting in a classroom, sweating their bollocks off, you know, while we've been . . . I mean look at the things we can look back on, fighting on the Pakis, fighting on the JA's (Jamaicans). Some of the things we've done on teachers, it'll be a laff when we look back on it.

School seems to be good for a 'laff' and not much else. Judging by the following reactions of the lads to a lecture on the need for discipline at school and work, they obviously see little connection between school and the type of work they will do.

> *Spansky:* He makes the same points all the time, Fuzz. He's always on about if you get a job, you've got to do this, you've got to do that. I've done it. You don't have to do none of that. Just go to a place, ask for a man in charge, nothing like what he says.
> *Joey:* It's ridiculous . . .

Paul Willis notes that in later years, some of the 'lads' do come to regret their failure to realise that education did offer a possible escape from life as a manual labourer. But to what extent does the school system give the 'lads' a fair chance? Basically, Willis sympathises with their spirited rejection of the label of 'failures'. He appreciates, far more than Bourdieu seems to, that, in terms of their own class position, their way of life makes sense. It does so because most of them will, in fact, remain working class.

M. O'Donnell, *A New Introduction to Sociology* (Harrap, London, 1981) p.114–115

EXERCISE

Select a book from the library which contains an account of a sociological study. Allow yourself a set period of time e.g. 5–10 minutes to survey and gather the gist of what it is about. Now write down what you have learnt about the book in that time. You can often surprise yourself at how much you can relate about a book even after such a brief cursory survey.

C. DIFFICULTY OF SUBJECT MATTER

Reading varies with the level of difficulty of the subject matter. You will probably find the more abstract theoretical discussions in books more demanding than straightforward accounts of research findings.

EXERCISE

Read the following passage from a book about sexual divisions in schools. Record and make notes from what you have read and time how long it takes.

D. The faceless bunch: gender divisions in coeducation

It was argued earlier that the experiences boys and girls have in mixed classes contribute to their evolving views about their own, and the other, sex. When boys are more outspoken and manifestly confident—and especially when teachers take more notice of boys—pupils tend to see this as evidence that boys in general are more capable, and more highly valued, than girls.

Interviewer: Which of these pupils gets asked questions most often by the teacher?
Female pupil: Well, Terence does. And Johnny. And Mr Howard asks Rob a lot of questions as well.
Interviewer: And which pupils join in discussions or make comments most often?
Pupil: Rob says a lot, and Julian, and Paul, and Johnny too. They all make a lot of noise, all those boys. That's why I think they're more intelligent than us.

The down-grading of girls in their own eyes and those of their male classmates is confirmed by other parts of the interviews. Both teachers and pupils ranked the members of each class according to their success in the subject. Before comparing the rank orders made by teachers with those constructed by pupils, the following hypotheses were set out: first, that girls would know where they stood in relation to other girls, but would place boys higher in the rank order than teachers had done; second, that boys would give an accurate account of the rank order of boys, but would assign girls a lower position than teachers had done; and third, that the net effect of pupils' "errors" would be an over-estimation of the academic standing of boys, and an under-estimation of that of girls. Since pupils (according to their own comments) rarely share either their marks or judgements passed on them by teachers with pupils of the other sex, the sexual distribution of classroom interaction is one of the few clues that girls have for judging the performance of boys, or boys, of girls. Therefore it was predicted that, even in cases where teachers rated the girls as more successful than the boys, pupils would think the opposite was true.

The results support these predictions to a striking degree. In the 19 cases out of 24 where pupils' rankings were different from those of their teachers, all of the girls under-estimated their rank; all but one of the boys over-estimated theirs. Furthermore, two-thirds of these errors involve only classmates of the other sex—that is, girls down-grading themselves relative to boys, boys up-grading themselves relative to girls.

These data on pupil rankings, combined with comments of the pupils themselves, strongly support the contention that the prominence of boys in classroom interaction plays an active part in the regeneration of a sexual hierarchy, in which boys are the indisputably dominant partners. Girls appear to boys—and more importantly, to themselves—as less capable than they "really" area.

The devaluation of girls which is the typical consequence of interaction in these classrooms can be, on occasion, undermined. In the first place, when girls are forthcoming in class, boys appear to take them more seriously than before. The pupil in the following quotation, for example, spoke well of only one girl—Audrey—during the entire interview:

Male pupil: Audrey, hmmm. Well, I'd like to classify myself as a better person than her, but she takes a more active part in the history class. She speaks out a lot, even though the statements are a bit, well . . . She is certainly well read, there's no denying that.

Secondly, when pupils do have access to the marks awarded to classmates of the other sex (something which rarely happens), they are able to challenge the supposed relationship between outspokenness and ability.

Michelle Stanworth, *Gender and Schooling* (Hutchinson, London, 1983), p.43–45

Now turn to the next passage. Although it is similar in length, it will probably take much longer to read. Write down the problems the passage raises in terms of content, vocabulary and subject matter. Use dictionaries and textbooks to help you understand and provide a summary of the passage.

Attempts to Achieve a Synthesis Between the Action Approach and Structuralism

The four perspectives we have examined take a different view of the relationship between ideas and the social structure. For Marxism and functionalism the structure dominates the realm of ideas. For phenomenology and interactionism, ideas are relatively free of social structure. Social structure is nothing other than a combination of the beliefs and values of a number of individuals.

In many instances there are areas of overlap between the perspectives. They are not *completely* separate points of view. The phenomenologist Schutz has elements of structuralism in his theory, while Marx has elements of idealism in his. Some of the writers make a deliberate attempt to synthesise the perspectives. This is true of Karl Mannheim, of Talcott Parsons and of Peter Berger and Thomas Luckmann. Max Weber also tried to blend elements of structuralism with idealism in his work. In *The Protestant Ethic and the Spirit of Capitalism*[69] he shows how a new religion and its modes of thought may simply arise almost at random in any society, propagated by a charismatic prophet. These religions may have important effects on the social structure. Protestantism, with its stress on hard work and saving, helped bring capitalism about through the accumulation of capital, the willingness to work among the population and the belief that waste and inefficiency is wrong. The idealism here is clear, however Weber also says that the development of Protestant beliefs, after their beginnings, was influenced by the socio-economic structure. Moreover he says that if ideas are to be adopted by large numbers of people in society there must be a correspondence between those ideas and the social conditions of the day. Inappropriate religions, doctrines, ideas and values will fade away and be forgotten if this is not the case. This is an example of the structuralist element to be found in Weber's work. Social phenomena are produced, according to Weber, by an *interaction* of knowledge and socio-economic structure. Neither determines the nature of the other, both are relatively free to move in any direction.

How successful are the attempts to synthesise competing perspectives? Peter Hamilton, in discussing Berger and Luckmann's effort, is quite dismissive.[70] He believes that functionalism and Marxism are irreconcilable. Berger and Luckmann in fact go for the functionalist view without admitting it. Religions are not ideologies as far as they are concerned, because ideologies, in Marx's sense, operate in the interests of some and against the interests of others. In Berger and Luckmann's scheme of things the role of religion is to sustain the universe of meaning (the socially constructed reality) of any given society. Just as the universe of meaning is shared by all, so all share the religion. Berger and Luckmann have no conception of conflicting groups in society.

If there are fundamental tensions between functionalism and Marxism, what of the microscopic, actor-based, approach of phenomenology on the one hand and structuralism on the other? We saw that the attempt to reconcile *these* two viewpoints got Mannheim into difficulties. Phenomenologists are happy to concede that no truth or reality exists other than that which is created in a given social context.

As a corollary phenomenologists can do no more than describe the reality of a particular society, they cannot explain it in any sense. For structuralists, like Marx, there *is* an objective reality which can be studied and explained. Mannheim is left in the position of trying to reconcile the two views: the impossibility of establishing one truth and the potentially fruitful scientific quest for it. His compromise, relationism, has been the object of heavy criticism.

Paul Trowler, *Further Topics in Sociology* (UTP, London, 1985), p.39–41

Directed reading

You probably found that the previous passage was difficult to read because of the words and terminology used and the subject matter. A further feature was that you were not directed in your reading, that is, no sense of purpose was given. This can be provided when checklist questions are asked after a passage of reading as in the following example:

> The notion of an underclass was first developed in the United States, where it was used to refer to that section of the population which seemed permanently trapped in a situation of poverty and unemployment. Although the term is not necessarily confined to black people, it had particular relevance to those people living in the black ghettoes like Watts, which erupted into violence and riots in the 1960s. Briefly, the sense of hopelessness and despair in these ghettoes was transformed into desperate action and protest, a dramatic expression of their feelings of marginality. Likewise, some British commentators (Young and Lea, 1982) have described the 'marginalisation' of black people as a major factor behind the British 'race riots' of the 1980s. Young and Lea suggest that the black population has been squeezed to the very margins of society, and this has denied them the normal channels for resolving their grievances. Unlike the white working class, they are distanced from traditional trade union and political party activity.
>
> This theme of marginalisation is pursued also in Rex and Tomlinson's study of Handsworth. What Rex and Tomlinson argue is that there has not been any marked sense in which ethnic minorities have gained access to those key political, educational, economic and cultural institutions which would enable them to compete on equal terms with whites. Despite their characteristic working-class employment profile, it does not make sense to describe ethnic minorities as part of the working class; rather, they constitute an underclass. Rex and Tomlinson allow that the concept of 'underclass' does not imply that everyone within it is unemployed, but they do point out that ethnic minorities are subject to higher unemployment rates. Some evidence for this is supplied by the 1981 *Labour Force Survey* (see table overleaf).
>
> However, the distinctiveness of the 'underclass' position persists even for those who are employed, and this distinctiveness is captured in the idea of a *'dual labour market'*. A dual labour market is one which shows clear divisions between two employment groups: the primary market (characterised by high pay, security of employment, and good training and promotion prospects) and the secondary market (characterised by low pay, insecurity of employment, and few opportunities for training or promotion). The expectation is that the underclass are highly concentrated in the secondary market, and this creates a vicious circle: the stigmatised racial minority can only land jobs in the secondary market; and their over-representation in this market serves to reinforce their inferior social status. Again, the *Labour Force Survey* gives some indication of this pattern of under-representation in the more desirable jobs.
>
> Michael Haralambos (Ed.), *Sociology: New Directions* (Causeway Press, Ormskirk, 1985)

EXERCISE

Read the above passage and answer the questions.

(1) How was the term 'underclass' first used in the United States?
(2) Why is the term particularly appropriate for black people?
(3) What is meant by 'marginalization'?
(4) Summarize Rex and Tomlinson's findings.
(5) What is a 'dual labour market' and how does this affect black people?

The majority of what you read will not be directed in this way so you need to develop the skill of asking your own questions and answering them as you read, so that you gain a fuller understanding.

D. DEVELOPING YOUR READING SPEED

(1) READING SPEED

> 'I took a speed reading course, learning to read straight down the middle of the page, and I was able to go through 'War and Peace' in 20 minutes. It's about Russia'
>
> Woody Allen.

As you progress through the course, you should become more familiar with sociological writing, so you will gain confidence and your speed of reading should increase correspondingly. Systematic study reading schemes like the SQ3R method described previously can help you to improve your reading capacity, but you do not have to adopt such an approach rigidly. It can be used as a guide to help you in the art of reading and can be amended to suit your own reading style. Reading with a sense of purpose and flexibility instead of reading everything in the same close detail will mean that eventually you will surprise yourself at how much your reading speed has improved when compared with the start of the course.

(2) THE RIGHT FRAME OF MIND

Reading will not register as effectively when your mind is on other things or you are distracted by noise. Work at concentrating on your reading and nothing else. The best way to concentrate is to set yourself slightly too short a time and race against the clock e.g. 'I'll read this 40 page chapter in half an hour'. You then work hard, rather than ambling along, and you can reward yourself with a drink at the end of the half hour.

(3) VOCABULARY

The earlier section in Chapter 1 on the language of Sociology dealt with the technical vocabulary or jargon of the sociologist. In the early stages of the course, you will encounter unfamiliar words and terms (e.g. alienation, socialization, positivism, functionalism). Do not be put off by such terms. Use them as tools for understanding key sociological debates and arguments, themes and issues. Refer back to the section in Chapter 2 for guidance on Dictionaries, Encyclopaedias, and developing your own glossary of terms.

Another aspect is that, as well as the language of Sociology, there will be a more general sense in which more complex or unfamiliar words will be encountered which applies to any advanced course.

Early in the course when you read you may have to use a dictionary to help you from time to time, but don't become over-reliant on one. Try to grasp the meaning from the context of the passage in which the word occurs. Repeated encountering of such words registers more effectively than trying to remember a dictionary definition. The tendency at first is to concentrate on the unfamiliar word rather than the meaning of the overall sentence or passage. Try to make an educated guess, then check with a dictionary. You may well surprise yourself at how near to a word's meaning you have come.

EXERCISE

Consider the passage on Positivist Sociology. Read the passage and underline words you do not understand. Which are jargon terms and which new words? Try to guess the meaning of the unfamiliar words from the context, and check afterwards from a dictionary.

Positivist sociology

The first distinctive sociological perspective sprang from the work of August Comte (1798–1857), who coined the word 'sociology' from the Latin *socius* and the Greek *logos*, in 1837. Comte believed that the scientific discipline of sociology was the result of a natural progression or development of human thought through three stages. In the first stage, thinking was theological or fictitious. In the second stage it was metaphysical or abstract. In the final stage it was scientific or positive. At this third stage all phenomena are looked upon as subject to natural laws that can be investigated by observation and experimentation. Comte believed that the social world is like the natural, physical world. It is made up of objective facts, independent of individuals, just waiting to be discovered. So, for Comte, social life, people and society, should be treated in the same scientific manner as biological organisms. The parts should not be studied on their own but each element should be studied in the light of the whole system, using scientific methods of analysis to produce accurate, quantified data.

When people and society are subjected to this scientific analysis, Comte believed, sociology would become the positive basis of social and political action, providing the basis for reforms. Comte wrote during the period of social and political upheaval following the French Revolution and the rapid social and economic changes of the Industrial Revolution. He believed that sociologists would be like secular priests bringing a new order to society. They would depend not on divine inspiration but on scientific knowledge, which would be used to predict in order to control. The social order was no longer deemed to be God-given but would be changed and improved by men on the basis of their understanding.

This was Comte's 'positive philosophy' and the essence of positivism. In addition to its origins in Comte's term, 'The name "positivism" derives from the emphasis on the positive sciences—that is on tested and systematic experience rather than on undisciplined speculation' (*International Encyclopaedia of the Social Sciences,* 1968). Thus it is closely identified with traditional scientific method, which is described in Chapter 3, pages 57–8.

So positivist sociology, rather than examining the way individuals perceive the social world around them, assumes that society is an objective thing, 'out there', waiting to be examined, analysed and understood like the natural world, rather like a biologist looking at an ant hill or at a bee hive.

P. McNeill and C. Townley, *Fundamentals of Sociology* (Hutchinson, London, 1981), p.18

E. EXPANDING YOUR VOCABULARY

It has been estimated by linguists that everyday gossip has a vocabulary of 2000-3000 words and that the average person has a latent vocabulary (i.e. words he/she knows whether or not they are used) of 20,000-25,000 words. For study at advanced level it has been estimated that a minimum vocabulary of 25,000 words and, ideally, around 40,000 words is needed.

EXPANDING VOCABULARY CONSCIOUSLY OR DIRECTLY

Expand your vocabulary by wide reading of magazines, newspapers and novels in your spare time. Do crosswords and play word-games like 'Scrabble'. When you write essays, use Roget's Thesaurus, a compendium of words of similar meanings, to find alternative words so that your writing becomes less repetitive and limited in vocabulary and hence more colourful, varied, sophisticated and correspondingly more interesting to read.

EXPANDING VOCABULARY UNCONSCIOUSLY OR INDIRECTLY

This is more difficult to give guidance on, but you will find through interacting with your peers and friends on your college or school courses, through hearing your teacher or tutor, through discussion and tutorial work and other related activities, that you will soak up these influences. Your vocabulary will expand without your necessarily recognizing it. It is interesting to compare your early essays and notes in a course with work in the later stages. You should clearly see an improvement, not just in content and style, but in the ability to handle language and an increase in vocabulary which comes from gaining confidence and an understanding of the subject.

FINAL NOTE

Now return to the preliminary exercise at the beginning of the chapter and evaluate your approach to reading for advanced Sociology.

NOTE-MAKING

CHAPTER 4

'The palest ink is better than the most retentive memory' Chinese proverb.

'The sound is forced, the notes are few!'
Blake 'To the Muses'.

The right note

Every academic year, millions of university students attend countless lectures, and industriously make many reams of notes. But is this really an effective way of communicating information and ideas, or was the cynic who defined education as "the process by which the notes of the teacher become the notes of the student without disturbing the minds of either" just being realistic? Kenneth Kiewra, of Kansas State University, has been trying to find out (Human Learning, vol 4, No.1, page 73).

Kiewra studied 100 education students. He played a 20-minute videotape of a lecture, and asked some of the students to take notes, some just to listen, and some not to attend at all. Then, 48 hours later, those who took notes either reviewed these, or re-read them and four pages of notes from the lecturer, or just thought about the lecture. All the rest of the students either read the lecturer's notes or thought about the lecture. Finally, the students were all given an 18-question multi-choice test on topics dealt with in the lecture.

Rather intriguingly, Kiewra found that the best test results came from the students who reviewed the lecturer's notes, including those who had not acutally seen the lecture at all. Unfortunately, those who used the traditional student technique—namely, taking their own notes and reviewing them—did relatively poorly.

Kiewra thus suggests that university and college lecturers should be aware of their students' problems in this area, and make a real effort to provide them with adequate notes. This might well help people like the Cambridge student who was heard to say, "I've just been to Professor Blank's lecture on communication, and I didn't understand a bloody word."

New Society,
11 October, 1985

'I prefer dictated notes from a teacher, you know where you are then don't you?'
(1st year A level student).

'I read and try to remember as much as I can'
(1st year A level student).

'I was always led to suppose that no educated person ever spoke of notepaper'
Nancy Mitford 'The Pursuit of Love'.

In pre-advanced courses, notes are often copied from a blackboard or dictated by a teacher. This emphasis on taking notes (sometimes referred to as spoon-feeding) often makes it difficult for advanced level students to work on their own with a book or an article and make their own notes as some of the students quoted above indicate. The ability to make good notes is essential for advanced level work.

There are two main advantages to sound note-making practice:

(1) Making notes keeps you ACTIVE while you are learning. Note-making is a creative process which requires concentration, clear thinking and organization and exercises your memory by re-phrasing in your own words.

(2) Making notes provides a valuable WRITTEN RECORD and REFERENCE SOURCE for retrieval whenever required throughout the course.

Nobody has a perfect memory, so it is of little use to assume that reading or classwork need not be accompanied by the making of notes, even when at the time you feel you have understood and can remember everything you have read or heard.

There are several situations where you will find it necessary to make notes; in class; to accompany your reading from books, articles and similar sources; from a television documentary; from a lecture; and sometimes from your own thoughts about a sociological issue.

A. CLASS NOTES

Teaching style/method.

In the early stages of the course you will be able to find out about your teachers' teaching styles and methods.

(1) Do they dictate notes?—If so, don't 'switch off'. Concentrate and try to undertand them at the same time as copying. If there are any difficulties in understanding, ask questions. Always read through as soon as possible after a lesson, make your own comments, underline, highlight sections, make the gist easily recognizable for later study.

It has already been suggested that at this level of study you will probably be less 'teacher-directed' in your work, so dictated notes may be less used than formerly.

(2) Do they lecture or talk about particular issues?—Usually important points which you should specially note are dictated, written up on a blackboard, or shown on an overhead projector screen. Teachers will often break up the talk with examples and illustrations, references to particular studies or by asking questions which lead to discussion. Listen out for key points and note those down. Don't try to make notes on every word.

(3) Do they encourage discussion in class?—When this occurs, always try to participate. This may be difficult at first, particularly if you are not used to discussion, but, as the course proceeds, you will gain confidence. Make notes as the discussion proceeds, listen to what your fellow students say and the teacher's response, and try to summarize what is going on. Try not to let your note-taking prevent you from participating.

(4) Do they use handouts?—In recent years the use of handouts in class has increased and to a large extent has replaced dictated notes as a method of teaching.

(a) *Detailed Handouts*

Handouts can be detailed and the teacher may guide you through them stressing key points and issues. If so, underline or highlight sections and put notes or comments in the margins.

EXERCISE

A class handout where a student has underlined what she regards as key points.
Read the passage—would you underline the same sections?

POST-WAR ARGUMENTS CONCERNING TRIPARTITE SYSTEM OF EDUCATION WHICH LED TO THE ESTABLISHMENT OF A COMPREHENSIVE SYSTEM

In theory, an essential part of the philosophy of the tripartite system was that the three kinds of schools, Grammar, Technical High, and Secondary Modern should be 'different but equal'. According to this idea, nobody should be regarded as inferior or a failure if selected for a Secondary Modern. In practice this did not work for several reasons.

Most parents, especially the middle class ones, wanted their children to attend Grammar Schools. Complaints about the results of selection tests at 11 became common. It was also more difficult than expected to select three types of children at 11 years. Studies revealed that there were many 'bright' children who failed to pass at 11, while a few studies showed some who did and became misfits. Educationists and psychologists began to cast doubts over the use of tests which were used as a final judgement at the age of 11. They suggested that these were not accurate because a person's I.Q. can change.

The supposed advantage of a partnership with the government by which local authorities were able to be different from each other, in fact turned out to be a serious disadvantage. It was soon found to be more a matter of geography than intelligence whether or not a child got into grammar school. Over the country as a whole, 20% of 11 year olds attended grammar schools, but in some areas places were available for less than 10%. In other areas, over 40% of places were available. This led people to question the fairness of the selection process.

Another kind of unfairness that was pointed out, especially by sociologists, was that, although the position had improved since the war, and fee-paying had been abolished, the chances of a working class child going to grammar school were still much lower than those of a middle class child. (see Douglas, Jackson and Marsden, Floud and Halsey, Plowden Report, etc.)

Finally, the idea of 'parity of prestige' was brought into question. Olive Banks pointed out that employers and adults generally valued the products of each type of school differently, grammar schools being associated with intelligence and academic ability, and secondary modern schools with ineptitude and failure. Banks' argument was that society gives higher prestige to lawyers, doctors and managers, who are likely to be the products of public and grammar schools, than to carpenters, bricklayers or dustmen, who are likely to have attended secondary moderns. A logical consequence of this was that the schools themselves would also be given high or low prestige. Consequently children were deemed to have 'passed' or 'failed' the 11 plus and correspondingly required to attend a superior or inferior school.

EXERCISE

Use the above passage and your textbook(s) to answer the following:

(1) What was the basis of selection for the three types of school in the tripartite system?
(2) Which of the three types of school never became properly established? Give reasons.
(3) Outline the arguments against the tripartite system.
(4) Explain in your own words the meaning of 'parity of prestige'.
(5) Why was the comprehensive system seen as a better alternative?
(6) Now the comprehensive system has become established have the problems of the tripartite system been eradicated? Give reasons including reference to sociological research evidence.

(b) *Linear Notes or Gapped Handouts*
An example of a linear handout used in class, where a student has filled in with notes/comments

SOCIAL MOBILITY

In the last 25 years information on mobility has been based on a survey carried out by Glass in 1949. This study showed that:

(a) Most mobility was short ranged. – movement between 1 or 2 class groupings

(b) There is a barrier to movement across the manual/non-manual line. Little transfer from working to middle class

(c) There is a high degree of self recruitment at the top of the social scale. Elite positions – reinforced by background, public school, Oxbridge etc.

The Oxford Mobility enquiry carried out in 1972 with a sample of 10,000 adult males tested some of Glass' theories, each respondent was asked questions about their own occupational and educational biographies plus information about their fathers, mothers, wives, brothers and friends.

Mobility from what to what:

The Oxford group looked at movement between 7 social classes, based on market and class position of the individual, the classes were:

SERVICE { (1) High grade professionals/admin.
(2) Lower grade professionals, high grade technicians, lower grade admin. }

INTER-MEDIATE { (3) Routine non-manual, sales personnel.
(4) Farmers, self-employed etc. – note this could contain same occupations as (6) e.g. plumber.
(5) Lower grade technicians, and supervisors of manual workers. }

WORKING { (6) Skilled manual workers.
(7) Semi and unskilled manual workers. }

This differs from Reg. Gen.'s Index

For a full account of these 7 classes see "Social Mobility and Class Structure in Modern Britain". J.H. Goldthorpe – page 39–42

Goldthorpe sometimes groups these into three broader classes

A – classes 1 and 2. The service class.
B – classes 3, 4 and 5. An intermediate class.
} Are these what was once the middle class?
C – classes 6 and 7. A working class.

Long or short range mobility

Short range mobility would be moving

From class 1 or 2 to class 3, 4 or 5
" " 3, 4, 5 to class 1 or 2, or 6 or 7
" " 6 or 7 to class 3, 4, 5.
} see (a) above

Long range mobility would be moving

From class 6 or 7 to class 1 or 2 Son/daughter of labourer becomes Doctor
" " 1 or 2 to class 6 or 7 Doctor's son / daughter becomes labourer. – This would be very rare.

CONT.....

These are usually intended as a guide through the main points which your teacher wishes to cover. They are often in linear note form with headings, sub-headings and numbered points with space between for you to add detail as the teacher goes through the handout. Discussion can also be incorporated into this teaching style, so make notes as you go through the handout as the example shows.

(5) Do they show videos/films, play audio cassette tapes?—When this occurs in class make notes as you listen or watch and also make notes of points arising if there is discussion at the end.

During the class you should:

(1) recognize the way the teacher may use voice changes to stress key points;
(2) always note references to studies and names which your teacher says are important. Follow them up, find out more in your private study by borrowing the books from the library, reading the appropriate articles, and so on;
(3) summarize key points—either during or at the end of the lesson.
Whichever teaching style or method is used, try to grasp the key ideas and overall structure of the topic being dealt with and shape your notes around this.

After the class (in Private Study time)—

(1) Go over the notes again to make sure they are fully understood.
(2) Tidy them up. They may be understandable or readable now, but what about in six months time?
(3) If they are lengthy dictated notes do you need to make your own brief version, or, underline or highlight key sections?
(4) If handouts have been given out but not worked at in class, always read them as soon as possible, highlight, underline, add comments, make notes. Use private study periods for this purpose. Don't file handouts away intending to read 'at a later date' which often never comes!

B. NOTES FROM READING

Providing they are legible, well-organized and the main points are recognizable to you at later stages of the course, your notes made from reading books or articles are very much an individual thing. With practice you can develop your own style and presentation. Broadly, two main types of notes can be identified: LINEAR NOTES, sometimes referred to as SEQUENTIAL NOTES; and PATTERN NOTES, sometimes referred to as NUCLEAR or DIAGRAMMATIC NOTES.

Linear (sequential) notes

These are the more familiar form of notes to most students. They are usually presented in the form of headings, sub-headings and numbered points with the use of indentation and spacing to make points clear.

FEATURES OF LINEAR NOTES

Headings	—	Usually in block capitals, single or double underlining, or underlined in a different colour to stand out.
Sub-headings	—	These can be in capitals, less conspicuous than headings, single underlining or a different colour.
Numbered points	—	e.g. the main functions of the family as suggested by MURDOCK are: (1) .... (2) .... (3) .... (4) .... (5) ....
Indentation	—	used to present things under headings so headings are clear and stand out. Space between points and good, wide margins help with later additions.

When presented in the above form, the information can be quickly obtained as important points are made to stand out. Linear notes should act as an aid to memory, as something you can look at at various stages of the course and quickly identify key points and relevant information.

PROBLEMS IN MAKING LINEAR NOTES

> 'I find it difficult to make notes from a book, I don't know what to leave out and often end up writing nearly everything down.'
>
> 1st year A level student.

The above quote illustrates a common problem in constructing linear notes experienced by new students who are confronted with unfamiliar and sometimes difficult material. Many students make notes which are slightly abbreviated versions of the original. This is time-consuming and unnecessary. You need to develop the skill of picking out the key points from a section or passage and putting them down in an abbreviated and easy to follow format.

DEGREE OF DIFFICULTY OF READING MATERIAL

An obvious point to make is that reading material varies in the degree of difficulty or depth involved. Complex theoretical arguments will require more concentration than more descriptive accounts of studies of criminals, football hooligans, children in classrooms or factory workers. A book's layout can sometimes be helpful in that use is made of headings and sub-headings, the text itself is written in an easy to follow style and sometimes authors write as follows:

'There are four main objections to X's theory of Y. *Firstly, ..., *secondly,.......,' and so on.
*Look out for sign-post words.

Clearly it is relatively easy to 'translate' such a passage into linear note form, the heading would be OBJECTIONS TO X's THEORY OF Y and then your numbered points could be contractions of those offered by the author under 'firstly', 'secondly' etc.

EXERCISE

Make linear notes from the following passage *or* underline or highlight key points.

The 'functions' of poverty

In *More Equality*, Herbert J. Gans argues that 'poverty survives in part because it is useful to a number of groups in society'. Poverty benefits the non-poor in general and the rich and powerful in particular. They therefore have a vested interest in maintaining poverty. From this perspective, Gans outlines the following 'functions of poverty' for the non-poor.

Firstly, every economy has a number of temporary, dead-end, dirty, dangerous and menial jobs. The existence of poverty ensures that such work is done. Gans argues that 'poverty functions to provide a low-wage labour pool that is willing—or rather, unable to be unwilling—to perform dirty work at low cost'. Without the low paid, many industries would be unable to continue in their present from. Gans claims that hospitals, the catering trade, large sections of agriculture and parts of the garment industry are dependent on low wage labour. Raising wages would increase costs with 'obvious dysfunctional consequences for more affluent people'. Thus at one and the same time, poverty ensures that 'dirty jobs' are done and, by getting them done cheaply, subsidizes the non-poor sections of the population.

Secondly, poverty directly provides employment and financial security for a fast growing section of the labour force. In Gans's words, 'Poverty creates jobs for a number of occupations and professions that serve the poor, or shield the rest of the population from them'. These include the police, probation officers, social workers, psychiatrists, doctors and the administrators who oversee the 'poverty industry'. In Britain, the social security system employed some 80 000 staff in 1976 and the cost of administration amounted to £649 million. However altruistic their motives, Gans suggests that those employed to deal with the poor have a vested interest in poverty.

Thirdly, Gans argues that the presence of the poor provides reassurance and support for the rest of society. They provide a baseline of failure which reassures the non-poor of their worth. Gans claims that 'poverty helps to guarantee the status of those who are not poor'. It does this by providing 'a reliable and relatively permanent measuring rod for status comparison'. Since they are relatively powerless, the poor also provide an effective scapegoat for the non-poor. Gans maintains that, 'The defenders of the desirability of hard work, thrift, honesty, and monogamy need people who can be accused of being lazy, spendthrift, dishonest and promiscuous to justify these norms'. Gans argues that the poor function to reinforce mainstream norms since norms 'are best legitimated by discovering violations'.

From a somewhat different perspective, Gans has reached a similar conclusion to those who argue that poverty must be analysed in terms of class inequality. From both viewpoints poverty exists because it benefits the rich and because the poor are powerless to change their situation. Gans concludes that poverty persists 'because many of the functional alternatives to poverty would be quite dysfunctional for the more affluent members of society'.

Michael Haralambos, *Sociology: Themes and Perspectives (2nd Edition)* (University Tutorial Press, London, 1985), p.165–166

If you found this an 'easy' section to make notes from, why do you think this was?

The following extract provides an example of a clear layout with the additional impact of names and key points in heavy type, which makes for easy reading and note making.

Delinquency, Disorder and Contamination

. . . From the beginning, then, 'juvenile delinquency' described a law and order problem that was different from the law and order problem posed by adult criminals. Three issues were involved in particular.

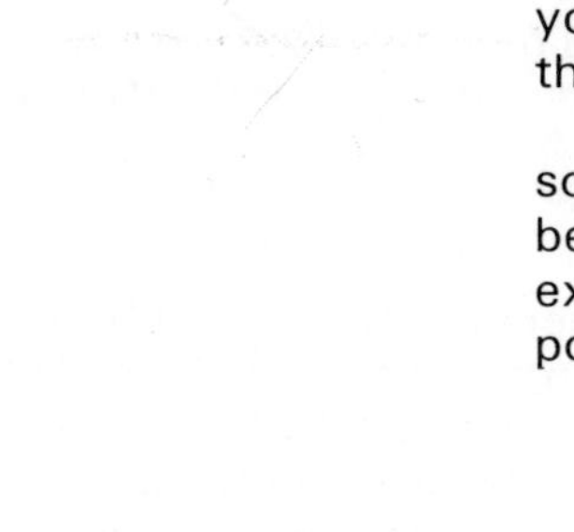

First, is delinquency a **collective** or an **individual** problem? The law defines crime in individual terms—this is the logic of arrest, trial and sentence—but much juvenile delinquency takes place in groups. Football hooliganism, for example, is a problem because of the activities of **groups** of people, but the law can only deal with those individuals 'unlucky' enough to be picked out of the crowd by the police.

Second, is delinquency a **rational** or **irrational** activity? Vandalism, for example, is usually described by newspapers as 'mindless', football hooligans are called 'animals'. How can a 'rational' legal system respond to irrational behaviour?

Third, should the treatment of delinquents emphasise **punishment** or **reform**? Do young people need a clear **deterrent** from delinquency, 'a short sharp shock'? Or is the problem one of poor socialisation so that what is necessary is re-education?

These issues have particularly concerned sociologists and if, as a result, the sociology of youth has been dominated by studies of problem youth, then this is because such studies are seen to have **practical** implications. If sociologists can explain juvenile delinquency then they can have a direct influence on the state's youth policy.

S. Frith, *The Sociology of Youth* (Causeway Press, Ormskirk, 1984), p.26–27

However, not all reading will be as straightforward as this example. Working with one or two partners, consider the following from one of the major A level Sociology textbooks, each take your own notes on it, and then compare them. Whose notes are most effective and why?

John Westergaard and Henrietta Resler

Westergaard and Resler argue that private ownership of capital is the major determinant of inequalities in income. The role of the state and the labour market are secondary, and largely influenced by the power of capital. Via taxation and welfare provisions, the state has done little to redistribute income. The benefits gained from the Welfare State by the working class are largely paid for by taxes from its members. What the wealthy appear to lose from taxation, they largely regain in tax concessions on private insurance policies, payments to company pension schemes and mortgages. Income differences which arise from the operation of the labour market are relatively small compared to those which result from the ownership and non-ownership of the forces of production. Table 6 shows trends in income distribution. Data on income are usually derived from tax returns, which provide only a very rough estimate and tend to understate high incomes. For example, they do not include various fringe benefits, nor do they account for income gained from tax evasion which may be substantial. Westergaard and Resler have therefore adjusted the figures provided by the Inland Revenue to include various sources of 'hidden' income.

In terms of the adjusted figures, the richest 1% received as much income as the poorest 30%, the richest 5% as much as the poorest 50%. There was a trend towards greater income equality from 1938 to 1949, which slowed from 1949 to 1954 and then virtually ceased. Westergaard and Resler conclude that, 'There are no indications of an inherent and continuing trend towards substantial redistribution of income within the capitalist economy of Britain. More recent figures based on tax returns show a small reduction in the concentration of income but they have not been adjusted to include 'hidden' income.

Table 6 Share of top income recipients in personal income from 1938 to 1980

			Groups of income units					
			Before Adjustment			*After Adjustment*		
		Received by richest	*1%*	*5%*	*10%*	*1%*	*5%*	*10%*
Estimated % share of total value of all personal income received by the richest 1% (5%, 10%) of all income units	1938		11½	—	—	15	—	—
	1949		6½	—	—	10½	—	—
	1954		5½	—	—	9½	—	—
	1957		5	—	—	9	—	—
	1959/60		5	—	—	10	20½	30
			Before income tax			*After income tax*		
		Received by richest	*1%*	*5%*	*10%*	*1%*	*5%*	*10%*
	1964		8.2	19.5	29.1	5.2	15.0	25.9
	1970/1		6.6	17.7	27.5	4.5	14.5	23.9
	1976/7		5.4	15.9	25.8	3.5	12.9	22.4
	1979/80		5.2	15.4	24.8	4.1	13.6	22.8

Sources: Adapted from Westergaard and Resler 1976, p.42, and from Talbe 2.3, pp.14–15 'Report No. 7 Fourth Report on the Standing Reference', *Royal Commission on the Distribution of Income and Wealth*, 1979, *Social Trends*, 1983, p.77.

Westergaard and Resler argue that the maintenance of inequalities of wealth and income is due to the power of the capitalist class. They maintain that, 'The favoured group enjoys effective power, even when its members take no active steps to exercise power. They do not need to do so—for much of the time at least—simply because things work that way in any case.' It is generally taken for granted, by members of society and governments alike, that investments should bring profit and that the living standards of the propertyless should be based on the demands of the market for their skills. In general, governments have favoured the interests of capital, assuming that the well-being of the nation is largely dependent on the prosperity of private industry. The relationship between the state and capital will be examined in detail in the following chapter.

Westergaard and Resler claim that the class divisions in British society are systematically generated by a capitalist economic system. They identify two major classes. The dominant class is made up of perhaps 5% and at most 10% of the population. It includes the major owners of the forces of production, company directors, top managers, higher professionals and senior civil servants, many of whom are large shareholders in private industry. The subordinate class consists of the bulk of the wage and salary earning population. Westergaard and Resler reject the view that the so-called separation of ownership and control in the joint stock company results in the rise of salaried managers who should properly be placed in a middle class. They argue that 'directors and top executives, in whose hands the major strategic policy decisions lie, are, in fact, owners of large stockholdings themselves'. Like the 'absentee owners', their main concern is the maximization of profit. As such the interests of owners and controllers are largely similar.

The general profile of inequality drawn by Westergaard and Resler is supported by a large body of evidence but their explanation for this inequality is open to a number of criticisms. They insist that private property is the basic determinant of class inequality. However, as Frank Parkin notes, this leaves unexplained the privileged position of top professionals and higher civil servants, many of whom are propertyless. What, asks Parkin, is the significance of private property in determining the high rewards of doctors and the low rewards of nurses, the large salaries of higher civil servants and the relatively small salaries of lower civil servants? Westergaard and Resler do not provide an answer. The view that private property is the primary determinant of the distribution of rewards in capitalist society may be questioned by evidence from socialist societies where the forces of production are communally owned. As a later section will indicate, there are marked social inequalities in East European communist societies. (See pp.91–95.) Westergaard and Resler fail to show that inequality in capitalist societies is generated by mechanisms which are distinct from those which operate in socialist societies. This throws some doubt on their claim that the key to the class system in capitalist society is the private ownership of the forces of production.

M. Haralambos, *Sociology: Themes and Perspectives (2nd Ed.)*
(University Tutorial Press, London, 1985)

ABBREVIATIONS

You should develop your own system as well as the well known ones

soc. socs. — socialist societies
inequals. — inequalities
cap. — capital, capitalism
caps. — capitalists
and so on.

Don't over-abbreviate particularly at first, or notes may become inscrutable. You will gradually find that familiar and regular usage will enable you to abbreviate increasingly: e.g.

emb.	=	embourgeoisement
w/c	=	working class or white collar (depending on context)
m/c	=	middle class
func.	=	functionalism, functionalist
fem.	=	female, feminist, feminine (depending on context)
sec.	=	secularisation
ind.	=	industrialisation, industrialised
mech.	=	mechanised, mechanisation
1p.fam.	=	one-parent family
urb.	=	urbanised, urbanisation
div.	=	divorce
off.stats.	=	official statistics
dev.	=	development, deviance (depending on context)

EXERCISE

Consider the following notes made by a student from an article. Are they satisfactory? If not, what alterations can you make? (You may wish to con sider factors like headings, sub-headings, indentation, spacing, abbreviation, etc).

society TODAY

A social science brief for schools and colleges 28 February 1980

WORK

Advanced industrial societies like Britain seem to be at a crossroads. Is our future to be with the silicon chip and a new age of leisure or with hyper-inflation and mass unemployment worse than that of the 1930s?

Work, and what it means to society, is one of the most important areas of study in social science. The topic is so broad that sociologists have divided it up into a whole range of specialisms—the sociology of occupations, of the professions, of industrial relations, of organisations and so on.

THE STRUCTURE OF WORK

In Britain most work is based on our industrial structure, whereby goods are mass-produced through factories and power-operated machinery. Industrialisation has led to the growth of cities, of mass communications and a complex transport network. It has fundamentally changed nearly every other social system—the family, education and religion.

Britain's industrialisation was on a capitalist basis. Businessmen set up factories, mines and mills in competition with one another. The control of capital and resources was in the hands of these private owners, and workers "sold" their labour to them. The main stimulus to economic activity was profit. Today we have what is known as a mixed economy. Some areas of industry belong to the government, others are individually owned. Others still are large corporations controlled by groups of managers on behalf of the owners, who may be foreign. The multi-national Ford Motor Company, for instance, is American-owned and operates in almost every industrialised country in the west. Its wage bill approaches the size of the Irish Republic's gross national product.

Britain's industrial structure is typical of most capitalist societies. There is a labour force of 26 million out of a population of 57 million. Compared with a century ago, more people make things than mine them or grow them, but there is an increasing movement into the service industries, too. These are the whole range of non-manufacturing industries, from transport to hairdressing. In 1851 22 per cent of the labour force was in agriculture; today it is less than 4 per cent. Employment in manufacturing grew by 150 per cent in the first half of this century, while employment in mining and quarrying fell by 20 per cent.

One of the biggest occupational shifts this century has been the growth of the "white collar" sector (clerical, managerial and professional people). This reflects the increasing number of women in employment rather than the displacement of men from manual jobs. Most men (about 60 per cent) are still involved in manual work.

Work, and its problems, are rarely out of the headlines.

Notes made on 'Society Today' Work article by a student.

Work

Structure of Work

1. In Britain most work is based on our Industrial structure whereby goods are mass produced thru factories + power-operated machinery. Industrialisation has led to growth of cities, of mass communications + a complex transport network. It has fundamentally changed nearly every other social system – family, education + religion.
2. Britain's industrialisation was on a capitalist basis. Businessmen set up factories, mills + mines in competition with one another. The control of capital + resources was in the hands of these private owners + workers 'sold' their labour to them. The main stimulus to economic activity was profit. Today, we have what is known as a mixed economy. Some areas belong to govt. Others are individually owned. Others still are large corporations controlled by groups of management on behalf of owners who may be foreign.
3. Britain's industrial structure is typical of most capitalist societies.
4. There has been an increased involvement in service industries. 5. One of biggest occupational shifts this century has been the growth of the "white collar" sector. This reflects the increasing number of women in employment rather than the displacement of men from manual jobs. Most men are still involved in manual work.

When completed does the following apply to your notes:

(1) Are they clear and easy to follow?
(2) Are there headings and sub-headings?
(3) Are there numbered points?
(4) Are recognizable abbreviations used?
(5) Did you find it easy to pick out information? Why?
(6) Will you be able to get the gist from the notes in 6 months time?

Pattern Notes (Nuclear notes, diagrammatic notes, concept trees, mind or mental maps).

This form of note-making should not be seen as an alternative or replacement for linear notes, but can be applied to other study activities as well as reading, for example analyzing questions or revision. This method of note making has only come to the fore recently, its origins being attributable to a combination of the work of the psychologist Tony Buzan, the author of 'Use Your Head' (BBC Publications London, 1974), and Gestalt psychology. In simple terms it is suggested that the brain does not think and problem solve in a neat linear way as the numbered progression of linear notes seems to imply. Rather, our thoughts are often random, incoherent and disjointed so that when we consider a problem and eventually solve it we do so by drawing all these apparently disconnected thoughts together into a PATTERN.

This pattern is constructed from what was a jumble of disorganized information, much as when we complete a jigsaw from a 'jumble' of what seems to be unrelated jigsaw pieces in a box. The crossword anagram, which requires the unscrambling of letters in a word or phrase, in order to make another word or phrase is a good example of how this process works. Sometimes you can attempt to solve an anagram and the solution is not forthcoming, then if you go away, carry out some other activity and return to the anagram the answer 'jumps out', so, GO COSY OIL becomes SOCIOLOGY. This establishment of a pattern from disordered information is referred to as a GESTALT which is a German word. The Gestalt school of psychology originated in Germany.

CONSTRUCTING PATTERN NOTES

Start with a blank sheet of A4 size paper placed horizontally rather than vertically as with linear notes. The topic selected is placed at the centre of the page in a bubble or rectangle. You then gradually work outwards from the centre, using more bubbles or rectangles connected by lines. Nearest to the centre, cover the most important connected themes or ideas, and move out towards the edges of the paper where eventually the more peripheral points or issues are dealt with. The creative and challenging aspect of constructing pattern notes is in the design of the pattern. This should include all aspects that relate to the central topic, and these should interconnect. Where possible, you can use cartoons or picture diagrams as these make a visual impact which is more recognizable at a later date.

Pattern notes require careful design and clear presentation so you need to proceed through the following stages:

(1) Choose the topic.
(2) Read up on the topic first and then briefly note key words and terms, theoretical arguments and issues, empirical research evidence and major contributions to the debate so that you get a broad overview of what the topic involves.
(3) Link the above together so that they can be represented diagrammatically in a way that makes it easy to recognize the key features of that particular topic.

COMPARISON of LINEAR and PATTERN NOTES

Compare the following two sets of notes on the topic of secularization which refers to the declining influence of religion in a society.

In Pattern Note form the debate about secularization could be presented as follows:

Compare to the linear notes.

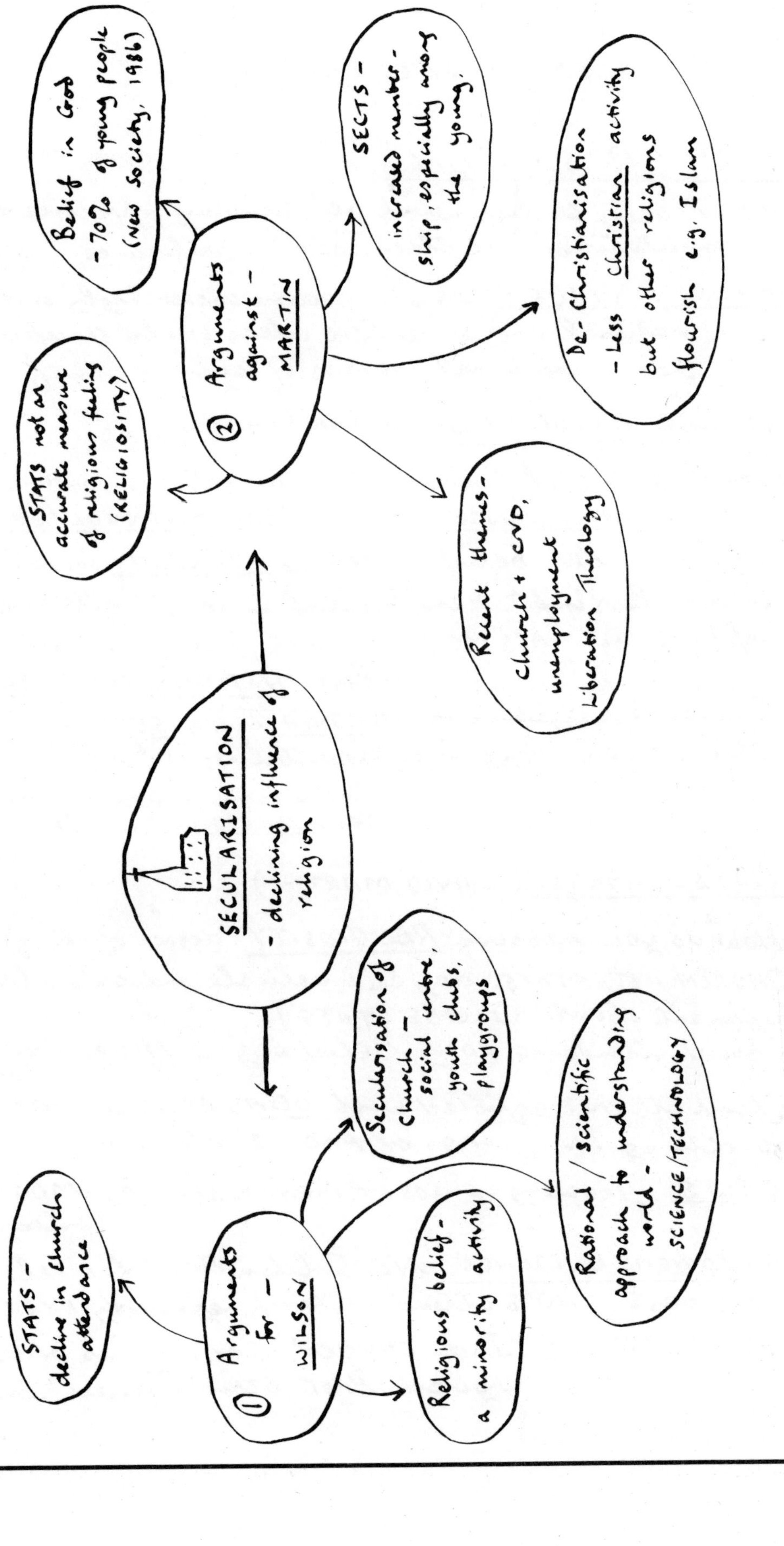

Compare the following linear note presentation of the arguments surrounding secularization with the pattern note presentation.

LINEAR NOTES ON SECULARISATION

SECULARISATION

DEFN: Process through which rel. thinking, practice + institutions 'lose their social significance' (WILSON)

THEOR. LINK: WEBER as soc. became increasingly ind., rational and scientific ideas would sweep away trad. + irrational sources of auth. + belief.

(A) PRO-SEC. ARGUMENTS (BRYAN WILSON)

(1) Decline in Rel. practice + participation in adv. socs. CHURCH ATTENDANCE STATS fallen INVOLVEMENT

(2) Decline in Rel. belief – less INTEREST in rel.

(3) Church less impt. + influential in soc. – other agencies replaced eg MASS MEDIA, SCHOOLS, WELFARE STATE – less INSTITUTIONAL INFLUENCE

(4) Church less a place of WORSHIP more SECULAR – Church runs Playgroups, youthclubs, clubs for elderly – has become a SOCIAL rather than RELIGIOUS centre

(B) ANTI-SEC. ARGS. (DAVID MARTIN)

(1) How do you measure RELIGIOSITY (degree of rel. feeling)? CHURCH ATT. STATS. may be unreliable indicators (see argument about SUICIDE STATS) Church attendance LOW Belief in God HIGH (New Society Survey 1985)

(2) Church att. not equated with BEING RELIGIOUS. Other sources eg TV 'Songs of Praise' etc.

(3) SECTS growing in nos. + membership eg MOONIES (Eileen BARKER)

(4) HISTORICAL EVIDENCE No 'Golden Age' for rel. in the past. 40% attended Church regularly 1851

(5) CAUSE + EFFECT Ind. 'caused' Sec. or as WEBER argued Prot Ethic 'caused' IND REV?

The pattern notes are less detailed than the linear notes but is the gist conveyed? If so, pattern notes have the advantage of visual impact as they are easier to scan, grasp key issues from and so on. They are less lengthy than linear notes.

PROBLEMS OF PATTERN NOTES

(1) Pattern notes may result in a confused jumble of information ('though this can also happen with linear notes).
(2) Making connections between points may be difficult.
(3) Complex topics may not easily lend themselves to such a format.
(4) Linear notes may be easier to translate into an essay structure.
(5) Over-simplification to make visual impact may lead to lack of depth and detail. (This could also apply to linear notes).

ADVANTAGES OF PATTERN NOTES

(1) Pattern notes are good for getting you thinking creatively about topics rather than mechanically writing points down, as may happen with linear notes.
(2) They are particularly useful during Exam Revision Periods (see Chapter 7)—you could make Pattern Notes from Linear Notes, providing strong reinforcement and a better memory aid.
(3) Visual impact stimulates creativity and imagination in usage.
(4) Easy to recognise key issues.

CONCLUSION

Pattern notes cannot be seen as a replacement for linear notes. They are a useful alternative way of presenting and simplifying topics and are particularly good for creative or thinking activity, such as initial preparation for an essay, decoding a question, and exam revision.

EXERCISE

Return to the passage p.76 and construct a pattern note from the information. Compare to your linear notes. Which do you find most useful and why?
There is an example of a pattern on p.84.

Sprays/Spider Notes

These operate on a similar principle to pattern or nuclear notes, but are usually made without books or other notes. They are useful when you are engaged in activities such as revising and recalling topics or decoding a question. Sprays involve you in 'brainstorming', which means drawing out as many ideas or thoughts about a subject or topic as possible, even if they may not at first appear to be directly related.

CONSTRUCTING SPRAYS OR SPIDER NOTES

There is a similarity in presentation to pattern notes in that it is usually best to work outward from the centre of a sheet of paper placed horizontally. In the same way, place the key term, topic, concept or idea in a bubble or rectangle at the centre of the page. Unlike pattern notes, sprays or spider notes can be 'sprayed' out from the centre in a more haphazard fashion, the idea being that as you think of ideas you follow them through, adding related points as you think of them, even when sometimes the connection is not immediately obvious. As with pattern notes, the difficult part is the interlinking of terms so you end up with a web-like' diagram as the term spider notes suggests. See p.20

You should quickly 'spray' out all possible information: words / ideas / names / references/ theoretical aspects/empirical studies that are connected. As you think of further connected issues, try to extend the line of thinking so that you add points towards the edges of the page. Work rapidly, firing out ideas as spontaneously as you can. If you dry up, return to the central term, think of other points and follow these to their conclusion. When you have exhausted all the possible avenues, try to take in the diagram as a whole and note repeated words or terms, make links between related words or terms and cross-reference wherever applicable. With this technique, you can sometimes pleasantly surprise yourself with the amount of detail you can draw out on a topic which you may have thought you had little or no knowledge of.

Not only can the three 'types' of notes in this section be applied to different study activities as described, but they can also be combined in useful and constructive ways. Take the situation of exam revision (see Chapter 7). Many students make

AN EXAMPLE OF A PATTERN NOTE

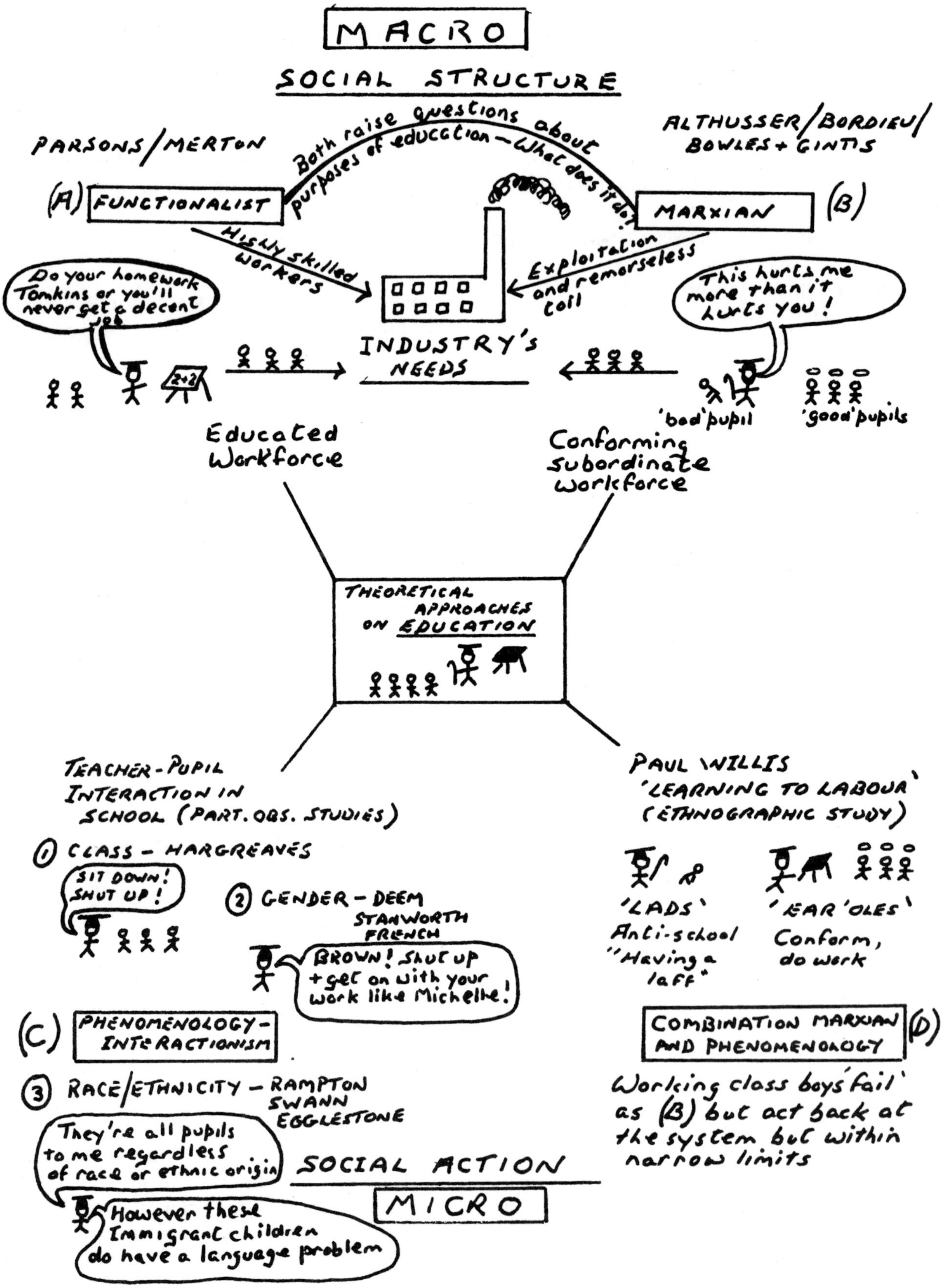

more condensed versions of their class or reading notes—notes from notes—until eventually they can be reduced to a card size and indexed accordingly. Such cards are useful and can act as a key-in or cue to the more detailed material. An alternative would be to approach revision in 3 stages:

(1) Make sprays when first considering a topic.
(2) Read and work from your course material, linear notes and books.
(3) Construct a pattern note.

This 3 stage approach has the advantage of combining creative thinking (sprays) with consolidation and detail (linear notes, course material) and provides easy reference and visual impact (pattern notes). It could well make the hard repetitive slog of revision more imaginative, interesting and variable, thereby being a more effective method of retaining information.

DIAGRAMS/ILLUSTRATIONS

These can be a useful way of highlighting a particular topic. They can sometimes alleviate the 'density' of a set of linear notes or add colour to a pattern note. Remember, visual imagery is a most effective form of communication.
Below there is a diagram used to introduce a section on Theories of Deviance.
Is this a useful way of presenting information?

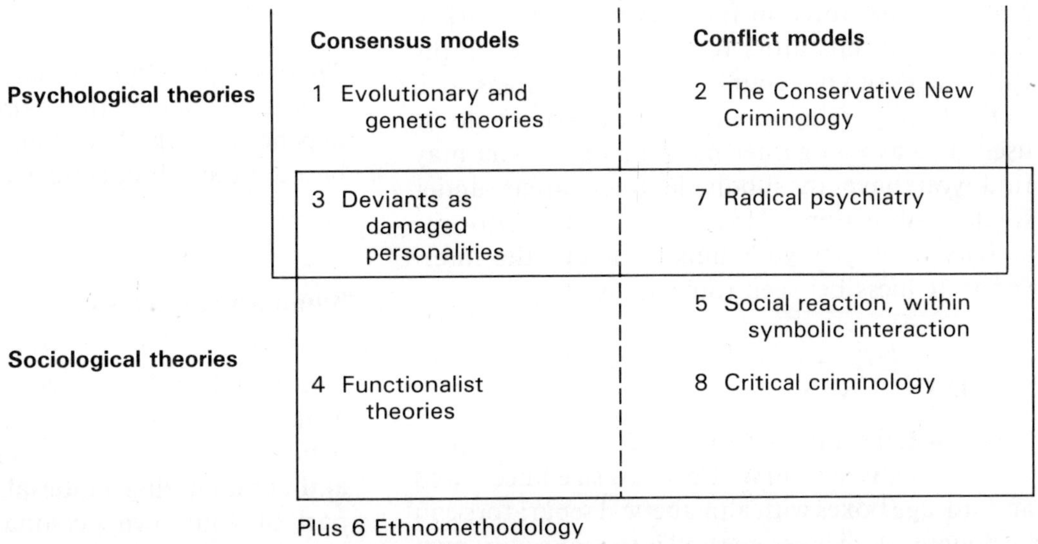

Figure 6 ***Catalogue of theories of deviance***

1 'Consensus models', which view society as either being based on a widespread agreement about what is right and wrong ('value consensus'), or as being in an imperfect state when such agreement is lacking. Given such a picture of society, deviance stands as evidence that some people are deficient or confused because they won't or can't share the values of others, or that 'society isn't working properly'. Such views of deviance are often called 'pathology models' because they entail the idea of deviance as an individual or social *sickness*.
2 'Conflict models', which view society as containing groups of people with different interests and values, and, usually, involve the idea that some groups are subjected to the interests of others. Looked at in this way deviance is unsurprising. It appears as part of an on-going struggle between people to get their own way.

P McNeil and C Townley, *Fundamentals of Sociology* (Hutchinson, London, 1981)

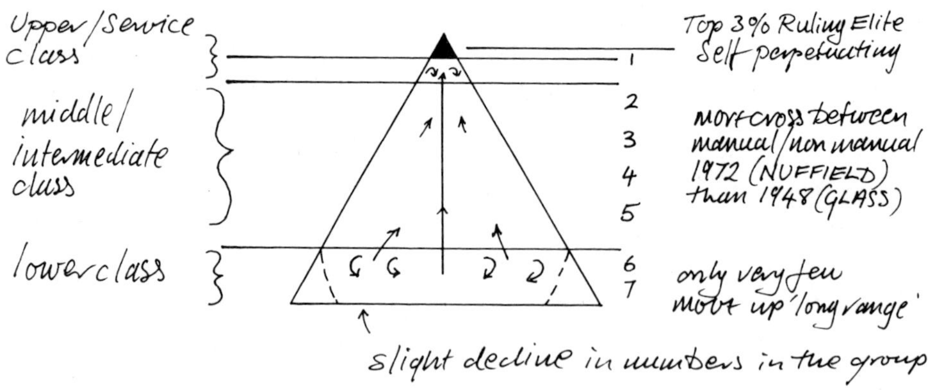

Diagram used by student to illustrate notes on social mobility.

C. STORAGE OF NOTES/RETRIEVAL SYSTEM

Notes can be stored in files under clearly marked headings on separators for easy reference. In the early stages of your course, broad topic areas such as the family, religion and stratification could be used, but as you gather more material, you may find you have to subdivide these areas under smaller subsections. This in itself is a worthwhile activity as it gets you thinking about the interconnectedness between topic areas.

CARD INDEXES

You can build up a reference source as you proceed through the course. Postcard size lined cards and storage boxes with alphabetical separators can be bought. A cheaper method is to make your own from thin cardboard such as cereal packets or washing powder boxes.

There are a number of uses for card index systems:

(1) As a GLOSSARY—an alphabetical collection of definitions of key words and terms dealt with during the course.

(2) As a KEY SOCIOLOGISTS INDEX—where key figures in the field of sociological ideas are filed alphabetically and a brief summary of their work is provided on the card.

(3) As an EMPIRICAL STUDIES INDEX—where brief summaries of research are provided. Could be filed under a subject area index, e.g. STRATIFICATION/WORK/GENDER / RACE-ETHNICITY, on separators.

(4) As a SUBSECTION OF TOPIC AREAS INDEX—where the separators deal with subject or topic areas as in (3) and, under each, subsections of that area are dealt with—possibly alphabetically e.g. under the separator heading GENDER you might have cards on BIOLOGY, CULTURE, EDUCATION, EMPLOYMENT, and so on.

There are possibilities that any of (1)–(4) could be combined under the same index. This could depend on whether your retrieval system was based on an alphabetical or a subject index.

Summary/Conclusion

You should make notes rather than take notes. Making notes is a constructive, creative activity, which involves you in reading, condensing, editing and summarizing material into a form which is part of your own personal activity in studying. You should never attend a lecture, read a book or article, watch a relevant TV documentary, read a handout or newspaper cutting without making notes. Notes form a permanent record which, when properly referenced or indexed in your files, becomes your central information or data bank, which is the basis of your knowledge of topics or subject areas.

Taking notes implies a more passive activity, where you automatically record information with little thought, so always think in terms of making rather than taking notes.

Notes can be used at later stages of the course as 'triggers' or 'cues' to memory for material on topics. So referring to your notes becomes the first stage in your preparation for writing an essay, and eventually, your revision and preparation for the examinations.

CHAPTER 5

WRITING SOCIOLOGY ESSAYS

> 'There will be a prize of half a crown for the longest essay irrespective of any possible merit' Evelyn Waugh, *Decline and Fall.*

> 'A man may write at any time, if he will set himself doggedly to it' Dr Samuel Johnson.

> 'I never really know what to put in or leave out of an essay' 1st year A Level student.

> 'The best way to support a sociological preference surely is to follow its arguments through, show that it works, answer the questions it sets out to answer, making it something that is sociologically exciting and worthwhile' R.J. Anderson, J.A. Hughes and W.W. Sharrock, *The Sociology Game* (Longman, London, 1985) p.161

Model answers

In this section there are no model or specimen answers for the following reasons:

(1) CORRECT OR RIGHT ANSWERS?
In Sociology there may be several ways of approaching a question so there is not one 'correct' or 'right' answer. Model answers could give the impression that there is.

(2) ROTE LEARNING OF MODEL ANSWERS
Model answers may tempt students into trying to learn such answers parrot-fashion, so they can be replicated in an exam, whether or not exactly the same question is asked. This would be disastrous, as it would show that the student had ignored the question and provided a topic-based 'write all I know about' answer. Examiners warn against such approaches:

> '. . . answers however good to questions that have not been asked will not obtain good marks'
> (Cambridge Examiners' Report: A level Sociology, 1984)*

(3) MODEL ANSWERS ARE OF A HIGH STANDARD
The model answer is often written by a Sociology teacher to a high standard (at least it would be hoped so!), which can be off-putting to a student who could find it very difficult to approach such a standard, more especially when writing an essay under examination conditions.

(4) ESSAY CONSTRUCTION
Model answers do not give you an indication of how to deal with a question, or the way into an answer, or how to construct an essay from a question title.

(5) INDIVIDUAL WRITING STYLE (Thinking in ink)
In some senses we all have our own idiosyncratic method of writing. A selection of essays written by different students, which are all of the same standard and cover similar material and points, would show differences in writing style between each. This is because when you write you are putting your thoughts on paper (thinking in ink), and thought is bound to be very much an individual thing.

USEFULNESS OF MODEL ANSWERS?
Despite the above comments, model answers can be helpful when used constructively as a part of the learning process. An example would be if you compared a model answer to your essay and noted the comparisons and contrasts in the content, structure, arguments and points covered, bearing in mind comment (1) above.

A useful book containing model answers as well as very useful additional commentary on the topics of the essays is J.K. Lane's *A Practical Guide to A Level Sociology* (Nelson, Walton-on-Thames, 1985).

WRITING AN ESSAY—STAGES

(1) Choose the question

↓

(2) Organize timetable for (3)–(6)

↓

(3) Analyse the question—decoding, making sure you have understood, interpreting accurately, asking questions around the question

↓

(4) Research—gather material—not too much but more than basic textbook + class notes. Use your questions to direct you. Look for the answers to give your reading a purpose

↓

(5) Plan your answer — INTRO / MAIN BODY / CONCLUSION — Paragraph, Paragraph, Paragraph, Paragraph, Paragraph, Paragraph

↓

(6) Write the essay—preferably at one sitting

↓

(7) Appraisal when marked—'I now realize/know that I should have included X, referred to Y, etc.'—very useful when considering essay at a later date for revision purposes, etc.

Introduction

The ability to write good Sociology essays is one of the most important skills you need to develop during your course, particularly as you are eventually tested on this in the final examinations. Writing an essay is a difficult, demanding and sometimes lonely activity, which requires high levels of concentration and motivation. Many students find it extremely difficult to make a start on an essay.

> 'I never know how to start, I think I just start writing on the question topic somehow'
> 1st year A level student.

So the student responds either by being a 'DIPPER' or a 'MAGPIE'. 'Dippers' are easily distracted and never really get down to the detailed preparation necessary for writing a good essay. They tend to rely solely on a section of one textbook and class notes and usually rush the writing of the essay at the last minute, i.e. the night before the deadline, so the resultant essay lacks the necessary depth and detail and uses insufficient resources (see Chapter 2). 'Dippers' have not really moved away from a pre-advanced style of essay writing. 'Magpies' on the other hand tend to do too much preparation. They read and make lots of notes and collect masses of information, the majority of which is never used when the essay is finally written. In some ways their preparation can be seen as avoidance of the task of actually writing an essay which they may find very difficult.

In this Chapter the aim is to show how, with careful planning and organization, by developing the skills of analyzing or decoding question titles and thorough researching of essay topics, you can become more effective at writing Sociology essays.

A. WHAT IS AN ESSAY?

An essay could be defined as a continuous piece of writing set out in paragraphs, which is a response to a question or title. At its simplest an essay comprises an INTRODUCTION, a MAIN BODY and a CONCLUSION. You should never write in a topic-based 'write all I know about' manner but should clearly demonstrate the following:

WHAT THE STUDENT SHOULD HAVE DONE	SKILL	PLACE IN ESSAY
(1) UNDERSTOOD the question you have answered	Analysing, decoding or dismantling the question	Introduction
(2) COLLECTED material in a conscientious manner	Research, ability to look more widely than textbook and class materials. Library work—variety of sources	Research for Main body
(3) MADE A PLAN from this material	Planning, good preparation	Before essay writing begins
(4) SORTED OUT (and ORGANIZED) material appropriate to the question	Organization Structure	Main body
(5) WRITTEN a CLEAR and COHESIVE answer, which is well structured, has appropriate content and shows a good style of presentation	Written communication, logical thought. Grammar, punctuation, paragraphing	Throughout the essay
(6) APPRAISED and EVALUATED your material and made clear its relevance to the essay title	Critical thought, presentation of arguments for and against—weighing and making judgement of arguments presented in essay	Conclusion

B. COURSEWORK ESSAYS

During your course you will have to complete regular homework essays which will require the use of books and course materials. Increasingly, as examination time approaches, it will be necessary to practice without the use of books and other sources by doing timed essays either in class or in private study periods. This is good preparation for the exams where you may have to write 4 essays in 3 hours. Essay writing progression could be represented as follows:

COURSE
(1 YEAR - 2 YEAR)
BEGINNING ——————————————→ END

COURSEWORK ESSAYS	REVISION PERIOD	TIMED ESSAYS	EXAM ESSAYS
Heavy reliance on secondhand sources: books, class notes, course materials. Highly derivative, sometimes material insufficiently understood. *Faults* Either (1) DIPPER: too short—lack of depth + detail, insufficient research, reliance on basic text + class notes. (2) MAGPIE: too long—much time spent amassing lots of information, majority of which not used. Inefficient planning, poor question decoding, "Throw enough mud at a wall and some of it's bound to stick" approach.		Ability to decode questions. Little or no use of texts and sources. Effective essay plans.	No books. Sound planning. Time constraint, 45 mins. Demonstrates wide reading, knowledge and understanding. Effective interpretation of question.

The purpose of essays

Essays are set regularly so that you have the chance to develop good written communication skills and are able to explain in writing your interpretation of a question. They are useful in that they let your teachers know that you have understood the material presented in class. An essay is a vehicle by which you can present and express ideas on a topic and demonstrate your knowledge of that topic. If you can talk or think clearly and logically, you should be able to do the same in writing. Essays help you to understand and learn about a topic by involving you in:

(1) thinking about sociological issues arising from essay titles;
(2) gathering material and information;
(3) reading and making notes as part of your preparation and research;
(4) examining in detail sociological arguments, controversies and debates;
(5) structuring an argument to a conclusion.

In the early stages you will spend more time in these activities than in the actual writing of the essay. You need to work at essays consistently throughout the course, so that by the time of the exams you are competent and confident in your written presentation.

Types of essay

(1) DESCRIPTIVE ESSAYS
These are the simplest form of essay and require the straightforward description of something. You would not be asked just to describe something in an Advanced essay and if the word 'describe' is used in the title (see Activity Words p.94) it will be accompanied by terms like 'and account for' or 'and explain', which require you to provide more than mere description.

(2) CREATIVE or IMAGINATIVE ESSAYS
These are often associated with English. We can all probably remember having to do such essays in our early school years as:

What I would do if I won the Pools

or

What I Discovered in the Locked Shed at the Bottom of the Old Man Next Door's Garden!

You would not be set this type of essay in Sociology. If you were, the title would possibly be:

What British society will be like in the Year 2000, but social forecasting has not as yet been included, possibly because it is notoriously incorrect even when carried out by eminent sociologists!

A mistake some students often make in the early stages of a Sociology course is to assume that creative or imaginative insights are required in essays, so they pass judgements or opinions with little or no supportive sociological evidence. Sentences are introduced with phrases like 'I think that . . .' or 'In my opinion . . .', which a teacher has to correct by remarking 'based on what evidence?' This type of introduction is often used when a student is writing about controversial or sensitive issues such as racism, sexism, juvenile delinquency or divorce. Remember that you should always provide supportive evidence for your statements and avoid passing unsubstantiated judgements, as in Sociology you should aim to be as objective and scientific as possible.

This is not to say, however, that creative or imaginative thought has no place in a Sociology essay. During the essay there is scope for you to provide a different slant or angle on a sociological issue or topic, which, provided you can justify it and it relates logically to the matter in hand, will be rewarded with high marks. A simple example of the good use of creative or imaginative thinking in an essay would be if you illustrated a sociological concept like Deviancy Amplification (which refers to the way mass media like the press and television can create moral panics about issues such as mugging or football hooliganism), with an example of your own, as in the following extract:

> 'A more recent illustration of the way deviancy amplification works can be seen in the example of the disease AIDS which has resulted in a hysterical press scare campaign predominantly levelled at homosexual men with headlines like "Menace of the Gay Plague" featuring in our popular newspapers.'

You will need to display your mastery of basic sociological arguments, issues, debates, theories and research before you progress to a more creative approach. This comes at a later stage when you have grasped the core material and have the confidence to illustrate this by thoughts, illustrations, examples and criticisms, which you have arrived at from your own reflections on the topic.

(3) ANALYTICAL ESSAYS

'To analyse (dict): to resolve or separate a thing into its elements or component parts; ascertainment of those parts'. (Chambers Twentieth Century Dictionary). This is the type of essay you will be expected to write for advanced level work. It has already been said that you will not be simply asked to describe a sociological topic, theme or term, e.g. 'Describe the functionalist theory of stratification', but rather you will be required to analyse, which, as the above definition implies, means conveying your understanding of the topic by taking it apart, criticizing, evaluating, examining and exploring arguments or debates, so that the question on the functionalist theory of stratification would be presented in the form:

Critically assess the functionalist theory of stratification.
AEB, November, 1985.

It has already been indicated that Sociology is an argumentative discipline, which means that the majority of topics covered are the subject of arguments, controversy and debate, so you would be expected to demonstrate your knowledge of this in an analytical essay. Activity words like 'discuss' 'evaluate' and 'examine', which are dealt with in a later section in this Chapter, indicate that you are required to write analytically about a topic.

APPROACHES TO ESSAY-WRITING

	REASON	RESULT
(1) LAST MINUTE RUSH —the night before a deadline (see 'DIPPERS' p.88) COMMENT May seem reasonable, but need to recognize in the first year particularly the need to build a solid base of core material from wide reading, so essays require much groundwork and preparation to achieve the necessary level.	Low motivation. Easily distracted. Preoccupied with other concerns e.g. leisure activities, hobbies, etc. 'You won't have lots of books and material in the exam so my approach is good practice'.	Inadequate preparation. Sources: one textbook, class notes, handouts. Possible misreading, misinterpretation of question. Lack of depth and detail. Insufficient reading or research. Low grade or fail. Inadequate basis for good progress in the course. Low satisfaction and motivation.
(2) PREPARATION/ PLANNING	High motivation. Able to concentrate. Able to organize. Spread the work on the essay over 1–2 weeks to give time for proper research.	Sound preparation. Time to think fully about title. Thoroughly research. Wide reading. Sound grasp of theoretical issues, arguments, debates. Refers to named evidence, empirical research. Good basis for further progress on course. High satisfaction from good grades.

Essay timetable

On advanced courses you will probably be given an essay title 2–3 weeks before a deadline. As implied in the previous section, it is important that you organize, so that you spread the work over that period to avoid the 'last minute rush' approach which receives low marks. Thinking about the title, reading, researching your material, making notes and eventually writing the answer will all need organizing and will take time. Your preparation and planning can be carried out in daytime private study periods, but it is advisable to write your essay in one continuous session. The best time for this is probably in the evenings or at weekends where you can write the essay in one go, undistracted and free from interruptions. Writing the essay in this way is good practice, as you will eventually have to write in this way in the examinations.

Over the 2–3 week period you should organize your time and make sure you cover the following activities:

(1) Consider and analyse the title—
question decoding/dismantling

(2) Reading, making notes, research
   (a) from class material
   (b) from basic texts, readers, topic books
   (c) from library books and other sources
   (d) from journals, reference works, statistical sources

(3) Planning your answer:
Introduction
Main Body
Conclusion

(4) Writing the essay
(Try to complete in one session.)

C. INTERPRETING/UNDERSTANDING THE QUESTION—QUESTION ANALYSIS/ DECODING/DISMANTLING

> 'Taking the question to pieces, analysing its total meaning and its various component terms, remains the best way to start constructing an answer'
> (Cambridge Examiners' Report: A level Sociology, 1984)*

This is one of the most obvious activities in the task of essay writing, but is the one that is most often ignored by students. Your interpretation of the question is something you must clearly convey from the outset of every essay. Failure to answer the question set or misinterpretation of the title is one of the commonest of Examiners' complaints as the following comments indicate:

> 'It is vital that candidates are instructed not to answer questions they do not fully understand'
> (Cambridge Examiners' Report: A level Sociology, 1984)*

> '. . . there is clear evidence that candidates find it difficult to venture from their familiar learned packages of material to the actual questions set'
> (JMB Examiners' Report: A level sociology, 1983)

An essay should always be seen to be addressing itself directly to the question set. Remember—constantly think of the question rather than the topic. Too many students, particularly in the examinations, treat the question as a background issue in their desperation to pour out as much material on a topic as possible. This could be referred to as the 'throw enough mud at a wall and some of it is bound to stick' or the 'write all I know about' response.

You should explain your interpretation of the question title from the outset, preferably in your introductory paragraph(s). This will show whether or not you have correctly understood the question, which is the first thing the examiner wants to see.

Choice of essay

When you are given a homework essay, you may be given a choice from several titles, so your first task is to select the one you are going to do. Read the titles carefully before you make your decision, as some essay titles may be more obscure than others. This sometimes is the case when a quote is used. Compare the following essay titles:

'The police obviously have to make decisions, both individually and corporately, about which crimes and criminals they are going to proceed against and how many men to allocate to which law enforcement tasks.' What implications does this statement have for sociological theories of crime?

Is crime a working class phenomenon?
Cambridge, June, 1985, Paper 1.

Quite clearly the first title requires more thought and interpretation than the second, but do not immediately discount a title because of its initial impact. Careful consideration and analysis of the title could mean that you find you can provide a good answer. It may be better to select the less difficult titles in the early stages of your course, so you can provide the best answer possible. However, in the later stages it is advisable to tackle more challenging and difficult titles and subject areas as preparation for the possibility of such titles in the examination.

Once you have chosen a title, you should not just plunge into a pile of topic-based reading, the next stage is to consider the question set in more detail. Write down the title on a blank sheet of paper and underline activity or cue words such as 'discuss' or 'evaluate' (see below) and key terms, concepts or ideas which have to be evaluated and explained. It is useful to use the brainstorming technique with a spider web or spray (see p.83) where you can pour out as many ideas and thoughts you have about the question as possible.

Ask yourself:
'What does this title require me to do?' (Activity words)
'What is the title getting at?' (Understanding)
'What do I know that is relevant to this title?' (Key terms, ideas, issues, arguments, debates to be explained).

Activity or cue words (the instruction)

DESCRIBE—give a detailed account or description (see descriptive essays p.91).
OUTLINE—give a brief account or description.

'Describe' or 'outline' will seldom be used alone in an advanced Sociology essay title. When used, they will be accompanied by 'and account for' or 'and examine in detail' or 'and assess' or 'and evaluate' and similar instructional phrases, which indicate that more is required than simple outlining describing or defining.

Outline the contribution made by the sociology of knowledge to our understanding of any one area of social life.
AEB, November, 1984, Paper 1.

Describe the main types of sampling used in sociological research. What are the advantages and disadvantages in sampling? How can the disadvantages be minimised?
Cambridge, June, 1985.*

DISCUSS

Discuss the view that the isolated nuclear family serves the needs of the wider social system at the expense of its own members.
AEB, November, 1985, Paper 1.

Workplace technology spills over into non-work life. Discuss.
Cambridge, 1985, Paper 1.*

'Discuss' or 'discuss critically' is one of the commonest instructions used in essay titles. The first thing to note is that all discussions are critical. You are expected to explore or examine an argument or debate which may have several sides, each of which needs to be given proper consideration. A discussion can often be similar to a debate, where arguments for and against are considered. An everyday example may be a debate about vegetarianism, the two 'sides' being presented as follows:

VEGETARIANISM

FOR

Cruelty to animals.
Vegetarian diet healthier.
Food for animals could be used to feed starving.

AGAINST

Animals humanely destroyed.
Meat contains essential elements in our diet, which cannot be obtained from other foods.
Food fed to animals inferior, not fit for human consumption.

EXERCISE

Construct a similar discussion or debate about the use of Nuclear Power.
In Sociology a debate or discussion about whether the family is becoming unstable could be as follows:

UNSTABLE FAMILY?

FOR	AGAINST
High divorce rates.	Divorce has become more easily attainable. Previously, unstable marriages existed but divorce not an available option for the majority.
Increase in co-habitation among young people. Declining influence of religion.	70% divorcees remarry. Majority of population marry at some time or another. It is NORMATIVE.
Women more independent. Less need for male economic support. Feminism points to exploitation and oppression of women in family.	Majority of women have little alternative. Social pressures and expectations from others e.g. older family members. Still difficult for women to be financially independent. Women's earnings 70% of men's. Majority one parent families headed by women on the poverty line.
Fewer children per family.	Majority of families still have children. Women having children at later ages—establish careers first.

You could probably add your own arguments for and against to the above examples to show how a debate can unfold on a point by point basis. Of course it is not always the case that a discussion proceeds in such a manner. Points for could outweigh points against or vice versa. If this is so, it could be easier to put all the points FOR together, and all those AGAINST together.

When you have decided which side of the argument you will finally come down on, present the opposite arguments first, so that you can use your favoured side of the argument to refute them and to lead strongly into the conclusion. Try not to zig-zag between points for and against in such a way that the essay loses direction. In essays the more difficult concluding sections to write are those where the arguments are finely balanced which can often happen in Sociology.

Remember when presenting a case:
—always give a full account
—try to be as objective as possible

EXAMINE

Examine critically the uses and limitations of observation as a method of sociological research.
AEB, November, 1985, Paper 2.

Examine the contribution made to our understanding of suicide by research which had focused on the role of coroners' definitions and societal reactions to suicide.
AEB, November, 1985, Paper 2.

'Examine' is another commonly used activity word in essay titles. To examine something in an essay means that you are expected to set out the essential elements or themes of a particular issue and to show the relationship between these elements as in the above titles.

COMPARE AND CONTRAST

Contrast any two theories which seek to explain power in industrial societies.
London, March, 1985, Specimen Paper 1

Compare and contrast functionalist and conflict approaches to the role of schooling in socialization.
AEB, November, 1985.

This instruction involves an exploration of similarities (compare) and differences (contrast). When 'compare' is used alone, it may imply that more emphasis should be placed on similarities, and when 'contrast' is used, it may imply more emphasis should be placed on differences, but in all cases a knowledge of both similarities and differences between theories or arguments would be expected.

EVALUATE/ASSESS

Using relevant sociological studies, assess the role of the media in creating moral panics.
London, March, 1985, Specimen Paper 2

Evaluate the contribution made by the labelling approach to our understanding of differential educational achievement.
AEB, November, 1985, Paper 2

'Evaluate' or 'assess' means that you are expected to weigh evidence and provide a critical appraisal of the arguments for and against or the worthwhileness of an approach or issue.

Other common activity words or phrases

You may wish to practise by producing a plan for your answer to one or more of these:

IN WHAT WAYS? as in:

In what ways have sociological accounts of mental illness challenged accepted medical explanations of mental illness?
AEB, November, 1985, Paper 2.

WHAT IS THE RELATIONSHIP BETWEEN? as in:

What is the relationship between organizational size and workers' attitudes and behaviour?
Oxford, 1984, Paper 2.

DISTINGUISH BETWEEN as in:

Distinguish between 'professions' and 'occupations'. Is teaching a profession?
Oxford, 1985, Paper 2.

TO WHAT EXTENT? as in:

To what extent are British cities residentially segregated on the basis of social class?
Oxford, 1985, Paper 1.

WHAT? as in:

What do the official criminal statistics measure?
London, March, 1985, Specimen Paper 2.

Other questions

Are modern industrial societies strike-prone?
Cambridge, June, 1985, Paper 2.*

Why do people live longer in the advanced societies than in the underdeveloped societies?
Cambridge, June, 1985, Paper 2.*

How far is it possible or desirable for sociologists to be objective in their study of society?
Cambridge, June, 1985, Paper 1.*

This latter section contains briefer and more direct questions, but it must be stressed that it will be expected in all Sociology essays that you are aware that there is rarely a direct or uncontroversial response to a question. The key activities you are expected to take part in when writing an essay are:

CRITICIZING
ANALYSING
TAKING APART
WEIGHING EVIDENCE / ARGUMENTS / DEBATES } FOR AND AGAINST

EVALUATING—Making judgements as to strengths or weaknesses.

You cannot present a satisfactory advanced Sociology essay which does not contain elements of the above.

EXERCISE

Choose three of the above essay titles, and plan them out within a strict time limit. Give yourself ten minutes per title to draw up the structure of an answer.

Key words/terms/phrases

When you are decoding an essay title, it is advisable to underline key words, terms or phrases which need to be explained or defined in your introductory paragraph(s). You can write these down in the form of questions to be asked around the title.

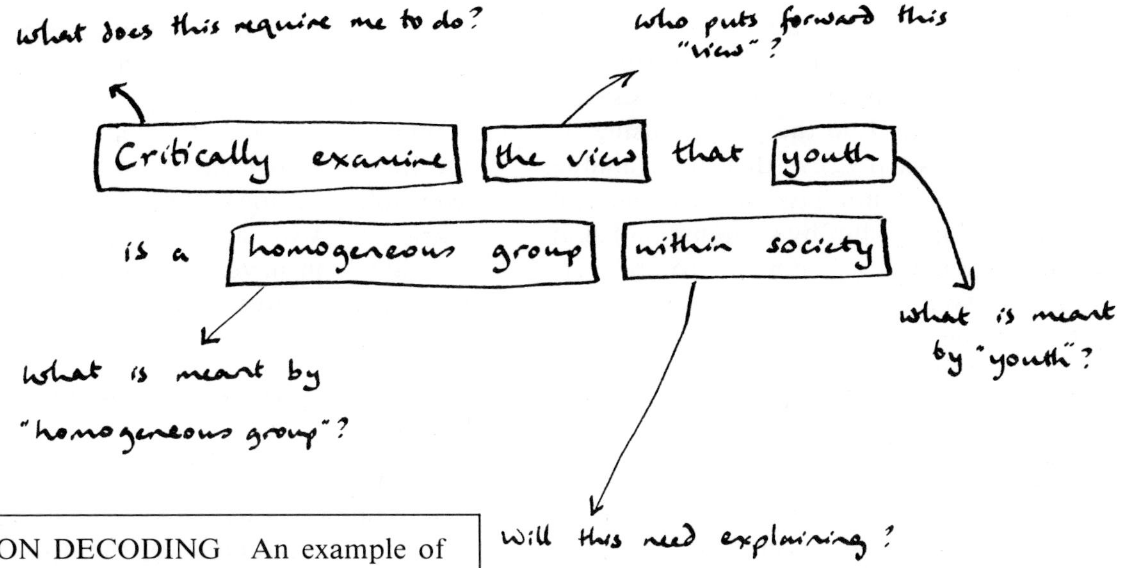

QUESTION DECODING An example of how you should construct questions around an essay title.

EXERCISE

Do the same with some of the essay titles given in this chapter.

Don't assume that the reader knows what you are talking about. Write as if you were explaining the terms to your student peers who know less about them than you do. You have to show evidence to the reader that you clearly understand the concept or theory that is the main theme of the essay.

In the early stages of the course you will probably need to consult dictionaries, encyclopaedias, reference works and glossaries fairly frequently. You are advised to compile your own glossary, so that you develop a stock of terms with which you will become increasingly familiar as the course progresses. Thus in the later stages you can confidently explain or define the majority of terms used in essay titles.

D. RESEARCH

When you are satisfied that you have some understanding of the essay title in relation to activity words and key terms, the next stage is to research for material for your answer which is aimed at the questions you have constructed around the title. Your starting point could be class notes and related material to see what information you have of relevance. You should then consult your basic textbook(s) and by using the Chapter contents, and/or the index, find relevant sections or chapters which you need to read and make notes from. Do the same with other course books such as topic books and readers. You should then go to the library and do the following:

1. Look for particular books referred to or recommended by your teacher. Use the Author Index (see p.22). If unavailable you can reserve the book or use the Inter-Library Loans service if it is not in stock (see p.21).
2. Consult the Subject Index (see p.22) to see if there is anything of relevance to key terms in the essay e.g. Divorce, Suicide, Poverty, Ethnicity, Comprehensive Education.

3. Use Reference Works, such as Dictionaries and Encyclopaedias of Sociology, Social Trends and relevant statistical sources to find out more about key terms in the title and to provide statistical support and back-up if necessary. Make notes from such works.
4. Look to see if there are any alternative basic textbooks, topic books or readers which might have additional material or present an alternative viewpoint or slant on a topic.
5. Look for appropriate empirical research studies. You may find these by perusing the subject index (see p.22). If they are available, you will probably not have time to read such works thoroughly, but by scanning and skim reading (see p.60), it is possible to grasp the main aspects of most studies and make useful notes on them. Concentrate on the Introductory section or chapter, which often sets out the terms, aims and objectives of the research, and the concluding chapter which sometimes contains useful summaries of research findings. Sometimes appendices contain useful information on methods used, examples of interview schedules or questionnaires, or statistical tables summarizing findings.
6. As indicated in Chapter 2, magazines/journals and other supplementary sources can be consulted for additional information, as textbooks quickly date.
7. If you use the library in the ways indicated in Chapter 2 i.e. as a learning resource centre, then you should develop a sound basis for your essay writing.

Too much information?

It is sometimes possible to accumulate too much material for an essay. This has advantages and disadvantages. One advantage is that if you have thoroughly covered the material and read and made notes, even if it is not all used directly in the essay, the information could be of use in other sections of the course, e.g. for revision purposes and related activities. Therefore you are building up your stock of Sociology sources as well as adding to your knowledge.

The disadvantages of amassing too much material are that you leave too little time for important tasks such as question analysis or decoding and the planning and writing of the essay. It is sometimes the case that continuing to gather information is a way of avoiding the actual task of sitting down with pen and paper and getting on with the writing. This is why it is important to plan and organize effectively by working to a proper timetable. Having a good plan and an idea of length will help avoid the problem of too much information and the last minute rushed answer, which is badly presented and disorganized in structure and style.

When you have completed the Research phase and gathered sufficient material, you now need to re-examine the title in the light of your reading and preparatory work and write a brief response to the questions you have asked round the title.—You are then ready to prepare an essay plan.

E. CONTENTS OF AN ESSAY

1. INTRODUCTION (1–2 paragraphs)
   - (i) Your INTERPRETATION/EXPLANATION of the title.
   - (ii) Key ISSUES/ARGUMENTS/DEBATES/APPROACHES/CONTROVERSIES relevant to title indicated briefly.
   - (iii) Key terms/words/phrases DEFINED.
2. MAIN BODY
   - (i) DETAILED examination of (i) and (ii) above—arguments for and against, supportive work and evidence, critical appraisal and evaluation. Named references.
   - (ii) RELEVANT EMPIRICAL EVIDENCE/RESEARCH FINDINGS to highlight/illustrate (2)(i). Named references.
   - (iii) SUPPLEMENTARY SOURCES—additional material from your own reading and research, plus experience, to highlight/illustrate. Using your 'sociological imagination'.
3. CONCLUSION

Your conclusions with reference to material in (1) and (2). Appraisal/evaluation of title in light of material in (1) and (2).

F. PLANNING YOUR ESSAY

It is best to plan an essay in pencil, so that as you prepare your essay framework you can erase and correct unwanted sections and tidy up the plan as it develops. A plan should be an outline or overview of what you intend to cover in the essay; it should be used as a guide to the structure and content. The advantage of a plan is that it prevents you getting sidetracked. However, it is not always necessary to stick to the exact letter of a plan, as the final draft may deviate somewhat from the original outline. This is to be expected, as in the course of writing, ideas and points can occur to you which you may consider to be important and of relevance to the essay. If, however, your completed essays vary too much from your plans, you perhaps need to reconsider your approach to planning as it may be inappropriate for the task.

A plan is the essay framework or skeleton, so a linear note format is advisable as this is more appropriate for the development of an essay. As suggested in Chapter 4, spider notes or sprays are useful for question decoding.

A SIMPLE VERSION OF A PLAN IN RESPONSE TO A QUESTION

QUESTION

.... Activity words, key terms/phrases underlined.

PLAN

1. INTRODUCTION — Interpretation of question; Key terms defined/explained; Reference to controversies, major debates, theories.

   1–2 Paragraphs

2. MAIN BODY (6–7 Paragraphs)

   Para 1 Explanation of Theory X
   Para 2 Supportive/non supportive evidence
   Para 3 Evaluation
   Para 4 Explanation of Theory Y
   Para 5 Supportive/non supportive evidence
   Para 6 Evaluation
   Para 7 Additional material (if appropriate) e.g. recent debates, research findings, supplementary material.

3. CONCLUSION — Weighing up the evidence. Show how appropriately you have dealt with title in main body. Make conclusions (could often be tentative, particularly if arguments balanced).

   1–2 Paragraphs

The above is a suggested 'model' for planning essays but there could well be variance from this, particularly in the way the main body paragraphs are dealt with, as these may not apply themselves to a rigid 'mechanical' formula for presenting your material. Writing essays is not a mechanical activity. It should be seen as creative and organic.

If you develop the practice of planning for your coursework essays, this will be particularly helpful to you in examinations when you are pressed for time. The ability to outline a plan quickly before you start each exam essay will be invaluable and will help you keep to the point. This should keep you within a manageable amount of writing for each answer.

It is advisable to plan in stages, first dealing with the essay as a whole, and then going into more detail via your Introduction/Main Body/Conclusion 'skeleton'. You can then break each section down into paragraphs.

The Essay Planning Process

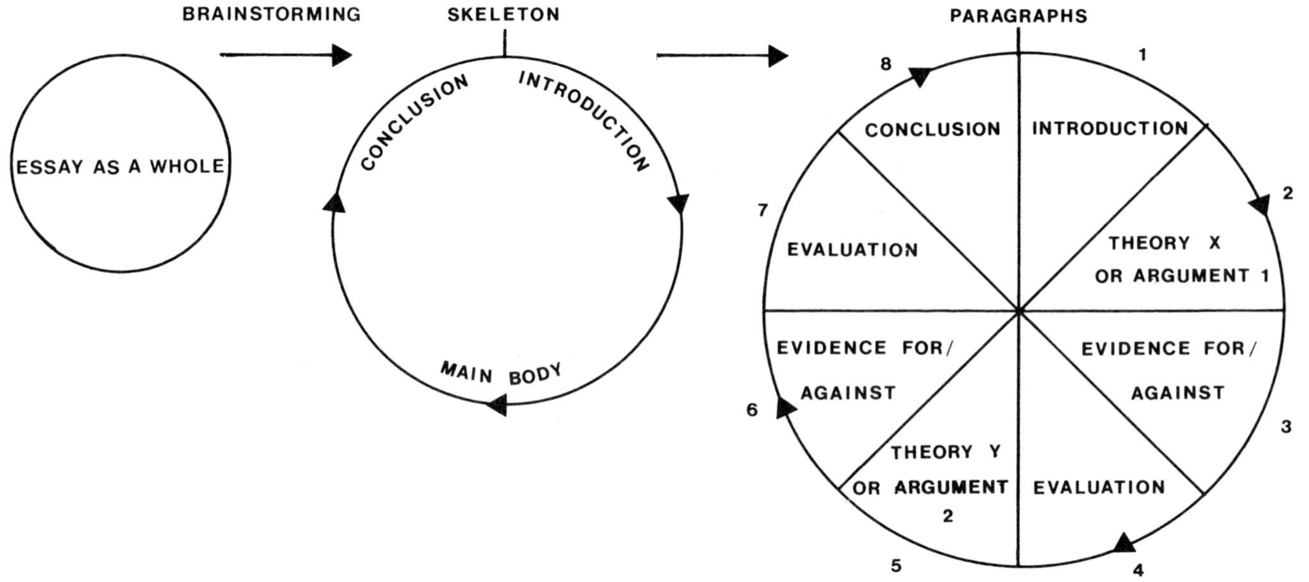

The models for an essay answer plan given above are reasonably straightforward. They involve presenting an argument and evidence for, as opposed to an argument and evidence against type of discussion. This will not always be the case as some topics involve more complicated discussion formats, so plans will vary in their level of complexity.

THE UNFOLDING OR DEVELOPMENT OF AN ESSAY AT THE PLANNING STAGE
Consider the following title:

Examine (ACTIVITY/CUE WORD) the view that there is an ethnically differentiated underclass (KEY TERM) in contemporary Britain. AEB, November, 1985, Paper 2.

1. **Introduction**

(a) Need to define 'ethnically differentiated underclass' (Key Term).

(b) Need to 'set the scene'—briefly refer to two main lines of argument in debate—(i) PRO: WEBERIAN approach (ii) ANTI: MARXIAN approach.

2. **Main Body**

(i) PRO

Weberian approach (Rex).

There is an ethnically differentiated underclass—Need to understand subjective aspects of skin colour within the context of a colonial/imperial past.

Britain has historical links with slavery that leads to attitude of dominance and superiority of whites towards blacks. Racism, exploitation, inequality, oppression of blacks is *culturally specific* to a colonialist/imperialist society.

Racism is subjective

(ii) ANTI
Marxian approach (Westergaard and Resler). Exploitation of ethnic minorities *class exploitation*. Not an ethnically differentiated underclass as such. All part of class structure of *capitalist society*. Racism, exploitation, inequality, oppression of blacks produced by their economic relationship to infrastructure of capitalism. Part of the proletariat who do not own the means of production.

Racism is objective

COMPARISON

Blacks in Britain .... 'Guestworkers' in Germany

W + R — there is no difference
Rex — there is a difference

EMPIRICAL EVIDENCE (This should be incorporated in your pro and anti theoretical points)

(i) FOR (PRO)

Blacks concentrated at bottom of socio-economic ladder—education (Swann Report, Egglestone) housing and jobs (Rex and Tomlinson).

(ii) AGAINST (ANTI)

Black professionals in Health Service
Swann Report indicated differences between ethnic minorities, e.g. Asians: educational achievement higher than West Indians and also Bengalis (part of Asian ethnic minorities) on a par with West Indians, so differentiation of opportunity within ethnic groups.

OTHER THEORETICAL INPUTS

a) Dual labour market Theory—ethnic minorities in secondary labour market (links with Rex) low paid, insecure, low status jobs.
b) Reserve army of labour—immigrant workers used in capitalist 'boom' periods—demand for labour (Marxian).

3. **Conclusion**

Strong arguments on both sides, both have empirical support.

Key aspect could be how 'tightly' you wish to define 'underclass'.

If exclusive category based on skin colour (Rex?)—then how come black professionals?

If looser, then skewing of inequality towards black ethnic minorities in particular provides some evidence for Weberian approach.

NOTE
The above plan is one example of how such a title could be approached. When you have studied and read up on this topic area you may well find another way of approaching such an essay. The ideas outlined are an indication of the way an essay can develop or unfold at the planning stage.

THE LAYERS (STRATA) OF AN ESSAY

(1) CORE/CENTRAL	(2) →	(3) OUTER LAYERS
Monochrome Priority Points Framework/Skeleton Outline/Overview	Colour Supportive Points Skin More detailed view, discussion + analysis	3-Dimensional Supplementary Points Clothes Flair, insight, colour + variety
UNDERSTANDING	DEPTH + DETAIL	BREADTH + ORIGINALITY
Show you have understood the question, know what the key issues and themes are, and the arguments and debates.	Add weight and depth to (1). Use of named references, research evidence, key figures and contributors to debate.	As (2) plus use of unusual or original material not in basic textbooks and traditional sources. Supplementary sources—media, literature, experience.

G. THE 'AUDIENCE' FOR AN ESSAY

Write as if you are addressing yourself to your Sociology student peers and as if you know more about the question than they do. Explain the question to them and deal with key concepts and terms. Don't launch into an essay as if you don't have to explain terms like symmetrical family, white collar proletarianization, underclass or underdevelopment. Yes, your teacher or examiner will know what they mean (you hope!) but you need to convince them you are fully aware of the meaning of such terms.

A useful activity is to read a completed essay aloud to a friend.

H. WRITING THE ESSAY

The Introduction

As indicated in the previous section, a good plan can simplify the task of writing the essay. All your essays should start with an INTRODUCTION (1–2 Paragraphs) where you 'set the scene' or 'set out your stall' i.e. you inform the reader as to your interpretation of the question, define key terms where necessary and give a brief indication of how you are going to respond to the question. Don't provide a shortened version or synopsis of your essay or reach a conclusion about the title in your opening lines. Show clearly your grasp of the key themes raised by the title and briefly refer to some of the main issues in relation to the question. In this way you can have a smooth transition into the main body of your essay. Consider the examples of introductions on page 103.

Many students find difficulty in introducing essays, particularly in writing the first two or three sentences, but once they have done this, they find it easier to proceed into the main body, so make sure you get plenty of practice in writing those crucial opening sentences. A good sound introduction can be the most important part of the essay. It is often scrutinized most by the reader and can virtually give you a pass mark. The old adage 'first impressions count' or what psychologists have referred to as the 'primacy effect' is something to bear in mind. You should aim to grab the attention of the reader—try to elicit a response as follows:

"Good, this student understands this question and has set out the key themes or issues to be examined. I am now interested to see what he/she has to say and in how the essay will develop."

To borrow a phrase from media studies, the introduction should 'set the agenda' or provide your statement of intent, but don't overdo this and use a 'checklist' approach as follows:

In this essay I intend to do the following, firstly I will present Marx's views on the role of religion in society, then I will consider the modern supporters of this approach, and then I will look at the counter-arguments . . . etc., and in conclusion I will . . .'

The use of the personal 'I' and the checklist style shows a lack of confidence and maturity in presentation. It can be irritating to the reader as he/she doesn't want to be told what he/she is about to read. You need to have an introduction which captures attention and interest.

In summary, the introduction needs to explain to the reader what the title means, to provide an assessment or evaluation of the topic, and to give a brief overview of issues, theoretical and related matters, arguments or controversies raised by the title. Remember, the idea of an essay title is to stimulate or provoke you into thought concerning the subject of that title. A perceptive comment or statement which shows the reader that you are clearly aware of the issues arising from the title will give a good impression from the outset.

You should never attempt an essay unless you fully understand the title. Your introductory section will indicate whether or not this is the case. Consider the following example:

In what ways have sociological accounts of differential educational achievement changed in the last 20 years?

A student may decide (and this often happens in exams; see Chapter 8) that she will answer this question on the basis of knowledge of sociologists' explanations of differential educational achievement. So she devotes the majority of her answer to a discussion of the relationship between social class and educational achievement. If the student proceeds on this basis without dealing directly with the latter part of the question (which concerns how these explanations have changed in the last 20 years, thus raising issues of gender and race in educational achievements as well as changing theoretical and methodological orientations of sociologists working in this field) she will receive few marks. *Never* alter the meaning of a question to suit your own ends. Your answer at best will only be partially correct and will receive low marks. Your introduction will show from the outset your lack of understanding of the title, so, either choose another question if you are in the exam, or consult your teacher in the case of a coursework essay.

'A ''checklist'' approach is not necessary'

Do you think this is a satisfactory introduction to the essay?

How would you improve on this?

"Sociology is the science of society". Discuss.

This essay is going to discuss what sociology society and science mean, and then I will try and Explain what I think positivism is and which sociologists believed in it, then I am going to say what an interactionist view and which sociologists believe in that approach. I will then try and decide if I can if I think Sociology is a science.

The word sociology is made up of two terms the Latin word Socius which means the companion and the greek word ology which means the study of so the word sociology literally means study of processes of companionships, so sociology might be defined as the study of the basis of social membership, but no definition is satisfactory because of the diversity of perspectives which is characteristic of the modern discipline.

Compare this introduction to the previous one. What are its strong and weak points?
Note the difference in style.

'Sociology is the science of society.' Discuss

It would be logical to begin with the question; "What is sociology?" but this is not such an easy question to answer. It would not be sufficient to say that sociology studies human society because so do history and ecology, nor is it enough to say that it studies human social behaviour because so does social psychology. What we really want to know is; "What is the distinctive way in which sociology looks at man and society and their interactions?" This too is a difficult question to answer because every person has his/her own views about different aspects of life. In order to be able to come up with some kind of answer it is as well to look at various points and views on the matter.

When we think of science, we think of physics, biology, chemistry, so how can sociology be classed as a science? Well, a science is concerned with questions of fact and sociology fits into this idea. A science may be defined as a way of looking at and talking about phenomena so therefore may be distinguished by; (1) the reliability of knowledge, (2) accepting the results you come up with (3) being organised and having a knowledge, ie. knowledge based on observation and testing the facts...

"Sociology is the Science of Society"
Discuss

Confident clear introduction—'sets the scene' well. Somewhat rhetorical style, e.g. 'What is Sociology?', 'Why is this?' etc. but settles down to provide a sound basis for lead-in to essay, particularly in last sentence.

What is Sociology? "Sociology is the scientific study of human behaviour from the point of view of social groups and social interaction." It is interesting to note that in the above definition sociology is classified as a science. Why is this? What are the recognisable features of scientific method, and could they be successfully applied to sociology? Such terms as observation, conjecture and hypothesis could be quite readily used; however it is with difficulty that such terms as generalisation, relativity and objectivity are used. Is it at all possible to analytically study and even call a discipline a science where there is no static ground for verification? Before attempting to answer any of these questions, it's important to briefly look at the historical development of sociology, and the schools of thought that have arisen within it.

An Introduction which defines 'key terms' from the outset.

What do sociologists understand by the concept of "underclass"? To what extent is there an ethically differentiated underclass in Britain?

Sociologists use the term 'underclass' to desribe the apparent existence of a class beneath the working class. Not all sociologists believe that the term underclass is either appropriate or correct. In recent years, in Britain, the majority of immigrants (52%) have been white. In relation to their black counterparts, they seem to be more successful. Thus, is the underclass merely a product of racial discrimination or, do other reasons exist to explain why the black immigrant population should find themselves in a disadvantaged position in Britain?

The Main Body

If you have a good plan and you have written the all-important introduction which clearly sets the agenda, the main body of your essay should not present too much difficulty. It is advisable to work within a 6–8 paragraph framework, each one dealing with a specific point, argument or theory as outlined in your essay plan.

EDITING, CONDENSING AND SUMMARIZING YOUR RESEARCH MATERIAL

One of the necessary tasks when writing the main body of an essay is the editing of material gathered during your research. Sometimes you will have to be fairly ruthless and condense your notes from a particular book or article to 1 or 2 brief sentences, otherwise you will have an overlong essay which is dominated by too much detail.

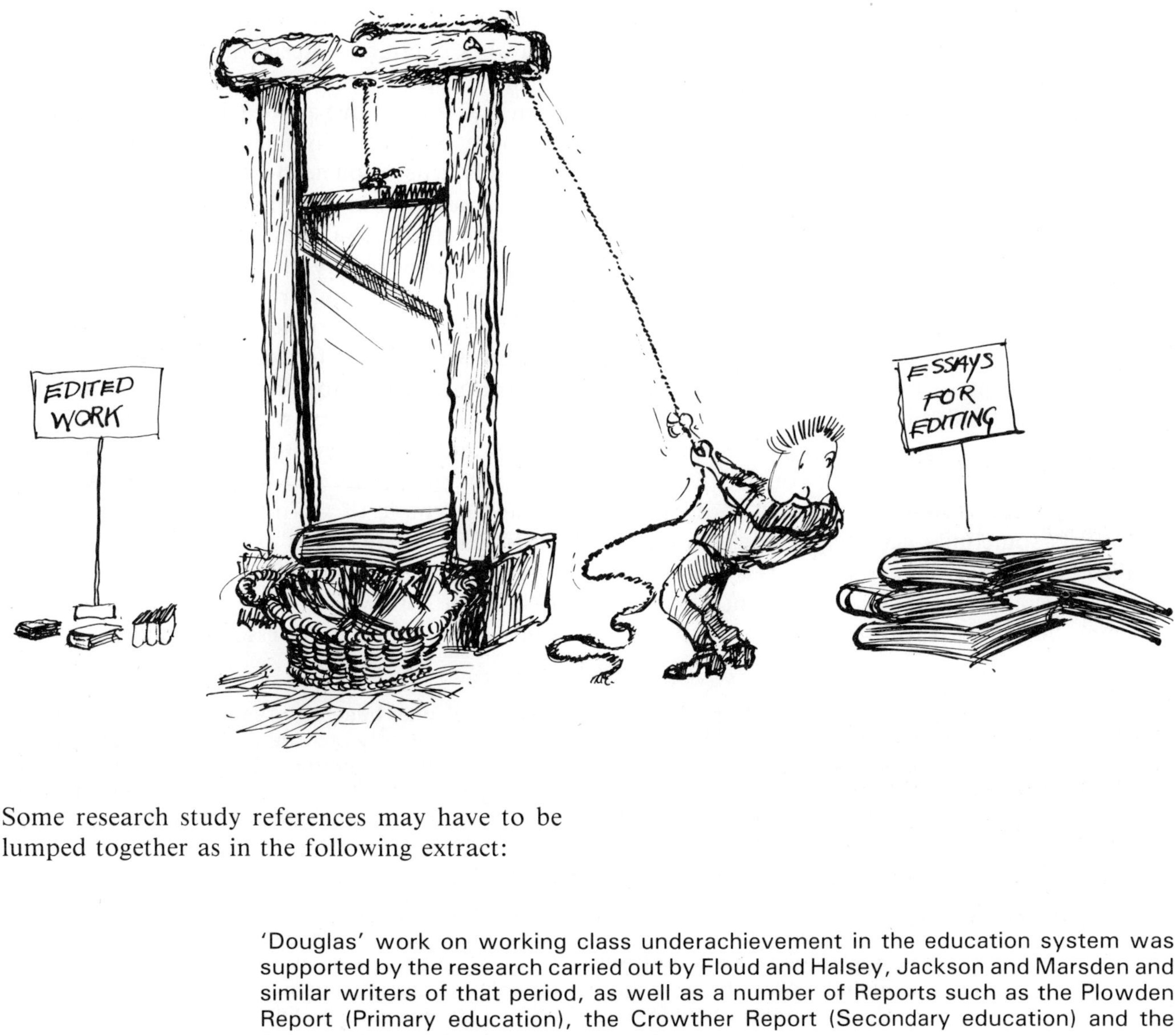

Some research study references may have to be lumped together as in the following extract:

> 'Douglas' work on working class underachievement in the education system was supported by the research carried out by Floud and Halsey, Jackson and Marsden and similar writers of that period, as well as a number of Reports such as the Plowden Report (Primary education), the Crowther Report (Secondary education) and the Robbins Report (Higher Education).'

This single sentence could be a condensation of 2–3 sides of notes. This is something you will have to get used to, as in advanced level essays you should work within the constraints of length (3–5 sides approximately) and, eventually in the examinations, time. Another argument for such a degree of summation is that it enables you to stick to central points in your essay without getting yourself sidetracked by too much attention to unnecessary detail. Consider the following extract:

'Jackson and Marsden in a study of 100 successful pupils at Huddersfield Grammar School between 1949–52 compared 10 middle class pupils with the remaining 90 working class pupils, two of whom were the authors themselves. As with Douglas, they found that home and family background were important factors in educational achievement. They found that the ninety successful working class pupils in their sample were somewhat different from the mainstream working class in that a high proportion had middle class extended family connections, or, had been middle class but because of business failure or similar misfortune were now working class by virtue of the father's occupation. These two groups were referred to as the 'submerged' or 'sunken' middle class. Other groupings were the sons or daughters of chargehands and foremen and those with parents who were involved in the Trade Unions and Politics.'

Two points to be made concerning this extract are that the study referred to is somewhat dated and that it has too much detail for the purposes of an essay. More recent sociological research on this topic has concentrated on factors besides social class, such as gender, and race and ethnicity. The concentration on the detail of one rather dated study in the extract above would clearly curtail the amount of space left in an essay of the required length to refer to such new developments.

However, in the light of the above advice it needs to be recognized that there are dangers in condensing and summarizing books or research studies, which can lead to distortion or misrepresentation of central ideas and arguments. Make sure that you have done full justice to a work you are referring to, especially if it is complex, detailed or abstract.

Students sometimes get bogged down in over-detailed accounts, because the rest of their material is somewhat thin. The amount of detail you may be required to provide on a particular work can vary according to the theme of the essay. If a work contains material that is central to some of the key arguments or points you wish to make, then you should give a more detailed account. An example of this is in questions on sociological methods, where you need to go into some detail on a few studies, or in some instances treat one study as a case study. If a question concerns the use of the participant observation method of research in Sociology, it is important that you indicate familiarity with some studies where such a method is used, with a view to examining the advantages and disadvantages of that method. You could show your familarity with the study by using quotes and references to particular sections which highlight the points you wish to make. An often quoted example of a study using the method of participant observation is William F. Whyte's *Street Corner Society* (Chicago Press, Chicago, 1943). The following extract indicates how such a study can be used in an essay question:

'Although Whyte's 'Street Corner Society' was based on research carried out fifty years ago, it remains of interest because it not only provides an account of slum life in an American city but it contains much detail concerning the problems and issues Whyte had to confront when conducting his research using the method of participant observation. These difficulties are not faced by positivistic sociologists using social surveys and similar quantitative data collection methods.

One example occurs when he relates the difficulties he had in telling the group studied his purpose in being among them. He could not give too much detail as this could possibly have altered their behaviour toward him. After one or two awkward attempts at explanation, he found the gang members themselves had developed their own explanation that he was writing a book and this sufficed.

More recent participant observational studies such as Eileen Barker's study of the Moonies religious sect, James Patrick's Glasgow gang study and Laurie Taylor's study of professional criminals, provide similar examples of how difficult it is for sociologists to become a part of a group being studied.

Taylor was introduced to the criminal underworld by John McVicar, an ex-bank robber he had befriended. This form of relationship between researcher and introductory companion is similar to that with Doc in Whyte's study and with Tim in Patrick's study. Such relationships could all be seen as potentially problematic with regard to the research outcome as each confederate acted as a sort of 'go-between'. The question arises as to whether the accounts offered to the researchers, when they were not actually witnessing certain events were accurate, unembroidered or unembellished. With reference to Taylor's study there were some reports in the media (note good use of media resources by student here—see Chapter 2) that John McVicar had said that Laurie Taylor had himself been 'conned' by some of the criminals he had met because they had coloured their stories and accounts for the sake of interest, and to give them a sense of excitement. Such criticisms can be seen as raising difficult problems for participant observational research.'

ACTIVITY

Compare the above extract with the previous one on education and note how sometimes in answers a greater degree of detail needs to be provided to highlight specific points concerning an essay topic. You should be aware of such factors at the planning stage of your essay, where you could consider how much detail from studies is necessary, and the number of studies to be referred to, so that you have a good idea of the amount of editing and summarizing that needs to be done.

PARAGRAPHING

As indicated previously the main body of your essay should have about 6–8 paragraphs, each centring on a specific point, argument, theoretical approach or aspect of a debate.

TRANSITION

In the same way that the Introduction 'leads in' to the main body of the essay, so should each paragraph logically connect to the next one. The last sentence should link with the first sentence of the following paragraph (called transition) as in the following extract:

'. . . the functionalist explanation of the link between education and increasing technological complexity in the workplace suggests that the education system provides the future work force with the necessary levels of education required to work with the new technology.

However, (Transition link word) an alternative view comes from Marxian approaches such as that of Harold Braverman. He argues that advanced technology does not require an increasingly educated and skilled labour force, rather, the technology deskills and creates fewer jobs. This effectively transfers control and power away from workers as in craft production, to managers and capitalists, an example of this being the introduction of robots to car assembly lines . . .'

RELEVANCE CHECK

It is useful before starting each paragraph to consider whether the point you are about to make is of relevance to the essay title. This avoids the dangers of getting sidetracked or going off at a tangent. Effective planning should lessen the need for this but it is a good habit to cultivate particularly when you are working under exam conditions. Consider the response to this question:

In what ways have feminist writers challenged earlier sociological accounts of the family? AEB, June, 1985.

'. . . so Oakley and other feminist writers are highly critical of sociologists of the family who suggest that the increased numbers of married women who work has resulted in their husbands dramatically increasing their share of domestic and household tasks.

Women also face problems at work in that they are usually either concentrated in all female occupations with low pay and status e.g. shop assistants, or, when they are in the same occupations as men they are usually in the most junior positions e.g. 44% of secondary school teachers are female but only 1% of secondary school heads are female.' (Transition is OK but is the second paragraph relevant to the title?)

The Conclusion

Your final section is as important to a good essay as the introduction. As well as first impressions counting, so do last impressions, a phenomenon referred to by psychologists as 'recency effects'. A sound and well constructed conclusion can leave a good impression which could even make up for some deficiency or omission in the main body of the essay, so a good concluding paragraph can sometimes 'rescue' an essay.

The most difficult aspect in concluding a sociology essay for most students is that conclusions rarely contain a direct answer to the question set. Even in a question as direct as *Is crime a working class phenomenon?* the answer is not a simple 'yes' or 'no'. It has already been said that sociology essays are always about arguments, controversies or debates which cannot be neatly packaged in a 'this one is better than the others' format. If you do arrive at such a conclusion, then clearly the main body of the essay would need to include fair representations of opposing arguments, good reasoning and logical argument as to why one particular explanation, or theoretical approach is more satisfactory than another.

A conclusion to an essay does not compare with a final chapter of a 'Whodunnit' novel when the detective tells the assembled house guests who murdered Lady Blenkinsop, based on his deductions from clues and various pieces of evidence.

The nearest comparison would be if all the guests had in some way contributed to Lady Blenkinsop's demise, thus leaving no simple answer to the question!

Consider the two concluding paragraphs which follow. Try to evaluate them yourself before you read the commentary beneath.

Title: Examine the view that there is an ethnically differentiated underclass in contemporary Britain.

Thus, it may not be sufficient to lump all black people together and to say, "here we have an underclass". As with all groups blacks are spread throughout the occupational structure, although there can be little doubt that most of Britain's blacks lie unenviably at the bottom of the labour market. Capitalist entrepreneurs and blatant racists are largely responsible for this inequality, however by our very passiveness, we inevitably help to preserve the status quo. It seems that Marxists underestimate the conflict between races. The low status of blacks can only be ended by direct attempts to overcome this abhorrent situation. We are all to blame.

This conclusion starts off well but ends by being far too opinionated and speculative. Note the last sentence. Does this mean anything and does it have a place in a Sociology essay?

How different then are the stances taken by Weberians and Marxists? It is clear that they all agree that black people do occupy a subordinate position in British society, whether as part of the working class - as proposed by Miles et al - or as a sub-proletariat - as proposed by Rex et al. Moreover, each thesis acknowledges the disadvantages faced by black workers (and black people in general) which can give rise to distinct forms of action viz: the Broadwater Farm Estate riot, the Honeyford protest etc. The main differences, then, between the two theses, appear to lie in the factors which gave rise to the subordinate position of black people, not in the conclusions they reach.

Finally, whilst black people do appear to predominate in the lower stratum of society, it should be acknowledged that black women like Angela Davis have highlighted their triple oppression. So, British black women like Beverley Bryan are beginning re-write the underclass thesis in feminist terms.

This is a much sounder conclusion, which interestingly raises further ideas at the end to illumine the title.

Structure and Style

> 'Serious concern is felt at what many judge to be steadily declining evidence of the ability to structure an argument. Frequently the sequence of points reveals no underlying logic; points are listed with no attempt to connect them or even to order them in terms of some scale of priority, even implicitly. Thus, by contrast, the balanced, structured, inter-related answer tends to gain credit even when its content is comparatively thin'
> (JMB Examiners' Report: A level Sociology, 1984)

The STRUCTURE of an essay concerns the manner in which you present your material moving from:

(1) Question analysis and decoding, and the defining or explaining of key terms in your INTRODUCTION;

to (2) the MAIN BODY where you provide a discussion, examine theories, arguments or debates supported by appropriate evidence where possible;

and (3) finally providing a CONCLUSION where you evaluate the title and weigh the evidence and arguments presented in the main body.

3. A further aspect of essays besides Content and Structure is the STYLE of presentation.

The marker or examiner of an essay will not directly deduct marks for poor spelling, incorrect grammar, punctuation or untidy presentation, but this does not mean that 'anything goes'. The key point is effective communication and a poor style in an essay can be a barrier to this. A more indirect factor with a badly presented essay is the impression it gives the reader. The mis-spelling of names or technical terms is not too serious, but consider the impression given by the following:

'. . . among the founding fathers of Sociology DIRKHIME (should be DURKHEIM), stressed the pluralistic (should be POSITIVISTIC) or scientific approach, VABER (should be WEBER) the importance of seeing the world through the eyes of the actor, 'WURSTAIN' (should be 'VERSTEHEN'), and MARKS (should be MARX), the scientific nature of his analysis of the evolution of a capatalist (should be CAPITALIST) society to the eventual sociological (should be SOCIALIST) society.'

The above section could well be making some sound points concerning the theme of the essay, but consider the negative impression given to the reader by the mis-spellings and incorrect terms which indicate a lack of familiarity with central sociological figures and concepts.

> '. . . candidates ought to be able to spell correctly key concepts such as consensus and bourgeoisie, just as they ought to be able to spell correctly well known writers' names such as Marx and Durkheim.'
> (JMB Examiners' Report: A level Sociology, 1983)

You should avoid colloquialisms, slang, hyperbole or over-elaborate metaphors, as in the following examples:

'Marx came down like a ton of bricks on capitalism' (!)

'there is no way that interactionists accept . . .'

'the functionalist approach is incredibly riddled with flaws . . .'

'. . . it only goes to show that when it comes to inequality and poverty "it's the same the whole world over" as the saying goes'.

When writing, always think of ACCURACY, BREVITY AND CLARITY. Don't be verbose or pompous in your expression and don't try to impress with lots of complex terms and jargon which you don't really understand.

Often a wordy and complex style of writing is an attempt to cover inadequate content. (Think of this when you next hear a politician speak!).

One way to appraise your writing style is to read a complete essay aloud and imagine how it would be received by your fellow students.

Handwriting

Always write clearly and legibly. It is pointless providing a brilliant answer if the marker has difficulty in reading it. As with incorrect grammar and punctuation, it is a matter of the impression given. If your handwriting is bad, for example if your friends have difficulty reading it, then you need to pay attention to improving it early in the course. Your handwriting will probably be worse under exam conditions when you are under pressure. Place yourself in the reader's position and imagine what it would be like when marking a pile of essays late at night to encounter a scrawled answer which is almost impossible to read. If poor handwriting is something you cannot correct, for example, because of disability, consult your teacher. Arrangements can be made with the examination board for someone called an amanuensis to write for you.

Content may be reasonable, but the handwriting may give the reader a headache.

Emile Durkheim believed in a consensus throughout the strata of society which brings them all together, in order to serve each other and maintain the stability of society. This perspective is based on the idea that there is an agreement relating to the fact that some people occupy higher positions than others and that this is acceptable to the majority. Social stratification is thought right and natural by those at both ends of the social scale.

Structural functionalists argue that because stratification exists and it works it must be justifiable.

Plagiarism

This means the direct copying of another person's work without acknowledgement and is something which should NEVER be done. If using a direct quotation, you should name the source and use quotation marks. If you are paraphrasing or summarizing you should also name the source.

In advanced level Sociology much of your work will be derivative, using second hand sources such as textbooks, articles, studies and similar course materials. This is to be expected as you are advised always to back up or support your arguments and ideas with sociological references. (Remember the sociologist always asks 'Says who?' or 'Based on what evidence?'). As you progress through the course, you become increasingly familiar with the major issues and can provide your own versions without the need for quoting passages verbatim.

Quotations

An aspect of style in essays is the use of quotations to highlight or illustrate your discussion or a point you are making. You should not use quotations in isolation, as if their inclusion is self-explanatory, rather they should always fit in with and be relevant to the context as well as being an integral part of the point or statement you wish to emphasize, as in the following extract:

> '. . . industry demanded an educated workforce from the manual to the managerial levels so educational provision had to be made for all from the late 19th Century and has expanded so much that, as Haralambos says, 'it is one of the major growth industries of the last 100 years'.'

Use short, to the point quotes. Lengthy passages are not necessary. In the exam they will probably overtax your memory and may divert your attention from the more important aspects of the essay. Don't use quotations to impress, use them to amplify and illustrate when necessary.

Sources/Bibliography

When you have completed a coursework essay, you should provide a list of sources or a bibliography of articles and books used for the essay. This enables the reader to see the range of your research and reading and perhaps to advise on other sources which could be followed up. It is also useful at later stages of the course when you re-read your earlier work. You may wish to check or follow up some reference made in an essay, so it would be annoying and time consuming if the reference was not recorded by author, title and page numbers.

Essay Checklist

Before handing in your essay, evaluate it as follows:

(A) CONTENT

1. Have I effectively analysed or decoded the question title?
2. Have I really understood and absorbed all the concepts discussed and considered?
3. Have I really understood the varying contributions, researches and studies encountered during my preparation for the essay?
4. Have I used supplementary sources which can add colour, depth, interest and variety to the answer?
5. Can I express in my own words the key themes and arguments to show understanding to my teacher or other students?

(B) STRUCTURE

1. Is the structure of the essay reasonable?
2. Is everything relevant to the title?
3. Have I stuck to the point without getting side-tracked or waffling?
4. Have I developed the discussion, main ideas, themes and arguments in a satisfactory way with smooth transition from one point to another?
5. Is the conclusion sound and linked back to the title?

(C) STYLE

1. Is my essay presented in a good style without clichés, colloquialisms, slang, pretentious language or repetition?
2. Is there accuracy, brevity, clarity and correct grammar, spelling and punctuation?
3. Have I avoided value judgements and opinionated personal statements?
4. Can I show the reader of my essay that I am able to approach questions in a logical, carefully argued style, and not present him or her with a mere rehash or rearrangement of course material?

Appraising and evaluating your marked essay

When a coursework essay has been marked and returned, it is important to consider both the mark and the comments that have been made. Usually the greater the number of comments, the lower the standard of essay, but don't be disillusioned when this occurs. You should see the comments as constructive criticisms. A useful exercise when you receive a marked essay is to write your own self-appraisal in the light of the mark and the comments made. This could be along the following lines:

'In this essay I should have ...... and .... In future essays on this topic there is a need to be aware of x, y and z. I need to watch the wording of my sentences which can sometimes be clumsy, and take care with paragraphing and layout . . .'

This form of self criticism or evaluation should help you to improve your essay writing and it will be useful for revision purposes in the later stages of the course. Something can be gained even when the essay is not a good one. Often students file essays away and do not reconsider them. Such essays can be useful in the ways suggested, but you should not attempt to memorize essays for exam purposes. Sometimes re-reading essays you have written earlier in the course can boost your confidence as you see how much you have improved in terms of the depth and detail of your essays, your written expression, vocabulary, ability to reason and argue logically, and so on.

Finally, remember that the coursework essay provides you with your main chance of personal or individual tuition from your teacher, so you should take advantage of this. Be prepared to ask about marks or comments you do not understand.

A final comment

Despite the title of this book and the way structured advice on essay writing has been given, it has already been suggested that essay writing should not be seen as a mechanical process, the rudiments of which can be explained by taking the activity apart piece by piece. There is not a clear or correct 'formula' which can make you into a good essay writer. Good essay writing is a mixture of the advice given here and your own creative thinking and flair, which often requires hard individual work and effort. Despite this, essay writing can be rewarding, particularly when, (1) you have completed the essay ('Now I can go out for a drink, listen to that record or read that novel. I deserve it!') and, (2) you receive your marked essay back with a good mark and approving comments from your teacher. May this always be the case!

CHAPTER 6

ALTERNATIVES TO ESSAY WRITING

The majority of examination boards use the essay question as the main form of assessment, but in recent years alternative question forms have been introduced. The largest A level Board, the AEB, introduced a compulsory stimulus-response question into the examination in 1982. The London Examination Board now includes compulsory stimulus-response questions:

AFTER WORK
Farewell to the Working Class
By André Gorz
Translated by Michael Sonenscher
Pluto Press £3.95

A few weeks ago I caught a glimpse of what looked suspiciously like the *post-industrial* future. I was driving through the Rhondda, once the greatest coal-producing valley in the world. There wasn't a pit in sight. Most of the slagheaps had been landscaped; the mountainsides reforested. It was as if King Coal had never been. The narrow terraced streets ribboning out along the valley floor had a curiously beached air: like the community they house, they seemed to have been robbed of their raison d'etre.

Coalmining in this part of South Wales was always more than just a job. It shaped a whole social and political culture. With unemployment in the region now running at over 17 per cent there is just nothing to take its place. In Blaenclydach, where my grandfather was a miner, the Marxian Club still exists, but it's become just another watering-hole and the bar-talk is of snooker on the box and latest videos. Politics is a dirty word.

It is precisely this situation—economic decline coupled with *changed perspectives within the working class*—that André Gorz addresses in his brilliantly heretical 'Essay on Post-Industrial Socialism'. "Farewell to the Working Class" spectacularly inverts conventional socialist wisdom about the current crisis. It claims, for instance, that far from demanding a return to full employment—a chimera according to Gorz, given the inroads already made by the new technology and the fact that investment now destroys more jobs than it creates—socialists should be pressing for a reappraisal of the whole notion of work itself. Drawing on a largely lost tradition of utopian Marxist thought, Gorz argues that work is always and in itself alienating, and ought therefore to be abolished. And, now for the first time in human history, the existence of the new microchip technologies makes this a realistic demand.

Instead of rationalising production in such a way as to make some workers permanently unemployed, there is now the opportunity, says Gorz, to reduce the amount of time everyone in a society spends working. This would have the dual advantage of ensuring that all its members both receive wages and were given more time to engage in their own autonomous self-determined activity.

Clearly, much of this is anathema to traditional Marxism, which on the contrary tends to stress the heroic nature of labour.

The Listener, 26 May, 1983

1. (a) "Coalmining in this part of South Wales was always more than just a job". (Line 8). Explain briefly, in your own words, what this means. *(4 marks)*

   (b) What is the meaning of "post-industrial"? (Line 2) *(4 marks)*

   (c) What sociological evidence is there to substantiate the claim that there are now "changed perspectives within the working class"? (Lines 14/15) *(7 marks)*

   (d) Making reference to sociological theory, explain why Gorz's book might be considered to be critical of traditional Marxism. *(10 marks)*

   (Total 25 marks)

(LONDON SPECIMEN PAPER 1985/4)

The JMB in its 1985 examinations moved towards a stimulus-response question format throughout most of the two examination papers, thereby reducing the number of essay questions overall. However, at present the JMB is very much an exception among examination boards, and it is still the case for the forseeable future that essay questions will dominate advanced Sociology examinations.

A. STIMULUS—RESPONSE QUESTIONS

What are stimulus-response questions?

There are three main forms of stimulus-response question: the written extract from a book or article; the statistical table; and the diagram or graph, the book extract being the most common. The AEB has only used book extracts in its stimulus-response questions so far.

The purpose of stimulus-response questions

As the name suggests, the idea is that you are presented with some material which stimulates you into thinking about some sociological issue or concern, on which you are then asked questions. Stimulus questions demand much from students in that they cannot readily be responded to with a rehearsed answer, as may be the case with essay questions ('though remember the inadvisability of the rehearsed answer for any examination question). One of the major difficulties is that you are required to think like a sociologist about issues arising from the given material, which can be difficult under exam conditions.

Answering a stimulus-response question

Stimulus-response questions require as much thorough preparation as essay questions. It is essential that you practice answering such questions throughout your course. The first activity in answering a stimulus question is to skim or scan read the material to get the gist or the general sense. You should then read the questions, which are usually in three or four parts, noting the mark weighting for each. This is important as it gives you an idea of how much time should be given to each section. (See below for further advice on this). You should then return to the passage for a second more detailed reading. Pick out and underline any phrases quoted in the questions and underline or note any related or relevant points of interest.

Planning

The importance of planning your answers has already been stressed with reference to essays, and, if anything, it is even more important to plan for stimulus-response questions. Without a well-ordered plan, the structure of your answer could be chaotic with overlapping points made in each part or section, lengthy responses to a question which gains only a few marks, and so on.

When an answer is badly planned and organized, some students may try to cover up for this by not marking sections or even dividing the answer up and labelling the sections afterwards(!) If an answer is not clearly labelled in sections, the examiner has a difficult task and is likely to discount anything that is not readily recognizable as an answer to a specific part or section. Therefore it is very important that you devise a tight plan for each section when you have considered the whole question.

The mark weighting guides you not only as to how much time to spend on each section, but also the amount of depth and detail it is necessary to provide for the marks allotted. This should also give you an idea of the length of your answer.

EXERCISE

1. "My aim is to provide an overview of the sorts of considerations that sociologists take into account when designing research and deciding which methods to use. These considerations can be thought of as falling into four groups. First, what is to be the researcher's *standpoint* in relation to the research? Is the researcher going to do the research, evaluate the research done by other people, or commission someone else to do the research? Second, what is the researcher's *approach*? Is the aim to produce positivist, interpretivist, ethnomethodological or structuralist explanations of whatever aspects of the social world are under study? Third, what *strategy* is the researcher adopting: a case study, a sample survey or an experiment? And fourth, what *techniques* is the researcher going to use to collect and analyse data? For example, will it be an observation or an interview study? Will the data be quantified and statistically analysed or used raw in illustrative quotations?"

(from *Principles of Method*—PETER HALFPENNY)

(a) Name two *techniques* used by researchers, other than those in the passage. *(2 marks)*

(b) What does the author mean when he talks of data being "used raw in illustrative quotations" in sociological research? (lines 15–16) *(5 marks)*

(c) Explain what is meant by the term "case study", and why sociologists might accept this strategy. (line 11) *(8 marks)*

(d) Examine the relationship between a researcher's *approach* and her or his *technique*. *(10 marks)*

AEB, November, 1985, Paper 1

Underline key sections of the passage and sections from the passage used in the questions. How much detail should be in each section (a)–(d) and approximately what length should the answer to each section be?

If a section merits less than 4 or 5 marks, it is usually definitional or of the type that requires you to list or name several things. The response can be short and in note rather than full sentence form. For example, if you are asked for two alternative methods of data collection to participant observation, the *naming* of two alternatives is all that is required. It is pointless to expand on such answers by giving detailed definitions, discussing problems arising from such methods or giving accounts of studies using these methods. In low mark sections, only give directly what is required and nothing more. Over-long answers show indecisiveness, inability to be guided by instructions and may make the reader suspect that you are covering up for your lack of knowledge in other more important sections. There is also the danger of overlapping and providing material which is more appropriate to other sections. One or two named terms, methods or definitional sentences will, if correct, merit the same marks as half or three quarters of a side of written material.

Question sections given more than 5 marks require more detailed responses, so that if a three part (a), (b) and (c) question is allotted 5, 8 and 12 marks respectively, you should calculate on approximately half a side for section (a), a side for section (b) and one and a half sides for section (c), which gives an average answer length of around three sides. Slightly less, possibly two or two and a half sides total could suffice if the answer was of a good standard. Answers to stimulus-response questions could well be shorter than those to essay questions, because stimulus questions involve more reading and preparation time.

When you have decided on the approximate length of each section with respect to mark weighting, and made sure you have understood what each section requires in relation to the material provided, the next stage is to set out a plan for your answer. This should be straightforward with low mark sections, but with longer answers it is more difficult. You cannot provide a mini-essay in the sense of an introduction, a main body and conclusion as with a full essay, but you would need to have a structure with paragraphs to distinguish points or arguments and a logical sequence which fits together in a coherent manner.

SUGGESTED GUIDELINES FOR APPROACHING A STIMULUS-RESPONSE QUESTION

"A social scientist is always a person with his own personality, idiosyncracies and faults. One suspects that as a participant-observer he makes more impact on the people he studies as an individual person rather than as a researcher. Most scientists disturb what they observe to some degree, but in the case of the social psychologist or sociologist the extent of this distortion is relatively larger. A different researcher in the same social situation would make a different impact on the people and they would react to him in different ways. No doubt different discoveries would be made, different aspects emphasized, different interpretations elaborated, even though the central analysis might be the same. Yet more important than this is the extent to which the same single researcher can influence the situation by the roles he adopts. In my own case, the history is one of a conscious manipulation of roles to avoid and control conflicts at different levels in the situation at different stages. There is little doubt that a more consistent adoption of roles would have given me a somewhat different perspective of, and insight into, the social system of the school. As social scientists we assume that a common core of material and interpretation would result, especially if this is based on data collected by 'objective' methods which can be treated statistically. Yet the failure to make explicit the limitations and difficulties of participant-observation would be a failure to assess, however unquantitatively, the margin of error incurred by this method of social investigation."

(*Social Relations in a Secondary School*, D.H. Hargreaves 1967)

1. (a) Hargreaves refers (line 19) to "data collected by 'objective' methods which can be treated statistically."
   (i) What are these methods? *(2 marks)*
   (ii) What does Hargreaves mean by "objective" in this context? *(4 marks)*

   (b) Why do researchers who generally favour an interpretive approach to the study of social life tend to adopt participant observation as their research method? *(9 marks)*

   (c) What are the "limitations and difficulties of participant observation" (lines 20–21) to which Hargreaves refers? Illustrate your answer with examples taken from published research studies. *(10 marks)*

AEB, November, 1983, Paper 1

APPROACH

(1) Scan/skim read the passage.
(2) Read the questions (a), (b) and (c).
(3) Return to passage and mark quotes used in questions. Read in more detail. Mark key points.
(4) Note mark weighting of sections, sub-sections—this gives you an idea of how much time to spend, length, depth and detail required.

AN EXAMPLE OF A STUDENT PRACTICE PLAN FOR A STIMULUS-RESPONSE QUESTION
(The student has included some commentary on approach.)

(a) (i) Structured questionnaires/Formal Interviews (2 methods = 2 marks - don't elaborate, just name)

(ii) "Objective"
Sociologist as outsider, no involvement or commitment. Unbiased, impartial, neutral. Adopting a natural science approach to study of behaviour - "Consider social facts as things" (Durkheim)

(b) Research Method = Part. obs.
Discuss within INTERPRETIVE APPROACH ∴ not simply methods i.e. advantages/disadvantages of Part. Obs.
RATHER Interpretive Sociology using Part. obs. as a method.

INTERPRETIVE SOCIOLOGY → PARTICIPANT OBSERVATION
(i) What is imp. in a sociological explanation
+
(ii) Human behaviour involves consciousness, meanings + motives - these studied effectively only by taking part.

Briefly contrast and compare with objective or positivistic techniques eg. Structured questionnaires or Formal interviews - both work from pre-existing categories decided by researcher.
Conclude that interpretive sociologists see their research as having more validity than positivist research.

(c) '<u>Limitations and difficulties of part. obs.</u>'

(i) <u>Time</u>, <u>Expense</u> } economics

(ii) <u>Starting the research - getting introduced.</u>
William <u>Whyte</u> - Doc - accidental meeting.
James <u>Patrick</u> - Tim - gang leader met in Remand centre where Patrick teacher
<u>Laurie Taylor</u> - John McVicar - Sociology student Durham Prison.

(iii) <u>Involvement</u>
How do you remain detached, avoid being 'duped' or 'conned'?

(iv) <u>Danger</u>
Could be risk of this if violent gang or crime study.

(v) <u>Sample Size</u>
Usually very small eg. 12 working class males in Paul Willis' "Learning to Labour".

(vi) <u>Problems of generalisation</u>
uniqueness of study
Individuality of research - 'personality, idiosyncrasies and faults' (lines 1-2)

(vii) <u>Isolation</u>
Feelings of estrangement - <u>Whyte</u> - several examples of this

(viii) <u>Ethical Problems</u>
Is it right to use people for research purposes?

Writing your answer

As with essays, an efficient plan should mean the actual writing is not too difficult. Your writing style will have to be shorter and crisper than in an essay, but similar points can be made as to presentation, grammar, spelling, accuracy and the need for brevity and clarity in expression.

The following are some points to bear in mind when tackling stimulus-response questions:

1. The aim is to get you thinking sociologically about issues arising from the extract given.
2. You need to show that you understand the relationship between the theoretical approaches and methods used by sociologists.
3. You need to show that you are aware that the methods of sociological research often involve practical and theoretical constraints concerning the subject of enquiry, size of sample and so on.
4. You need to show that you are aware that sociological theories or perspectives do not have clear cut boundaries between them, so avoid the dangers of labelling one sociological study in contrast to another.
5. You need to show that you are aware that in practice studies often use several sociological research methods and do not stick to one type or approach; so methods can be pluralistic.
6. It is important that you can provide appropriate examples of empirical studies to highlight or illustrate your answer. Don't just rely on studies cited in textbooks. Make sure you read and have details on a number of appropriate studies throughout your course (as indicated in Chapter 2), which may be unusual or are not very well-known.
7. It is more difficult to provide rehearsed answers for stimulus-response questions, but some recent examiners' comments indicate that this tendency may be creeping in on the part of some students and causes them to score very poorly.

As with essays it is essential that you address yourself directly to the questions asked.

EXERCISE

1. The methodology was deliberately eclectic*, involving the routine perusal of agricultural and population census statistics, a search of historical sources (both documentary and oral), participant observation and a survey investigation. Since many of the concerns of the study involve the interrelationships of farmers and farm workers and of farm workers with each other, it was apparent from the outset that a degree of participant observation would be necessary. However, the almost complete lack of any sociologically relevant data, even of a sociographic* kind, made it desirable to conduct a survey. In effect, the survey and the period of participant observation increasingly came to complement each other: insights gained from participant observation could be checked against survey data; on the other hand much of this data could often only become meaningful through the experiences gained from living with a farm worker and his family in a tied cottage for six months and gaining first-hand knowledge about the work and community situation.

H. NEWBY, The Deferential Worker.

*Glossary
Ecelectic—drawn from various sources.
Sociographic—social descriptive.

(a) "In effect, the survey and the period of participant observation increasingly came to complement each other . . ."

Newby is suggesting here that these two methods, though basically different, can be used together to advantage. Explain the basic differences between these two methods and discuss the potential advantages of their being used together in one study. (11)

(b) Distinguish between primary and secondary sources of data in sociological research, giving examples of each. (6)

(c) Discuss the advantages and disadvantages of using *population census statistics* in sociological research. (8)

AEB, November 1982, Paper 1

Show in detail how you would answer this question paying attention to content, length, structure and organization.

ACTIVITY

Work with fellow students on stimulus-response questions, making and exchanging plans, discussing possible answers and explaining why you would answer in a particular way.
Further help and guidance for AEB stimulus-response questions can be found in;

CLARKE, E.A. and LAWSON, T., *Stimulus Questions in A-level Sociology* (University Tutorial Press, London, 1984).

MYERS, D., *Stimulus-Response Questions in Sociology—A Guide for A-level Students.* (Longman, London, 1984).

Other types of Stimulus-Response questions

Other boards apart from the AEB use alternative types of material such as statistical tables. If you are unsure as to how statistics and numerical data are used in Sociology, refer back and re-read the section in Chapter 2. Such questions can be fairly open-ended as in the following example:

HOW TO EXAMINE A STATISTICAL TABLE

In the light of the sociology you have studied, what sociological conclusions can be drawn from the information in the following table?

Economic Activity, Great Britain, 1921–1971

All ages over 15

Year	All Males and Females			All Males		
	Number occupied/economically active	Population	Activity rate† (1)	Number occupied/economically active	Population	Activity rate† (2)
	Thousands	*Thousands*	*Per cent*	*Thousands*	*Thousands*	*Per cent*
1921	19,357	33,339	58·1	13,656	15,672	87·1
1931	21,055	34,662	60·7	14,790	16,341	90·5
1951	22,610	37,908	59·6	15,649	17,862	87·6
1961	23,810	39,360	60·5	16,071	18,677	86·0
1966	24,857	40,041	62·1	15,994	19,030	84·0
1971	25,103	41,048	61·2	15,917	19,560	81·4

See the figures as 'trees'; aim to see the 'wood'. Stand back and get overall picture

Year	All Females			Married Females		
	Number occupied/economically active	Population	Activity rate† (3)	Number occupied/economically active	Population	Activity rate† (4)
	Thousands	*Thousands*	*Per cent*	*Thousands*	*Thousands*	*Per cent*
1921	5,701	17,667	32·3	733	8,434	8·7
1931	6,265	18,320	34·2	953	9,492	10·0
1951	6,961	20,045	34·7	2,658	12,228	21·7
1961	7,740	20,683	37·4	3,886	13,070	29·7
1966	8,863	21,011	42·2	5,063	13,296	38·1
1971	9,186	21,488	42·7	5,799	13,729	42·2

† Activity rate is defined as the proportion of those occupied or economically active to the total population — Make sure you read and understand this

Based on: Department of Employment Gazette, Census of Population

Source: Central Office of Information, Reference Pamphlet 139, *Occupations and Conditions of Work* (HMSO 1976), p. 42

Scan for gist. Note headings. Then examine numbers. Try to gain general picture. What years are being compared? Which groups of people? or types? (you should be able to identify three)
Are rates specified? What do they show?
KEY QUESTION—which of the economic activity rates 1–4 has increased the most and why?

The first point to reiterate is that you do not have to be mathematically adept to answer such questions. The main skill or ability needed is that of interpreting the information given by the table and picking out details and relevant themes in order to answer the question. In the above example, you should consider things like table and column headings, and, as with other stimulus-response material, scan or skim to gain the general gist of what is being conveyed. Treat the information given in a statistical table which is part of a stimulus-response question in the same way as you would a passage from a book, the obvious difference being that you are dealing with numbers rather than words. Aside from this, the aim is the same. As with a written extract, ask yourself what information is being conveyed. Look at the overall heading and column headings. Are comparisons being made, between, for example, a number of years, particular types of people, men/women, middle/working class, old/young and so on?

In the example, factors like comparisons between males and females, the proportions of those occupied or economically active compared to the overall population, and the span of years from 1921–1971 should all be considered. As the question title is open-ended, there could be several ways into the question, but the most appropriate would be that which focused on the economic activity of women as compared to men and, in particular, issues centring around the increased economic activity rates of married women. Knowledge of the sociological factors behind women's changing position and role in society should provide a sound basis for an answer on such stimulus material. The key point to recognize is the increase in economic activity rates of women as compared to men. Once you have done this and seen the significance, you have decoded the table.

Note that it is insufficient in such a question, despite its open-endedness, simply to describe the numbers or percentage changes in a written form as in the following passage:

'The table shows that between the years 1921–1971 the numbers occupied increased from 19,357,000 to 25,103,000, as compared to a population increase from 33,339,000 to 41,048,000, which gives an increase in activity rate from 58.1% to 61.2%. In the case of males the number occupied has increased from . . .' etc, etc.

This simple descriptive approach to the table is not what is required. You should use the information to stimulate thoughts on sociological issues, the key phrase reflecting this in the question title is, 'In the light of the sociology you have studied . . .'

A detailed description of the figures in a written form would be a waste of time as you need to be able to search through and select out key sections of the table in order to develop a particular theme or issue. In the example this could then be followed by reasons for significant changes in women's economic activity rates. These could be explained in terms of wider societal changes such as demographic trends, women's role and position and so on.

Another point to consider, as is the case with quotes or statements in titles, is an analytical or critical approach to information conveyed in tables. Are the figures likely to be accurate? What may they hide or not show about economic activity? Are all economically active men and women likely to be represented in the tables? What about women in the home? Are they not 'economically active'? and so on.

This sort of thinking is another necessary element in a response to such a question.

What sociological conclusions can be drawn from the information in the following table?

STRIKE INDICES, SELECTED INDUSTRIES, 1970–1980 (ANNUAL AVERAGES)

	Number of Strikes per 100,000 Employees		*Number of Days Lost per 1000 Employees*	
	1970–75	*1976–80*	*1970–75*	*1976–80*
Coal mining	63.2	100.2	9199	421
Docks	168.4	115.9	4187	1065
Iron and steel	41.1	28.4	1117	6938
Motor vehicles	49.2	37.4	3422	4494
Shipbuilding	43.3	22.1	2876	1023
Footwear	6.2	14.1	69	146
Furniture	10.3	8.4	70	68
Printing & publishing	6.3	9.3	178	757
Gas, electricity, water	4.2	5.7	202	130
Railways	5.0	4.4	130	267
Distribution	2.2	1.9	17	20
All industries	12.4	9.4	569	567

This table is reproduced from P. Edwards, 'The Pattern of Collective Industrial Action' in G. Bain (ed.) *Industrial Relations in Britain.* (Blackwell)

EXERCISE

Following the guidelines offered in the previous example, write down how you would respond to the table given and provide an answer plan.

QUESTIONS TO CONSIDER IN YOUR RESPONSE

What is the gist of the information being conveyed?

What years are being compared?

What types of industry are being compared?

Some industries seem to have fewer strikes and working days lost than others. Why might this be the case?

Why might the statistics be inaccurate indicators of strikes or working days lost?

For what reasons might an employer not be willing to publicize a strike?

The example below is a more directed statistical source question. Provide an answer plan, and, if possible, compare it with that of a fellow student.

2 Study carefully the bar chart and the statistical table below and answer the questions which follow.

I HOUSEHOLD SIZE IN A TYPICAL URBAN AREA

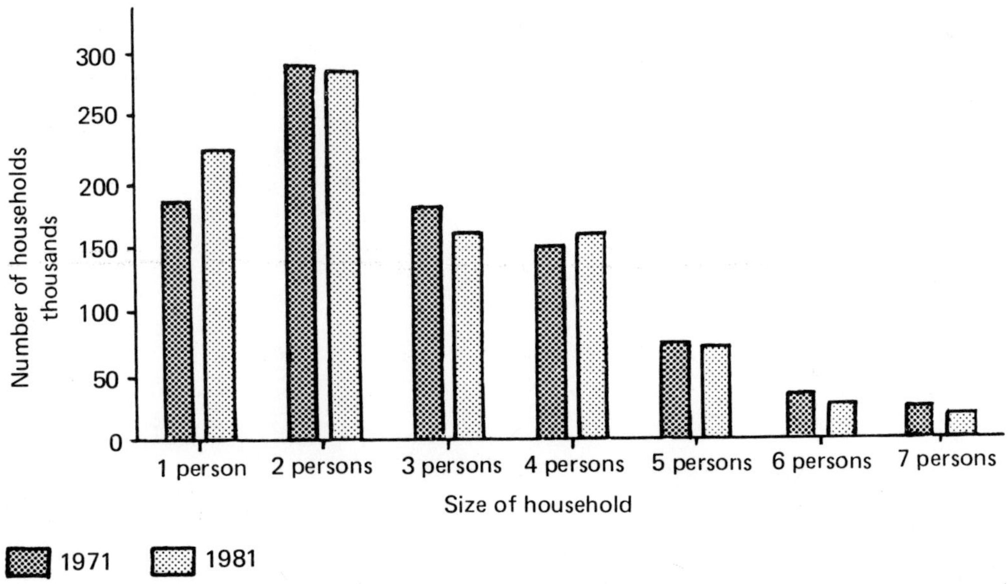

II INCIDENCE OF CORPORAL PUNISHMENT IN THE FAMILY

Scores on corporal punishment index* by social class (percentages)

	Social class					
Scores	I & II	III non manual	III manual	IV	V	All
High	21	27	34	31	40	31
Medium	30	33	29	32	33	31
Low	49	40	37	37	27	38

* Index based on mothers' replies to questions concerning the frequency with which physical punishment is used when child misbehaves.

(a) Suggest **one** proposition that can be derived from the bar chart, and **one** proposition that can be derived from the figures in the statistical table, if they are taken at face value. **4**

(b) Taking the chart and the table in turn, identify the various factors which may have influenced the nature of these statistics. **8**

(c) Use evidence from research studies to demonstrate the weaknesses inherent in such statistical data. **6**

(d) How might a sociologist defend the use of official and other statistics as a basis for theory and generalisation? Of what use might official and other statistics be to sociologists and official agencies such as government departments? **7**

25

JMB, June, 1985, Paper 2

Conclusion

This section has dealt with the variety of alternatives to the essay question that have emerged in recent years. For most exam boards the passage from a book or the statistical table is the main stimulus used. You may be reasonably confident with passages but less so with statistical sources. Try to see both in the same light, i.e. as source material for triggering ideas and thoughts about a sociological topic. In this sense numbers are conveying information in a slightly different way from words in a passage, so you don't have to be a mathematician in order to answer such questions. All that is required is the ability to get the gist of the information featured in the table, so you can provide a satisfactory written answer to the questions asked.

CHAPTER 7

REVISION

Dictionary definition:	'to look at again' 'to study anew'

Revision is usually associated with the last few months or weeks leading up to an examination. It should, however, be an activity which is carried out from the beginning of any course. This means that at regular intervals, for example on completion of a section or subsection of the course, you go through material covered so that it is re-inforced and more firmly imprinted in your memory. Regular revision of coursework also gives you a chance to eradicate difficulties or misunderstandings as they occur, rather than letting them get bypassed and lead to confusion later. An advanced course covers a lot of ground, so it is necessary to keep on top of things by making sure you thoroughly understand everything at the time it is studied. Continuous revision will enable you to do this.

So, what in effect is commonly called revision should perhaps be more correctly termed exam preparation or exam revision. With regard to the literal meaning of the word, 'to look at again', this is perhaps unfortunate as it implies a passive approach. Generations of students have used the exam preparation period as a time to read and re-read books, files of notes and other course material in an attempt to learn by heart masses of information, which they hope to be able to reproduce in their examination paper. Consider the large numbers of students during the months of May and June who sit in libraries throughout the land glumly flicking through files of notes, whereas it would be far more constructive if they involved themselves in more active revision tasks of the type outlined in this section.

A. REVISION AS REHEARSAL

Taking part in a play, musical concert or competing in a sports event are activities which all require thorough preparation and rehearsal. This could involve weeks or months of painstaking work, some of which could well be monotonous and repetitive, but this is recognized as essential for optimum performance.

Try to see your revision or exam preparation in a similar light. You need plenty of rehearsals—question decoding, answer plans, timed essays, answering full papers. If you were acting in a play it would not be enough to sit and read your lines over and over again. You would need to practise saying them aloud, acting the part of the character at the same time, so that your eventual portrayal would not just be a wooden repetition of words from the script, but a living, three-dimensional presentation of your role. Similarly with your revision for exams, see this period as preparation for your 'performance' in the examination when you are in the 'spotlight', showing the examiner (your 'audience') your prowess. If you approach the exam in this way, you should be well prepared. Unfortunately many students do not 'rehearse' adequately and so do not do as well as they should.

Exam preparation materials

Paper
Pens (range of colours, highlight pens)—aim is to make revision highly visual.
Pencil and rubber—notebook for brainstorming, random thoughts, ideas (a pocket notebook could be useful to carry around with you for recording as ideas occur).
Cards—for Card Index
Past exam papers—very important
Syllabus
Class notes
Handouts
Personal notes
Marked essays—very important, lessons to be learned from comments, but not intended as something to be learned by heart.
Textbook(s)—at this stage used mainly for quick reference.
Other course books—to look up points, etc. Do not undertake new reading.

Timetable and organization

You need to think in terms of a ten to twelve week intensive period of preparation, so the few weeks leading up to the Easter vacation are, in the case of summer exams, probably the ideal time to start. First you need to collect together and organize your course material. One of the initial tasks is to make sure your notes and related information such as handouts are complete, so fill in any gaps that may have occurred through absence at any time during the course. Prepare a revision timetable, so that you have a reasonably clear idea of the amount of time you have available each week. Some full-time courses allocate a specific 'stand-down' revision period in the summer term, but this is less often the case for part-time courses.

The precise number of hours per day spent revising is difficult to specify.—Don't overdo things by working twelve or more hours per day, so that you are exhausted by the examination. Work at your own pace in short time periods, 40 minutes - 1 hour, with short breaks, and finish work when things cease to register and you cannot concentrate any more. Exercise and a good night's sleep should prepare you for the next day's work.

Choosing exam topics

A full-time course should mean that you will eventually cover more topics than is necessary for the exam, where there is plenty of choice. For example, in Paper 1 the AEB gives a compulsory stimulus-response question in Section A, and then twelve essay titles in Section B from which you have to select three. In Paper 2 you have to answer one question from three titles in Section A, and three questions from twelve titles in Section B. Other boards offer a similarly wide choice, the intention being that the student is expected to cover certain core areas such as theory and methodology, but beyond that you are given the chance to specialize in key topic areas, so that you can provide detail and depth in your study.

Given the range of choice you have, there should be little difficulty in choosing four questions and answering them well. You will not be at any disadvantage if there are questions you cannot answer, except perhaps in the first few moments after encountering the paper, when the more pessimistic or perverse side of you will possibly only focus on such questions! If you have worked consistently and made good progress throughout the course and have prepared yourself, you should have no difficulty in finding four questions on each paper that you can answer well. So don't panic!

How many topic areas should I cover?

One of the early tasks in the exam preparation period is to decide how many topic areas you are going to concentrate on. Too few could mean problems in the exam if unusual or difficult questions come up. Too many topic areas might result in your knowledge of them being superficial and lacking the necessary depth and detail for advanced level answers, as well as possibly overtaxing your memory. Also it can increase feelings of panic if you have too wide a choice of questions you could answer.

Central or core topics

For most examination boards at advanced level, it is essential that you have a sound grasp of core sociological areas such as the following:

1. Sociology in relation to science (objectivity, values, ideology in Sociology).
2. The history and origins of Sociology. (You may not be asked specific questions on this but it is necessary background).
3. Key theoretical approaches or perspectives (particularly for the Associated Examining Board).
4. Sociological methods and debates arising from their use (methodology).

Some of these core areas are highly complex and involve abstract ideas or concepts, but it is necessary for you to have a thorough understanding of them if you are going to meet the required standard. Concentrated effort and work on these sections will bring rewards later, when you start to see the interrelatedness of topic areas such as the family, education, women's role in society, or religion, to the debates raised in the core sections of the syllabus.

Other topic areas

Before deciding on these, it is useful to consult past examination papers, which can be obtained from your teacher, the library or from the appropriate examination board. This might be difficult if there has been a recent change in exam format. In such a situation specimen papers should be available from teachers or the exam board itself. Past examination papers should help you to decide on topic areas, as they show the types of questions which can be asked. Other factors such as the centrality of a topic (i.e. is it always dealt with either on one or both papers?) can be considered also. An examination paper does not have to include every topic or area covered in the syllabus;

sometimes the sheer number of them precludes this. So some topic areas can be omitted or, more usually, included as part of a question on another area, the following question being an example.

Examine the relationship between the sociology of religion and the sociology of knowledge.
AEB, November, 1985, Paper 1.

It is useful here to re-emphasize the dangers of seeing Sociology as a collection of topics. You need to recognize the interconnectedness and interrelationships between all the topic areas in the syllabus. For example, questions on social class could relate to education, family, work, voting behaviour and so on. However, specialization and the exam format of four questions mean that topic areas can be a reasonable organizing principle for your exam preparation.

In addition to the central or core areas already discussed, it is advisable to concentrate on five or six additional areas from the syllabus. Fewer than this could mean restricted choice in the exam, which could create problems with difficult or obscure questions. Too many topic areas covered leads to superficiality. Five or six topic areas allows for a reserve or emergency. For example, you may have revised the topic of religion and religious sects but have difficulty in fully understanding the whole of a question. Consider the following title:
To what extent can the growth of religious sects be seen as a response to conditions of social disorganization and change?
AEB, June, 1985.

The latter part of this question, referring to conditions of social disorganization and change, may give you difficulty. Remember you should never answer a question unless you understand it fully, so in this case you should select another question.

Which topics?

The following factors should help you decide:

1. INTEREST
Do I find this topic area interesting or stimulating? (If this is the case, you are more likely to want to read widely and research the material thoroughly.)

2. UNDERSTANDING
Do I fully understand all the theoretical aspects, arguments, debates, and key concepts and issues relating to this area?

3. KNOWLEDGE
Is my knowledge of this topic area sufficient to answer questions with the necessary amount of depth and detail? Am I fully conversant with all aspects of the topic? Can I provide examples, illustrations, named references, and empirical research support for this topic? Does my knowledge go beyond basic textbooks, class notes and other course material?

4. SYLLABUS
Have I consulted the appropriate syllabus and/or notes for guidance to give me a clearer picture of what I am expected to know?

5. PAST QUESTIONS
Have I familiarized myself with previous questions, and do I fully understand what is required from them?

6. COURSEWORK
Has my coursework for this topic received good grades and favourable comments from my teacher?

7. TIME AND LENGTH
Can I answer questions on this topic under the time and length constraints imposed by the examination? (You should avoid choosing a topic where you might get bogged down in detail.)

8. MORE THAN ONE QUESTION ON A TOPIC AREA?
Some topics, such as the family and education, are likely to have a question on each of the two papers, so you may have to decide whether to answer both. If you do, this has the advantage of allowing you to specialize to a greater depth, but there are also some drawbacks. Such topics are popular with many exam candidates, so you need to bear in mind that answers will have to be of a high standard. Examiners like to see a candidate being somewhat adventurous and it gives a good impression if you are adept at answering questions on newer or unusual topics such as development or health and social policy, which are not chosen by many students. (You may know more about them than the examiner!!)

It is more important, however, that you give the best answers possible, so don't choose a topic with which you would have difficulty. Part-time students may well find that the topics covered in their courses are from the more mainstream areas of the syllabus in order to give a reasonable choice from the examination paper.

In summary, make sure your choice of topic areas is firmly grounded on syllabuses, past papers, textbooks, course materials, notes, and coursework, so that you have a clear understanding of what they involve. Topic choice is crucial so make sure you choose well.

Examples of one topic area producing a question on each paper:

EDUCATION

AEB, November, 1984

Paper 1
Question 6 *'The power of education systems to transform societies has been much exaggerated'. Discuss.*

Paper 2
Question 8 *'Education plays a major part in preparing males and females for their traditionally different social roles and therefore helps to maintain a division of labour based on sexual difference' Explain and discuss.*

DEVELOPMENT

Cambridge, June, 1985*

Paper 1
Question 7 *Why do many societies remain 'underdeveloped'?*

Paper 2
Question 10 *Why do people live longer in the advanced societies than in the underdeveloped societies?*

B. USING PAST QUESTIONS AND EXAMINATION PAPERS AS A REVISION AID

You should familiarize yourself with past questions on chosen topics. Carry out the following activities:

1. Make sure you can analyse or decode such questions effectively. Underline activity words, key words or phrases and explain them.
2. Make rough answer plans. This is especially useful as a timed activity.
3. Answer questions under exam time and length constraints.
4. Answer full examination papers in three hours to see how you cope in terms of your strengths and weaknesses.

In this way you use exam papers actively, rather than taking the approach which involves glancing at exam papers saying, 'I could have a go at that one', or, 'I can't do that one'. If you think you can answer a question, you should always test this either by making a plan or answering in full. This is the meaning of ACTIVE as compared to PASSIVE revision.

C. REVISION ACTIVITIES

1. You should always revise using blank paper for notes and thoughts as you work through material.
2. Brainstorm on topics using sprays or spider notes.
3. Condense your course material, notes, etc. Make notes on your notes, using large headings and subheadings.
4. Provide dramatic and colourful presentation, underlining and highlighting wherever possible. Use cartoons, diagrams or illustrations, all for visual impact.
5. Make pattern notes wherever appropriate.
6. Use cards with alphabetical or subject indexes to write summaries of key words, concepts, particular theories, research studies, debates and arguments. These can be a useful reference source which you can carry around with you to glance at on a bus or train journey, in a queue, the dentists' waiting room and so on. Such activity should make the recall of material easier.

D. REVISION SYNDICATES

A revision syndicate is formed when you get together with a group of friends in order to work on past exam questions, exchange ideas and information, make essay plans and discuss them, etc., so you feed off and mutually reinforce each other's knowledge and learning.

The following section contains a number of more structured activities which your syndicate could carry out. As well as learning from them, you could well find them fun to do!

E. REVISION ACTIVITY

COMMUNICATION Many teachers will tell you that a good way to learn something is to try and teach it or to communicate what you know about it to another person.

ACTIVITY 1

Get together with one or two other students from your course and each choose a different topic. Using your notes, diagrams, graphs, handouts etc., take turns at playing teacher. You must try to explain clearly to your students the topic you have chosen. Use visual aids to help you. Don't simply read points out as if you were practising lines for a play, but explain each point in your own words.

Encourage active participation in your 'lesson'.—Ask your 'students' questions and get them to ask you questions. Ask them if they have understood what you have been saying. Is there anything they would like you to go over again? Tell them to stop you if necessary in order to elaborate a point. It is surprising how ideas and knowledge stick in one's memory once they have been aired verbally.

ACTIVITY 2

This is similar to (1) but more formal. Imagine that you have been asked to deliver a lecture to a group of first year Sociology students on one of the topics on your course.

1. PREPARATION

Using your notes, draft a lecture on your chosen topic. Be as clear and concise as you can and concentrate on a sound and logical structure.

The following can act as guidelines:

(a) Where should I take my starting point from?

(b) Can I separate the lecture into an introduction, a main body and conclusion?

(c) Are there any terms or concepts my audience may not be familiar with? How can I explain these?

(d) Which examples (if any) should I use to illustrate a point?

(e) Have I underlined any points I may wish to give verbal emphasis to?

(f) Have I numbered each point and page?

2. PRESENTATION

Stand behind a table and arrange your notes in front of you in order. You can either deliver the lecture to friend(s), fellow student(s) or anyone prepared to listen, even the dog!

You can even record your lecture on tape.

Remember to make your lecture as lively and as interesting as possible.

(i) Pause every so often for effect.

(ii) Vary the tone of your voice.

(iii) Emphasize important points.

Now play back the tape, if you have recorded your talk. Ask yourself:

'Did I communicate the essence of what I wanted to say?'
'Were there any omissions?'
'Would there be a better way of stressing certain key points or issues?'

NOTE

Effective oral communication can have valuable repercussions on written communication such as essays, because it can help you to organize your thoughts and ideas and clarify understanding by expressing them aloud.

When it comes to examinations many students know their stuff, but fail to communicate it effectively on paper. It is helpful therefore to practise the simple art of communication to an imaginary audience. In an examination your real audience is, of course, the examiner, that shadowy grey figure looking over your shoulder!

ACTIVITY 3

GIVING THE EXAMINER A FACE

Practise giving him/her a face, to make the examiner real to you. Address your writing to this imaginary person when you are writing timed essays without books during the revision period. Use this approach when you take the full examination.

ACTIVITY 4

LETTER TO A FRIEND

A useful exercise, which will also help you with your revision, is to imagine that a friend has written to you asking for as much information as you can supply on one of the topics that you are revising. Using your notes, write a letter explaining that topic to your friend. To make it realistic set the letter out properly with an address, date etc. It is suprising how much easier written communication of knowledge, information and ideas becomes if you have a mental picture of the person who is reading it (see Activity (3) above).

ACTIVITY 5

THINKING LIKE AN EXAMINER

Get together with a friend studying Sociology. Both of you should choose a topic or section of the syllabus and spend some time revising. Then meet each other either in the library or you might be able to find an empty classroom (lunchtime is the most likely period). Your friend should then give you a question from a past paper on your chosen topic and you should do the same. You could give each other more than one question on more than one topic area, depending on the time you have available. Then answer the question(s) allowing 45 minutes each to include question decoding, planning and writing.

Exchange your answers and mark them on a scale A to E (or include F if necessary!) As you mark, you should consider whether the question has been understood, the structure, content and style, and the evaluation before awarding the mark.

When the marking is completed, you should then discuss the assessment with each other. Your friend might in your judgement be over flattering, and you should be willing to be self critical:

'No, it's not worth a C, I didn't cover . . . or . . .' Alternatively, you may think your friend has undervalued your essay, so be prepared again to present your case. Using this bargaining or negotiating process, you should be able to arrive at a fairly realistic mark. If there is strong disagreement, consult your teacher. It may be a good idea to do this at first anyway, until you get used to 'thinking like an examiner'.

If you are still speaking at the end of several weeks of this activity, then you must have a real friend!

A less time consuming variant of the above is to produce timed answer plans in about ten minutes.

ACTIVITY 6

EXAM SIMULATION—THE 'DRESS REHEARSAL'

You have already been advised to answer past questions without books or notes under timed conditions, as well as attempting full examination papers in three hours. This exercise helps you to prepare psychologically for the physical experience of the exam. There are several things you can do:

(1) Find out the location of a typical examination room and observe factors like the size of the room, the numbers of people likely to be in the room, the spacing of desks or tables and their size.

(2) You could find a desk or table of a similar size at home, or in school or college.

(3) Gather together the following—the writing equipment you intend to take into the exam; a past examination paper; an exam answer book (you may be able to borrow one from the college or school office or your teacher) or several sheets of paper of a similar type.

(4) Place these on the desk or table you have chosen.

(5) Sit at the desk or table and imagine that you are sitting your first examination with other candidates and invigilators present.

(6) Make a note of the following:
- Your immediate feelings and activities
- How you would make a start on settling yourself down to start the examination
- A plan of what you intend to do for the three hour period, with reference to time spent reading the question paper, choosing questions, brainstorming, planning, writing and a final reading of the paper.

(7) Evaluation
In the light of (6) above, what are your feelings?

—Is there anything you are doing which can be corrected? For example, are you tempted to start writing as soon as possible without proper consideration of the question(s) or planning?

—Is your heart pounding or are your hands shaking?
If so, try deep breathing exercises. If you are very nervous, try writing down what it is that is causing you to be nervous. If it is the unknown aspect of the questions on the examination paper, think to yourself—'I have seen past papers. I know the sort of questions on topics that have come up; I know about these topics; therefore I can do well.'

As well as having the benefits of helping you to come to terms with the physical experience of being in an examination, this exercise could be seen as your own sociological research. The title could be;

'A Participant Observation study of a Sociology examination candidate'(!)

Handy hints

(1) Provide yourself with incentives and rewards varying from the trivial: 'I'll have that bar of chocolate/play that record/read that magazine, when I have thoroughly learned and understood this section' to the more substantial: 'If I do a good solid week's work next week, I'll buy that record I like'. You will have saved money by staying in to work anyway.

(2) Write out a list of topics that you intend to revise and mark each with a large tick when you have covered it.—This is psychologically good for you, as it gives a clear picture of achievement.

Exam revision checklist

(1) ORGANIZE
- Revision Timetable—10-12 weeks
- Course Materials
- Class and Reading Notes
- Handouts
- Textbooks and related sources
- Coursework

(2) CHOOSE—consult syllabus, past papers
- Core Topic areas—essential, compulsory questions
- Key Topic areas—5 or 6—know them well

(3) REVISION ACTIVITY
Active not passive
- Brainstorming
- Notes on Notes
- Pattern Notes
- Spider notes/sprays
- Card Indexes

} VISUAL impact for effective memorizing
—Cartoons
—Diagrams
—Illustrations

(4) SIMULATE EXAM CONDITIONS
- Question decoding
- Answer plans
- Timed answers—also be aware of AMOUNT & LENGTH in 45 minutes
- Answer a full paper to identify weaknesses in exam technique.

(5) WORK WITH FRIENDS (A REVISION SYNDICATE)
- Discuss topics/questions
- Engage in activities/exercises outlined

(6) 'REHEARSE' FOR EXAM 'PERFORMANCE'
Make sure you know:
- Dates and times of exams
- Location of exam hall—the 'stage' for your 'performance'!
- Length of paper—usually 3 hours
- Number of questions to be answered
- If sections, compulsory questions?
- Stimulus response questions?
- Essay questions?

EXERCISE

Your friend at another college writes a letter to you which includes the following passage:

'Exams are something I don't think about, I put off thinking about them until the last minute and then I'm a nervous wreck!'

Write a letter in reply advising your friend as to how he/she could approach exams.

CHAPTER 8

EXAMINATION TECHNIQUES

The exam is not an unknown entity

If you have made good progress through the course; have done the necessary work; have been thorough in your revision; and have used your exam preparation period effectively, the exams should not present too much difficulty. Apart from the specific wording of questions you should know what to expect.

Known aspects of exam

You know:

1. the length of the exam (usually 3 hours);
2. that there are a set number of questions to be answered;
3. that there are stimulus response as well as essay questions;
4. whether some questions are compulsory;
5. about the inclusion of core or essential topic area questions.

Exam nerves

You will probably be slightly nervous but this is quite common. A little nervousness can be beneficial in that this can heighten or stimulate brain activity. Slow, deep breathing can help you to settle down before the exam. Too much nervousness, which may be detrimental to exam performance, invariably stems from a lack of confidence, which reflects incomplete or inadequate preparation and work during the course. Such problems should have been ironed out earlier. If you feel anxious prior to the exam, think calmly to yourself:

1. I have progressed satisfactorily through the course and completed the necessary work.
2. I am well rehearsed for the exam in that I have studied hard and used past examination papers and answered questions under simulated exam conditions.
3. I have selected topic areas which I know thoroughly and on which I can answer questions with confidence.
4. Apart from the actual wording of the questions, I know what to expect.

A. THE DAY BEFORE

Double check the time and place of the examination. Is it a morning or an afternoon; in the main hall, sports hall or other location? Complete all your revision activities early enough for you to have a good break and get a good night's rest. Don't stay up until the early hours. 'If I don't know it now, I'll never know it' should be your motto at this stage. Last minute revision and lack of sleep could lead to confusion and less effective exam performance.

Exam equipment

Writing equipment, pens and spare(s), pencil and rubber for planning and rough work. If you must bring along lucky charms, cuddly toys, etc., don't overdo this. There is a story about a student who arrived for an exam with so many that by the time she had set them all out the exam was over!

B. EXAM DAY

Arrive about half an hour before the exam starts to give yourself time to find the room and wait outside. Arriving too early can heighten tension. Try not to get too involved in detailed talk about particular topics with your friends, as this can disturb your concentration. Try to keep your mind clear and uncluttered by extra details.

Rubric (instructions on the exam paper, usually in heavy print or italics)

Example: *Answer 4 questions, 1 from Section A and 3 from Section B.*

Familiarity with past papers should mean that you are fully aware of what is required, but always check to make sure when you first see the paper. Examiners still remark on the surprising number of candidates who do not follow intructions given, for example answering two questions from a section which requires one answer. If this occurs, the examiner will mark one answer and ignore the other.

Rough Work

Brainstorming, random thoughts, names, answer plans, etc.

Be prepared to carry this out in your answer book, however untidy and disorganized it may appear. Use a pencil and rubber if you wish and before you hand in your script, draw a single line through your rough work and it will not be read. It is inadvisable to scribble or write all over the question paper as many students do. The result is often a jumbled mess, because there is insufficient space for such work and points relating to one question could get confused with points relating to another. Some boards, moreover, require you to submit all rough work in your answer book.

Which questions to answer?

Do not start writing as soon as the exam begins in the belief that you must write solidly for three hours in order to pass the exam. If you take this approach, you are likely to end up with badly structured answers which stray off the point, are disjointed and disorganized and do not deal directly with the question asked.

First reading (scan/skim)

You should scan or skim read the whole paper first with a view to deciding from the start which four questions you intend to answer. Devise a system of marking questions on topic areas you have specialized in. For example, you could tick those questions you readily recognize and fully understand, and you could use a question mark for those that appear to be in your specialist topic areas but that you don't immediately understand. You can mark other questions which you don't intend to answer with a X but this could be time consuming. So your marking system could be:

(Tick)	I recognize this, I think I can answer.
(Question Mark)	Relates to one of my specialist areas but I can't fully understand the question at the moment.
(Cross)	I have no intention of answering this.

Second reading (detail)

You should now concentrate more fully on questions marked with a tick or a question mark. Underline activity words and key terms to be explained. Make sure that those marked with a tick confirm your first impression and that you fully understand the whole of the question and not just a part of it. Reconsider the questions marked with a question mark; a more detailed look might indicate that you can provide a good answer. The difficulty may be to do with the way a question is worded, or a quote may need unravelling. Once this is done, you may be able to change a question mark to a tick.

Ideally at this stage you should have up to seven or eight questions marked with a tick, but it could be fewer if you have covered a part-time course. Your next decision is which questions to choose, the obvious point being to select the ones you can answer best.

Overlapping answers

Sometimes part of one answer may well be relevant to part of another. For example, there maybe a question on the family where you deem it appropriate to make points about women's changing role in society, and also questions on women and work where you judge it appropriate to include similar points. It is acceptable to cross refer in this case as follows:

'As was referred to in Q.3, the issues concerning women's changing role in society are vital to an understanding of their position in the labour force.'

The problem with cross-referring is that it can be time-consuming if you have to keep looking back to a previous answer. If you can choose another question, it may be advisable as it shows the examiner that you have not just concentrated on a few areas of the syllabus. Don't cross-refer from one paper to another.

Popularity of topic area

Examiners' reports indicate that questions on topics such as sociology and science, the family, education, women in society and poverty are frequently answered, whereas topics such as race and ethnicity, youth culture, the sociology of knowledge and community are less popular. You can gain indirectly from answering questions on some of these latter topics, in that, as previously stated, it shows the examiner that you have been willing to study areas of the syllabus that are more unusual and possibly more challenging. Clearly, the ultimate criterion is that you choose the questions you can answer best, so don't 'play the system' and attempt to answer questions on unusual areas which you do not fully understand or have not grasped properly.

Brainstorming/rough work

Once you have chosen the questions, you next need to examine them in detail. You may have already jotted down some points concerning each question, so you can now 'brainstorm' or 'spray' further points to expand on and add to key terms, words or phrases in the title. You can then either organize this rough work into a fairly detailed plan for each question, or have a brief plan for each with the intention of adding more detail before you start writing each answer. Whichever option you choose, it is advisable to have some detail written down for each question as you consider them at the start of the exam. This helps to avoid the problem of returning to answer a chosen question later in the exam and not being able to remember some detail or point which you had at your finger tips on first reading the paper. Always write things down from the first consideration of each question.

Planning

By this stage, effective planning for your coursework essays or stimulus-response questions, as outlined in Chapters 5 and 6, and practice at preparing answer plans during the revision period, should mean you are adept at planning answers. In the exam, time constraints will mean that you have to be quicker at setting a plan out. A good plan has the advantage of making the task of writing easier, as you have the logical sequence of points to be covered set out in paragraphs and in the form of an Introduction, a Main Body and a Conclusion. Look back at your plan often to make sure you aren't wandering off the point.

The first question

Most candidates answer their strongest question first and this is quite sensible, as a good first answer can give you a psychological boost for the rest of the paper and help to settle you down. It is inadvisable to choose your worst question first ('I'll get this out of the way') as this could possibly undermine your confidence. Some examiners have indicated that in many papers it is the second question answered which is a candidate's best response. This could be because the student has 'warmed up' after answering one question, and has gained confidence. If this is the case, my advice would be to answer your second strongest question first and your strongest second. You don't *have* to answer compulsory questions first. If you find such a question difficult, it may be advisable to leave this until a later stage, possibly until your third answer.

Timing and length

It is important that you fully answer the required number of questions. You should not make rough calculations along the lines: 'If I can provide two good answers, and a fair third one, I should be through, so a fourth answer is not so important'. Consider the following example of the allocation of marks for two candidates' exam papers:

Question	*Marks gained*		*Potential Mark*
	Sharon	Louise	
1	17	13	25
2	15	12	25
3	4	10	25
4	0	11	25
	36	46	100

Despite Sharon's having much better marks than Louise for two of her questions, her overall paper would be borderline and possibly fail, whereas Louise's more consistent grading over four questions would achieve a safe pass grade.

The advice is always answer the number of required questions as fully as possible. You need to allocate a set amount of time to each question.

Concerning the length of your answers, you will not have time to provide the amount of detail you can put into a coursework essay and this is why it is important to include plenty of exam answer writing practice in your revision preparation. You may find that, where in coursework essays you can provide several examples, illustrations or pieces of research to highlight a point, in an exam answer you may only be able to include one or two.

It is a useful exercise during revision, not only to time your answers, but to have an idea of the length of your answers so that you know how much detail can be provided. The majority of exam answers are between 400–800 words; that is two to four sides in length. Less than this usually means the answer lacks the necessary depth and detail, but a good interpretation of the question could still mean a pass grade for a short answer. Much more than five sides could reflect bad planning and poor structure, where the answer often strays off the point or there is unnecessary padding or 'waffle'.

Allow time for reading the paper, decoding and choosing questions, brainstorming and planning answers, as well as a final reading through of the paper to look for errors or mistakes, the insertion of details previously forgotten or any additional points to be added to strengthen an answer. Time spent on such activities is not wasted. A script with four answers of three sides, showing that the candidate has interpreted each question effectively and answered them well, is worth more than a script of 20 sides which is disorganized, full of mistakes and crossings out, and has not dealt with questions effectively. Aim for QUALITY not QUANTITY. To attain this you must spend some time thinking about and planning each answer, which means that you should not write solidly for three hours.

Examiners do not consider the length of answers, rather they look for:

1. understanding and correct interpretation of all parts of a question;
2. a sound knowledge of the themes and issues surrounding key terms in the question;
3. an awareness of the main theoretical, methodological and related debates wherever relevant to the question;
4. reference to appropriate empirical studies to support or question a particular line of argument, theoretical stance or debate;
5. the ability to provide a conclusion to the answer. This shows a considered evaluation or judgement concerning the issues and themes raised in the answer. Avoid 'sitting on the fence'. You will know by this stage that Sociology is a lively, active discipline which is full of controversies, debates and arguments, so you should be prepared to show the examiner that you are willing to participate.

Writing the exam answer

The time required for reading the paper, question decoding, brainstorming and planning should mean that you have approximately 35 minutes per question to write and read through your answers. If your preparation and planning has been thorough, the actual task of writing, as with coursework essays, should be relatively straightforward.

Structure and content

Remember that a good introduction, which shows you have clearly grasped the meaning of the title and are able to define and clarify the key terms and issues, is essential. Get points across in a direct no-nonsense manner, using paragraphs to make a logical transition from one point to another. You need to condense, précis or summarize the main theoretical arguments, but examine them in enough depth to do them justice. Include named references, quotations and relevant empirical studies where appropriate to support points or arguments. The necessity to refer to and summarize research studies in a manner which conveys their essence has already been referred to. This ability should be developed when writing your coursework essays. Don't leave your essay 'hanging in mid-air'. Don't forget to provide that all-important concluding paragraph which refers back to the title and introduction and leaves the reader with a good impression.

Style

As with coursework essays, accuracy, brevity and clarity are important, but in addition try to inject a sense of enthusiasm or flair into your writing. Don't be dull or turgid in approach. An example might be the inclusion of something topical from the newspapers or television, which is relevant to your discussion. Consider the following which might be applicable to some of the topic areas:

RELIGION

Has the Church recently spoken out against injustice? Is there any country where Church or religious leaders are criticizing government or state policy?

WORK/TECHNOLOGY

Are there any industrial disputes concerning the implementation of new technology? Is unemployment rising? What reasons are being offered? What are the latest arguments surrounding Youth Training Schemes?

MASS MEDIA/YOUTH CULTURE/CRIME AND DEVIANCY

Has there been a recent 'moral panic' about drugs, football hooliganism, young people, crime or deviance? Have crime statistics recently been referred to in the press?

POLITICS

What are the recent opinion poll findings on people's attitudes to politicians, political parties, nuclear issues, unemployment etc?

FAMILY/DEMOGRAPHY

What are the most recent figures on divorce, birth/death rates, population growth rates, average family size, working mothers, or the elderly?

WOMEN

Are there any recent articles on women's issues, such as work or related matters?

RACE/ETHNICITY, THE INNER CITY, THE POLICE

Have there been any recent issues concerning inner city areas, the police, or ethnic minorities?

In the pre-examination period, there may not be much time available for the consideration of news or current affairs, but try to keep in touch with such matters, as this shows the examiner that, as well as having a sound grasp of Sociology, you are able to draw in material to help make sense of the world around you.

EXERCISE

Go back and consult some of the question titles in Chapter 5. Write down any topical references which are relevant.

C. PROBLEMS THAT MAY ARISE IN THE EXAMINATION

1. The mental block

What should you do if you 'dry up' after writing half a side for an answer and cannot think of anything else to write? If you have thought about the question and planned your answer as described in previous sections this problem should not occur. However, if you do 'seize up' don't panic and carry on writing just anything, however irrelevant, in order to give a full answer. Stop, leave space and turn to another question. After a break, you may find that the 'block' has cleared and that you can carry on and write more.

2. Wrong question choice

If you have taken earlier advice, this also should not happen. Only answer questions you understand fully and prepare and plan your response properly. Wrong question choice usually occurs when a candidate unthinkingly rushes into an answer on the basis of an immediate recognition of part of an essay title without proper consideration of every detail. Examples of such an approach have been given in previous sections. Here is another:

Discuss the uses and limitations for sociologists of official statistics of crime and delinquency, and give an account of how sociologists have responded to these limitations. AEB, June, 1983, Paper 1.

On reading this, your attention might focus on the first part of the question which you immediately start to answer without properly considering the full title. When you come to this latter part, you may not be able to answer this, so that potentially your answer can only receive around half marks. It may also have the indirect consequence of annoying the examiner, because the question has not been fully answered. Examiners' reports often point to the large number of candidates who fail to answer fully the question set. If you have rushed in without thinking and written half a side or less, abandon the question and answer another.

3. Poor timing

If you allocate the time to be spent on each answer inefficiently and spend too long on earlier sections of the paper, you could well find yourself with twenty minutes or less to answer the last question. This should not occur if you are well organized, but if it does happen, you may have to decide whether to try and write a full answer in a rushed fashion, or to give a note or telegraphic form of answer. In either case, you could not gain the same marks as a full essay response, but if you can communicate the essence of the points you wish to make via linear notes, valuable marks could be received. Concentrate on showing you have grasped the issues arising from the question title and that you have interpreted it correctly, as well as briefly outlining the structure and main themes you would have provided in a fuller discussion.

NOTE However little time you have remaining you should at least attempt a final answer. As soon as you begin it, you break into a new block of marks, and even a few marks gained could make a vital difference either between one grade and another or, ultimately, between pass and fail. Consider the following example:

'Sociological theory and research methods are well nigh inseparable'. Discuss.

It is impossible to use methods without some sort of theory. Because you have to have a theory about how the methods work and what methods to use under particular circumstances. For instance, if you do participant observation research you must have a theory about how people react to an outsider, otherwise you might be misled. Or if you use a questionnaire you must have a theory about how people react to questionnaires and interviewers, so in this way theory and method are indeed inseparable.

Comment
Probably a fourth essay. Obviously, it is very short, but it makes one good point and it makes it well. It is certainly worth more than nought, but it is notoriously difficult to award very low marks equitably. Perhaps two out of twenty-five?
R. Gomm and P. McNeill, *Handbook for Sociology Teachers* (Heinemann, London, 1982)

However, if you have organized properly and have stuck rigidly to time allocated per question this situation will not occur.

4. A difficult paper?

The impression that a paper is difficult may occur on first reading, when the meaning of questions is not immediately obvious, particularly the ones on the topics you have specialized in. Suppose that you have concentrated on religion, the family and the media and the following questions are all on the paper you are facing:

1. *Examine the relationship between the sociology of religion and the sociology of knowledge.*
2. *Discuss the view that the isolated nuclear family serves the needs of the wider social system at the expense of its own members.*
3. *'While it is not difficult to find evidence of bias in the media, it is much more dificult to identify the causes of this bias.' Explain and discuss.*

(All three questions from AEB, November, 1985, Paper 1)

Closer examination of each question should show that question difficulties arise for different reasons. The question on the media uses a quote which needs thinking about and unravelling. The question on religion draws in another topic area. The family question includes a phrase 'at the expense of its own members' which needs explaining in your answer. Think about this—negative costs—the dark side of family life—exploitation and the oppression of women, the 'source of all our discontents', the 'destructive gemeinschaft' of the modern nuclear family etc.

The result could be that your initial impression of a 'difficult' paper is based on three questions which need some thought and consideration and it could be that there is only one you definitely cannot answer. In this case it could be the question on religion, because you are not sure how to draw in the sociology of knowledge aspect. It must be stressed that advanced level questions are rarely straightforward and that is why proper analysis and decoding is essential. However, if you cannot deal with a question fully, even if you know a lot about the topic area, choose another one. That is why you should always specialize in more topic areas than may strictly be required.

Finally if a paper is difficult overall, don't forget that this will also be the case for every other candidate in the exam, therefore concentrate and provide the best answers possible.

Exam Checklist

1. REVISION/PREPARATION

- Lead in to the exam should be months before, not weeks or days.
- Prepare thoroughly, use syllabus, notes for guidance and past papers, but don't 'question spot' or over-rely on certain questions or topic areas definitely being on the paper.
- Have more than the minimum necessary topic areas in case of difficult or unusual questions.

2. RUBRIC

- Before the exam make sure you are clear on the number of questions to be answered, whether the paper is in sections or contains compulsory questions.
- On receiving the paper, double check that instructions are the same as on previous years' papers.

3. MARK QUESTIONS

- Tick or question mark on specialist topic areas.
- Partial 'brainstorm' on reading, note relevant debates and issues, decode questions, underline activity words, key terms or phrases to be explained.
- Satisfy yourself that you can fully answer all parts of a question.

4. CHOICE

- Choose carefully the questions you are going to answer in the light of your knowledge and understanding.

5. BRAINSTORM

- Add more detail to initial thoughts—names, debates, central ideas and themes, theoretical approaches, empirical studies and other supportive material.

6. PLANNING

- Plan each answer—either all four in detail before you start writing, or brief plans with a view to additional material later. The latter approach is probably more satisfactory as it takes into account your first thoughts about a question as well as giving you a chance to add more detail when you are fully concentrating on the question before writing your answer. Careful attention should be paid to time allocation, however. Don't 'over-plan' and eat into your writing time.

7. WRITING YOUR ANSWER(S)

- Provide answers to questions. Do not spill out (or regurgitate) as much material as you can think of on the topic dealt with by the question.
- Answer questions clearly and accurately, showing full understanding.
- STRUCTURE
  - (i) *Introduction*—'set the scene', explain key terms, interpret the question. Point to the direction in which you intend to go.
  - (ii) *Main Body*—Paragraphs each dealing with a point, debates, arguments for and against. Relevant theoretical approaches and issues arising, appropriate empirical material.
  - (iii) *Conclusion*—Show how you have dealt with the question in the main body. Evaluate and appraise the question in the light of this.
- CONTENT
  Cover as much detail as possible. Show that you are aware of all the issues by discussing them. Include examples, illustrations from sociological and supplementary sources.
- STYLE
  Accuracy / Brevity / Clarity + Flair, e.g. use of experience or current affairs to highlight mainstream discussion.

8. OPINIONATED OR DOGMATIC ANSWERS

- Don't be opinionated, moralistic or appeal to 'common sense' in your answers. Avoid opening sentences with,

'I think that . . .'
'Everybody knows that . . .'
'It's common sense that . . .'
'We are all to blame for . . .'

- Don't use 'problem' or 'blame' when explaining issues e.g. 'the problem of working class underachievement in the education system is that the anti-school working class culture is to blame'.

Such usage of 'problem' and 'blame' is, to say the least, contentious, and indicates a lack of sociological understanding of educational processes.

9. 'MODEL' OR 'RIGHT' ANSWERS

- In Sociology there is never a clear 'right' answer as such. There can often be several approaches to a question, each worthy of consideration and in some cases you may answer a question in a way that is unusual and provide a response which has not been expected by the examiner. Providing it is sociological, well argued and justified it will be rewarded on the same basis as a more conventional answer. It could even gain extra marks, as it may indicate maturity and independence in your thinking.

10. 'THROW ENOUGH MUD AT A WALL, SOME OF IT'S BOUND TO STICK'

- Don't 'pad out' answers.—Only give what is relevant to the question. Six sides of irrelevance is worth less than one and a half sides of relevance, where the candidate indicates a clear understanding of what the question is about.

11. TIMING and LENGTH

- Answer the required number of questions as fully as possible.
- Pay attention to time: approximately 45 minutes per question, allowing time for decoding, planning and writing and reading through at the end. When the time for one question is up, leave it quickly and start another.
- Work within a set length which can be determined before the exam e.g. 'three sides is what I can write under exam conditions, so I have to get all my points across in this space'.

12. KEEP CALM (DON'T PANIC)

If you have worked consistently throughout the course, made good progress in your coursework and are well prepared for the exam, you cannot but do well and when the results are published you will have something to celebrate!

D. EXAM DO'S AND DONT'S

DO'S

1. Do arrive for the exam in good time, but not too early—hanging around waiting to be allowed in can be bad for you if you suffer from exam nerves.
2. Do have a light meal before an exam (not a heavy one). Concentration becomes difficult when blood sugar is low.
3. If you have suffered badly in the past from exam nerves, a counsellor or pastoral care tutor may be able to help. Talk to them. Get a beginner's Yoga book from your library and practice some simple relaxation and breathing exercises.

DON'TS

1. Don't feed off the exam nerves of others. If you have done your work, it does not matter if someone else has not done hers.
2. Don't take tranquilizers, alcohol or other drugs to calm the nerves. Most drugs impair concentration and anyway a certain level of 'nerviness' can be a good stimulant.
3. Don't worry if, when you arrive at the exam, you think you can't remember anything. This is quite common and passes when you receive the right stimulus, i.e. an exam question you understand. It can happen with your first cursory glance at the paper when a wave of pessimism might affect you. Think positive—'I have worked hard for this, I can do it!'

Finally, it is hoped that the study of Sociology is as challenging, exciting and interesting to you as it has been for countless students and teachers.

Good Luck, enjoy your course and studies and may you have every success!

ACKNOWLEDGEMENTS

The author and publishers wish to thank the following for permission to reprint copyright material:
The Guardian for Leader article, 14th March, 1986 and letter in reply from Phil Scraton, Centre for Studies in Crime and Social Policy, Edge Hill College, 18th March, 1986; also for Malcolm Dean's 'When Murder is a Family Affair', 20th September, 1985, and for statistics on newspaper circulation, 27th January, 1986; *Private Eye* for 'A Doctor Writes', 1982; T. Bilton and Macmillan for Tables 1.1 and 1.2 from *Introductory Sociology* (London and Basingstoke, 1981) pp.6 and 7; Mike O'Donnell and Nelson for the introduction to Reading 21, *New Introductory Reader in Sociology* (London, 1983) p.132 and for the extract from *A New Introduction to Sociology* (London, 1981) pp.114–115; Laurie Taylor and Allen and Unwin for the extract from *In the Underworld* (Hemel Hempstead, 1985) pp.26–27; W.F. Whyte and the University of Chicago Press for the extract from *Street Corner Society* (Chicago, 1943) pp.300–301; Ken Pryce and Bristol Classical Press for the extract from *Endless Pressure* (Bristol, 1979); A.D. Burgen for the extract 9A from *Comprehension Exercises in Sociology* (Stanley Thorne, Cheltenham, 1982) and Michael Banton and Collins for the extract from *Racial Minorities* (London, 1972) within it; *New Society* for 'Observations: Snakes and Ladders', 7th March, 1986 and for 'The right note', 11th October, 1985 and 'Work', 28th February, 1980; Peter Worsley and Penguin Books Ltd. for the diagram from *Introducing Sociology* (Harmondsworth, 1977); Steve Bell and *The Guardian* for the 'If . . .' cartoon, *The Guardian*, 1st February, 1986; Alex Hailey and Souvenir Press Ltd. for the extract from *Wheels* (London, 1973); Nick Hedges for photographs from *Born to Work* (Pluto, London, 1982); Maggie Murray and Format Photographers Ltd. for the photograph of Carshalton Laundry: NHS NUPE members; Posy Simmonds and *The Guardian* for the cartoon 'Who worries about the worriers?', *The Guardian*, 3rd March, 1986; Michelle Stanworth and Century Hutchinson for the extract from *Gender and Schooling* (London, 1983) pp.43–45; Paul Trowler and Unwin Hyman for 'Attempts to Achieve a Synthesis Between the Action Approach and Structuralism' from *Further Topics in Sociology* (UTP, Slough, 1985) pp.39–41; Michael Haralambos and Unwin Hyman for two extracts from *Sociology: Themes and Perspectives* (UTP, Slough, 1985) pp.77–80 and p.165; Michael Haralambos and Causeway Press for the extracts from *Sociology: New Directions* (Ormskirk, 1985) and from S. Frith, *The Sociology of Youth* (Ormskirk, 1984) pp.26–27; P. McNeill and C. Townley and Century Hutchinson for two extracts from *Fundamentals of Sociology* (London, 1981) p.18 and p.288; Peter Halfpenny and Longman Resources Unit for the extract from *Principles of Method* (York, 1984); D.H. Hargreaves and Routledge and Kegan Paul for the extract from *Social Relations in a Secondary School* (London, 1967) p.205; Philip Abrams and Weidenfeld for the extract from *Work, Urbanism and Inequality* (London, 1978); Paul Edwards for the Table 'Strike Indices, Selected Industries, 1970–1980' from 'The Pattern of Collective Industrial Action' in G. Bain (ed.), *Industrial Relations in Britain* (Blackwell); R. Gomm and P. McNeill and Heinemann Educational Books for the extract from *Handbook for Sociology Teachers* (London, 1982); The Controller of Her Majesty's Stationery Office for items from *Social Trends 16*, 1986.

It has not been possible in all cases to trace copyright holders; the publishers would be glad to hear from any such unacknowledged copyright holders.

The author would especially like to thank the following students for their assistance in the writing of this book:
Gail Barton, Mark Duerden, Lesley Fish, Gloria Ford, Judith Hale, Graham Henry, Sylvia Howarth, Lesley Hoyle, Tahir Idris, Lisa Jepson, Samantha Lambert, Stephanie Leigh, Jamila Mulla, Douglas Newton, Rebekah Northcott, Christine Ryden, Michelle Tomlinson and Alison Waters.